When America Still Had Children

First Edition First Printing May 2005
ISBN: 0-9765369-8-6
Written by O'Neal Henley.
Cover Design by Annette Galloway and O'Neal Henley.
Edited by Sheri Isbell. Copy editing by Annette Galloway.
Published by Main Street Publishing Inc., Jackson,Tn. Printed and bound by NetPub Corp., Poughkeepsie, New York.

For information on this publication write: Main Street Publishing 206 East Main Street, Suite 207 P.O. Box 696, Jackson, Tn. 38302. Websites: www.mspbooks.com and www:mainstreetpublishing.com. Phone: 731-427-7379   Toll Free: 1-866-457-7379

When America Still
Had Children

O'Neal Henley

Main Street Publishing, Inc. Jackson, Tennessee

Dedication

To all the friends and family who have gone to be with the Lord, who enhanced the lives of the Cotton Mill Boys in our formative years.

Acknowledgments

There are so many to thank for their help and encouragement. Margaret Williams, Faye Hardin, and Gary Cook, thank you for your help and encouragement. I thank my daughter, Suzie for her editing and suggestions. I thank my son, Hunter and my grandchildren for their excitement and inspiration as I read the book to them, but most of all I thank my wife Bren for the untold hours of typing and the encouragement and support she has given me.

Introduction

World War II had ended. Fathers, sons, and daughters were home. The communist were a threat to world peace, but from 1949-1955 the Cotton Mill Boys and Humboldt, Tennessee were the center of my universe. Humboldt was, and still is, a small town in West Tennessee. Its claim to fame is the West Tennessee Strawberry Festival and the home of all-pro Chicago Bear Doug Atkins. In the early 1950's it seemed to be much larger than it does today, but it couldn't have been, because Humboldt has grown to include many of the surrounding fields, wood lots, and farm land. Many of the places where we played, hunted, and explored are now shopping malls and subdivisions. There is even a new high school and park smack in the middle of Spangler's Woods.

We grew up in the part of town commonly referred to as the "Cotton Mill." It was in the Cotton Mill neighborhood that we spent our formative years, and what years they were! The lives of the Cotton Mill Boys were one adventure after another. The Cotton Mill Boys ranged in age from six to sixteen. We lived in a closely knit neighborhood where we all worked and played together. Summer, winter, spring, or fall - there was no time to be bored if you were a Cotton Mill Boy.

Most children growing up in America today are sorely lacking in their rearing because they are missing out on the kind of education received by the Cotton Mill Boys. It wasn't always pretty, but life taught us lessons every day. We were never spectators in the game of life. Our lives were all-out participation. We reached out to become a part of everyone and everything in our world. There were no TV's, Game Boys, or computers to distract us. The only thing that came between us and total domination of our world were chores, school, sometimes homework, and occasionally a radio show like "Sgt. Preston of the Yukon."

Map of the Cotton Mill

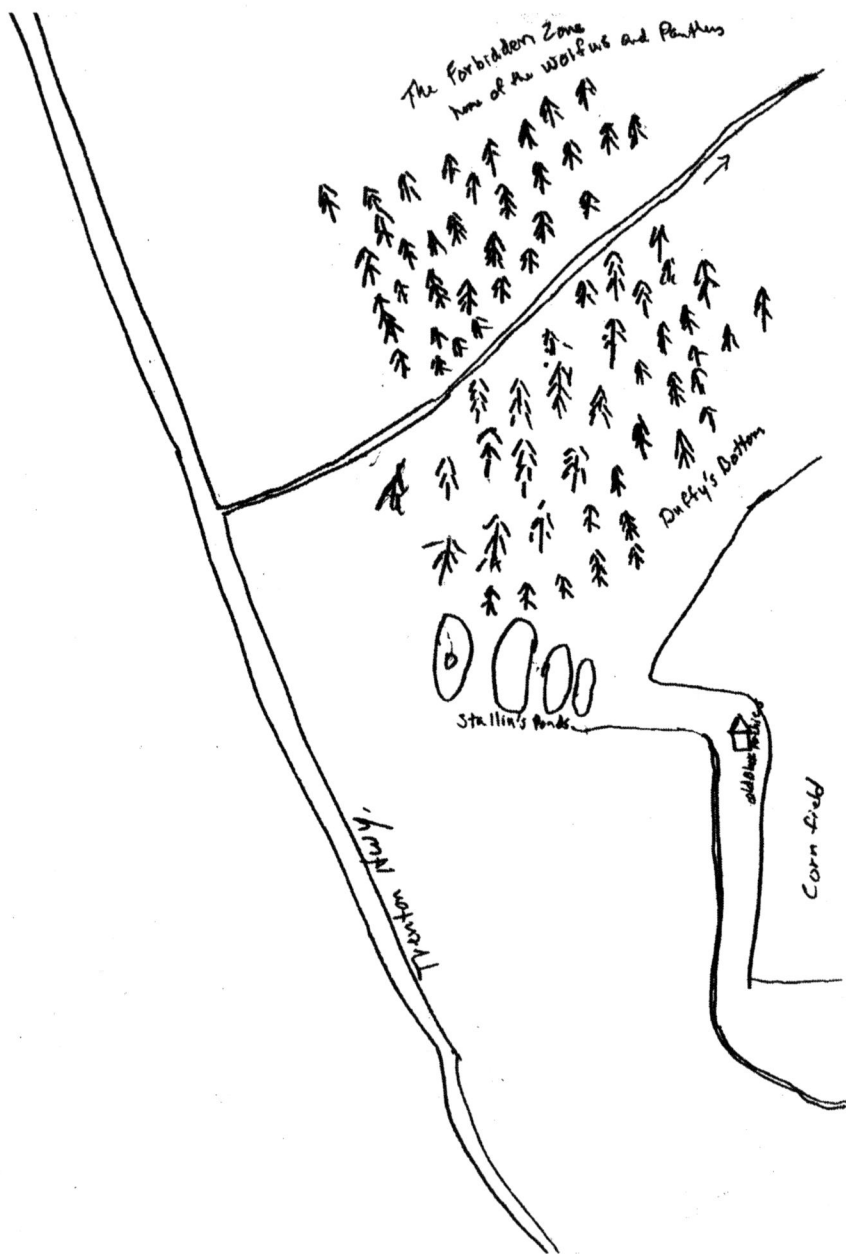

The Forbidden Zone
home of the Wolfius and Panthus

Duffy's Bottom

Stallin's Ponds

old school house

Corn field

Thatcher Hwy.

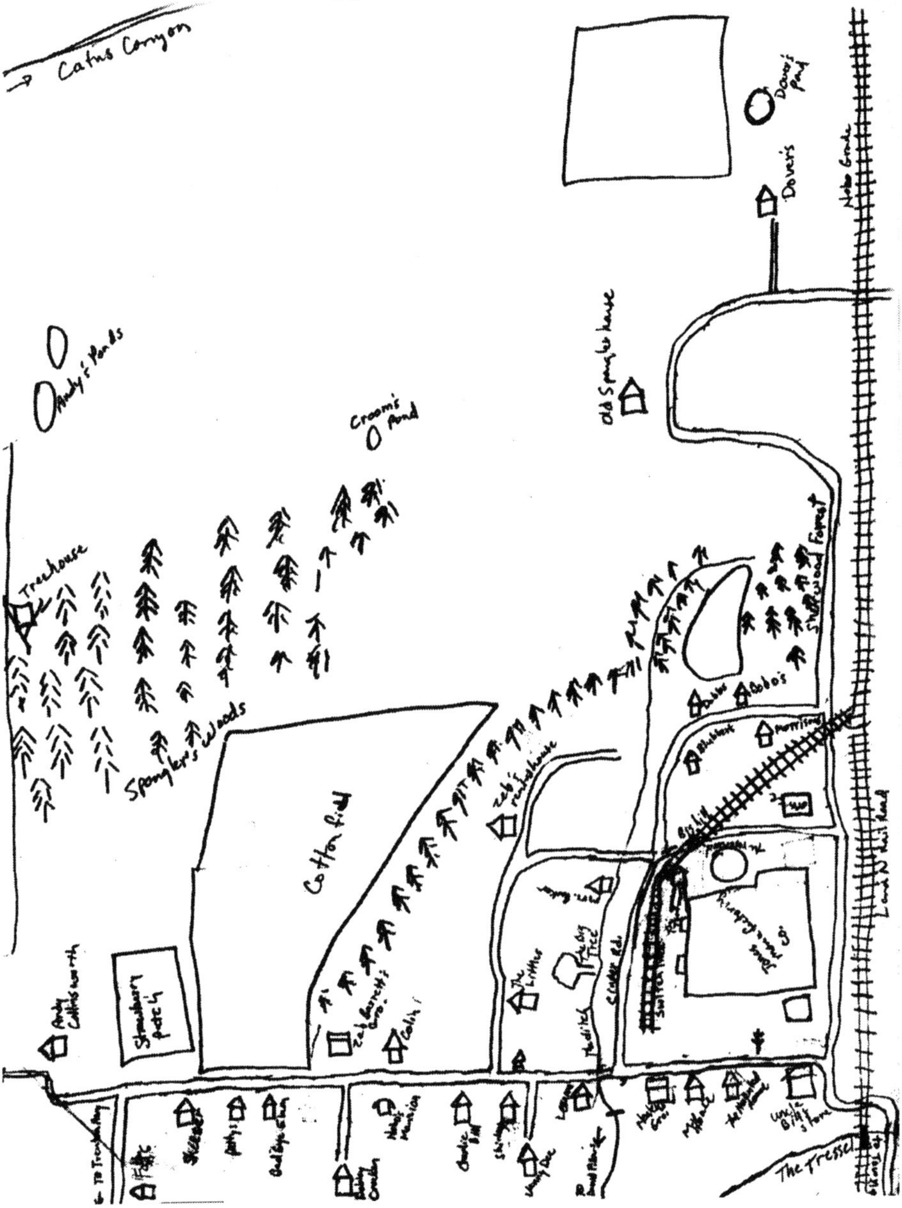

Catus Canyon
Dover's Pond
Dover's
Old Spangler house
Andy's Ponds
Croom's Pond
Treehouse
Spangler's Woods
Cotton field
Strawberry patch
Andy Collinsworth
Zeb Barrett's Barn
Bobo's
The Tressel
Uncle Bill's Store

The following characters, stories, and events are my recollections of the way it was while growing up at the Cotton Mill. Some of the characters may remember the events slightly differently than I, but most are vivid in my mind even after fifty years.

Contents

Introduction   9

I.   What's in a Name   14

II. The Chores   22

III. Summer Games   35

IV. Winter Games   93

V.   Acting Lessons   116

VI. The Cotton Mill Animals   136

VII. The Construction Projects   168

VIII. The Conveniences   186

IX. Sex Education Class   212

X.   Church   222

XI. The Thriving Metropolis   230

XII. Dares, Double Dares, and Double Dog Dares   244

XIII. The Nights   258

Epilogue   276

Chapter I: What's In A Name

The Cotton Mill was what most people in Humboldt called our neighborhood. To some it was used in a derogatory way, that is by those on the proverbial other side of the tracks. Our neighborhood was literally divided from the Humboldt city limits by the L&N Railroad tracks and we happened to be on the wrong side of the tracks.

I suppose that most of us who lived in the Cotton Mill neighborhood would be considered by today's standard to be below the poverty level, but we never knew it. As a matter of fact, we all thought we were pretty well off. After all we could always come up with enough money to buy whatever kind of ball that was in season, or go to the Saturday matinee, or finance most of the hair-brained schemes we came up with. In the spring there was always strawberry picking as a source of income. In the fall there was money to be made picking cotton and when we needed money at other times there was selling scrap iron and getting the deposit on drink bottles as a means of income.

The Cotton Mill, a textile mill that was established in the early 1900's, got its name from the factory that was the center of the neighborhood. Like many plants of its time, a mill village grew up around it. Most workers lived within a short walking distance of the mill. The original plant had shut down during the depression, but shortly after the war the Jones brothers, Ted Sr. and Ralph Sr., bought the plant and began to make mop yarn from waste cotton. It was an economic boom for the Cotton Mill. Many of the men and women in the neighborhood went to work for Jones Manufacturing

Company. My dad was already working for the Jones' in their downtown plant. He had started with them when he was 16 years old. With only an eighth grade education he advanced from his beginning job as a ball winder operator to plant superintendent before he retired.

The cotton mill employment provided many people in the neighborhood with economic stability, but for the Cotton Mill Boys it provided a playground like no other. There was a baseball field built by Ralph Jones Jr. This field became a football field in the fall. There was a basketball goal, a bit muddy when it rained, but that made it all the more fun. On rainy weekends when the mill was shut down, there was a whole warehouse full of mountains of stacked cotton bales to climb and play on. There were push carts in which to race. There were drink machines, if we could come up with a nickel. Oh yeah! There were even indoor toilets. There also was a vat that was used to dye cotton that made a pretty good swimming pool if you could catch it with clear water.

Outside the switch tracks were boxcars readily available for playing cowboys or army. Yes, we had it all and what made it even more fun was the fact that to use this playground we had to slip around and not get caught. If any one of our parents knew we were playing in the mill, it would have meant the belt or switch for sure. We kept our secrets from our parents well, and our exploits were only discovered a few times.

The Cotton Mill Boys owe a lot to the Jones'. Their benevolence provided a great place to grow up. The baseball field even had a backstop and a home run fence. Even the old Elm tree in deep center field provided shade from the July sun. It also was a favorite climbing tree for most of us. That is also where I got bit by Bobo's dog, but that's a later story.

There were other points of interest in the neighborhood. Uncle Bill's Store was located right next to the railroad tracks on Avondale Street. Uncle Bill didn't have any nephews that I know of, but everyone called him Uncle Bill. Cars from town could frequently be seen at Uncle Bill's. Mama said they were there to buy something called home brew. I wasn't sure what it was, but I thought it must be something like Coal Oil because I had seen men coming out with a jug!

1948 Tennessee 1949
SCHOOL DAYS

Colin had three sisters (besides Virginia Nell), Imogene, Pat, and Kay. Like me he was suprised with a younger sister when he was in Junior High School.

Zeb Barrett had a rival establishment up the hill. Zeb had a ranch style house next to the grocery store. He and his wife, Velma, had a son who was one of the Cotton Mill Boys. Colin Barrett was my age. He had an older sister, Virginia Nell.

She was the love of my life from the time I was six until I was ten. So what if she was five or six years older than I. She was my girlfriend and she played along. Then one day I saw her sitting on the porch with her real boyfriend.

Colin had three other sisters, Imogene, Pat, and Kay. Like me, he was surprised with a younger sister when he was in Junior High School. Zeb had more local customers than Uncle Bill. Mama would always send me up the hill to Barrett's Grocery to get bread or flour or meal and even an occasional Baby Ruth candy bar. Most of the time it would be a three-cent Baby Ruth, but sometimes when she was feeling generous she would let me get a nickel one. These were the businesses until Henley's Grocery was established in 1954, which was owned by my family and operated by my mom.

Another attraction at the Cotton Mill was the "big tree." The big tree was a huge red oak that grew on the bank of the ditch. It had a large metal cable tied around a limb high in the tree. The tree had long since grown around the cable. No one seemed to know when or how the cable got in the tree. Mama said she thought some CCC boys did it. This was the Civilian Conservation Corps established by Franklin Roosevelt to provide jobs for youth in the nineteen thirties. Regardless of how it got there, it made a great swing and provided transportation for countless "Tarzans."

The road across the ditch from the big tree was another landmark. It was black in color and had a very fine texture to it. It had been the recipient of cinders from the furnaces of both the mill and the steam locomotives that switched boxcars on the track at that point. The texture felt good to bare feet, and it also made an excellent surface for marble games. Most marble games took place on this road, either under the shade of the big tree or at the foot of the big hill.

The ditch was another well-known gathering place. It began behind Bobo Butler's house and went all the way to the

Forked Deer River. Bobo lived on the cinder road behind the mill. Bobo was legendary for his marble-shooting and bow-making. He and Skeezer were about the same age. Bobo had a brother my age, his name was Pee Wee. They had an older brother, Thomas, and two sisters, Becky and Titter. I think Titter was a mispronunciation of sister that stuck. Bobo's father was Claude and his mother was Doney. Bobo was a leader of the Cotton Mill Boys.

Bobo had a brother my age, his name was Pee Wee(above).

The ditch meandered through the neighborhood and came between our house and Leenova Hunt's house. Leenova was one of my earliest friends. He had a sister, Wonder and a little brother, Hilliard. Their parents were Cecil and Girtie.

Their outhouse was so close to the ditch that during high water it almost washed away. The ditch was a place to explore and even fish, but crawfish catching was one of our favorite sports in the ditch. We would take a five-gallon bucket and knock the bottom out. When a crawfish was spotted we would place the bucket over the "crawdad" and trap him. Then it was merely a matter of reaching in and grabbing the critter without getting pinched by his claws.

The tank was probably the most dangerous place, except maybe the reservoir. The tank was the water tank for the mill. I'm not sure how tall it was, but it seemed you could see clouds hanging around the ball on top. The tank was the subject of a lot of dares and double dares. A boy could become a man by climbing the tank. Legend has it that Zeb Barrett climbed to the top and locked his legs around the ball and played the guitar. I didn't see it, but I believe it happened. The tank became the gage for how strong your bow or BB gun was. If your BB gun could ring the tank (that is you could hear the 'plink' of the BB on the metal tank) from the big tree, you had a strong BB gun. If your bow could shoot a Golden Rod arrow over the tank, you had a great bow. Bobo Butler is the only one I ever saw do it.

I mentioned the reservoir. Like the tank it was the subject of dares and double dares. It was probably twenty-feet deep. At one time it was the water supply for the mill, but when the tank was built it became a fishpond. The water inside the reservoir was about five-feet deep and there was an island in the middle. There was an access to the island if one was brave enough to climb down a ladder and walk a board from the ladder to the island. Of course if you fell in you would be devoured by an alligator that supposedly lived in there. Mama said it was put there by the CCC boys in the thirties. I never saw it, but I did see a snake or two in there. The fishing was good enough that it was worth the risk of falling in and being devoured by an alligator or bitten by a snake, but I had to keep my pole hidden in the crawl space of the mill because Mama had made the reservoir off-limits to me.

Mama knew a lot about the history of the Cotton Mill. She lived there all her life. It was there she met my Daddy, James Herbert Henley, and married him. She was Maggie Alene Maitland before she married. I was one of the original Cotton Mill Boys. My sister, Gail, was four years younger than I. I had a surprise in the seventh grade when mother presented me with another sister. I must say I believe she and Daddy were even more surprised than I.

We had one other member of the family, my maternal grandmother, Little Mama. I adored her. Her mother was a full-blooded Cherokee and her features, as well as my mother's, reflected the Cherokee genes that had been passed on. It was probably her influence that had me yanking out the tail feathers of the chickens and putting them in a headband.

I was also fortunate that my paternal grandmother lived at the Cotton Mill. Daddy was the oldest of her children, then there was Roy, Joyce, Bo Jack, Doodler, and Skeezer. Mamaw Hallie, Doodler and Skeezer were the only ones still at home. My grandfather died before I was born. Mamaw did have an elderly man who boarded with her. Everyone called him Uncle Whit. He really was my great uncle on the Maitland side.

The railroad and the railroad trestle had a prominent place in our lives. The railroad was the shortest route to town or to school. We walked it almost daily. No doubt any one of the Cotton Mill Boys could have been a great gymnast on the balance beam. Most of us at one time or another had walked a single rail more than a mile to 14th Avenue without once loosing our balance and falling off. The railroad was not only the shortest route to town, it also served many other worthwhile functions. In early June we would head out up the railroad with a two-gallon water bucket. The prize we sought were the dewberries that grew along the sides of the railroad. In winter we would head up the same direction with our single-barrel 410 shotguns and every sooner in the neighborhood. Sooners were dogs that had sooner be one breed as the other. We were in pursuit of cotton-tail rabbits. We also used the rails and the train as a metal press. Ten-penny nails were easily flattened into arrowheads for our homemade arrows. It was also a good way to flatten a penny into a coin the size of a half-dollar, however we never found a use for them.

The trestle, which was the railroad bridge across the creek, was a benign place in the daylight, but in pitch black dark it became the haunt of ghost, monsters, and just plain old bad men. I can't remember anyone who would walk across the trestle at night by himself. We believed in safety in numbers so we always had at least one other person with us when we crossed it. The railway was also the main means of transportation for the hobos who frequently visited the neighborhood.

Chapter II: The Chores

All of the Cotton Mill Boys had certain chores. Some were the run of the mill kind, like mowing the yard. Most of the houses had little grass in the yards because of the constant traffic on the grass. There were bare spots where the girls played house and baked mud pies. There were bare spots where the boys dribbled a basketball until the earth was so compacted nothing could grow. There were bare spots in the front of the dog house where the dog was chained and ran back and forth barking at strangers or other dogs that passed by. All the traffic left little grass to be mowed.

The mowing of the grass was done with a push mower. The means of propulsion was the person pushing the mower. The reel type blades were turned by muscle power. There were no such things as riding mowers, at least not in the Cotton Mill area. Heck! There weren't even any gasoline powered mowers in the neighborhood until Daddy made one. I don't know if he saw one somewhere to go by or if he invented it, but it worked. An old motor off something and a series of pulleys and belts turned the blades he had made out of scrap metal. The handle looked like it came off an old push mower and the wheels probably came off an old buggy used to push cotton yarn around in the mill. I was the envy of the neighborhood for a while, then one day it quit running and I was back to push mowing again.

Besides mowing, there were some indoor chores, but the "he-men" of the Cotton Mill Boys would never be caught dead doing some of them. One was washing dishes. That was girls work. We wouldn't admit it but none of us would refuse when our mama said, "Wash the Dishes." I had one chore that I kept a deep dark secret. It was my job to carry out Little Mama's "slop jar." The slop jar was a potty-shaped bucket that set beside her bed and was used as a portable toilet. She was not physically able to go to the outdoor toilet so she used the slop jar and I carried it out each and every day and dumped it in the two-seater. That was my most dreaded chore.

Now that I think about it, there were some other chores I didn't much enjoy. In the winter we heated with an old Warm Morning coal stove. Someone had to keep enough coal and kindling wood by the stove to keep it going all night and fire it up high in the morning. Keeping the stove supplied with fuel became another of my daily chores in the winter. I didn't mind taking the hatchet and splitting kindling wood, but I did hate to climb the coal pile and handle the sooty stuff. Most of all I hated the precious daylight that I burned finishing the chore. It would rob me of at least thirty minutes of valuable hunting or playing time.

I was luckier than some of the other boys in the neighborhood. Some were still burning wood for heating and cooking. They not only had to gather in wood for the fire, but they also had to cut and split it. There were no such things as chainsaws at the Cotton Mill. All wood was cut with an ax and a crosscut saw. Anytime trees were cut, there was competition for the tree tops for wood. Anyone who had a tree that was sickly could bet someone would volunteer to cut it down and haul it off.

I competed for the broken bobbins that were scraped by the mill. They made excellent kindling. They were oil soaked and were just the right size to fit in the stove. They were easy to light with the oil on them and burned hot. This helped ignite the coal which I would lay on top of them. I checked the scrap pile often and hauled all I could get to my kindling pile.

The scarcity of wood made it quite valuable and that led to wood thieving. There was a certain man who had a good wood pile built up after some of the trees were cut at Spangler's woods. It was already January and he was still three or four cords to the good.

He noticed that his wood was disappearing faster than he was using it and expected foul play. One morning, after a snow, there were footprints around the wood pile made during the night. That cinched it. He had a firewood thief and he was going to get him if it was the last thing he ever did.

That night he sat at the window with a shot gun. He stayed up until one o'clock in the morning and no one showed up, so he went to bed. The next morning he checked his wood pile and sure enough, about a dozen sticks of wood were missing. He thought about staying up all night the next night, but it was just too hard to stay up and then go to work at 7:00 a.m.

Then he got an idea, which I later learned about from Skeezer. The man told Mamaw Hallie he was going to get the wood thief. He had a great plan, if a little explosive.

He took a piece of fire wood and, with his wood auger, he drilled a one inch hole from one end, almost to the other. The hole was then filled with gun powder. There must have been a thousand grains of powder in the piece of firewood. He then plugged the open end of the log with a cork and cut it off even with the log. The next morning several sticks of firewood were missing along with the powerful log that was on top of the pile.

It was close to noon that day when the whole neighborhood discovered who had been stealing wood. There was a loud explosion at the man's next door neighbor's house. People came running out of their houses to see what the terrible explosion was. Some thought the boiler at the mill had blown up. Others were just sure we were being bombed by the Russians.

The man who had set the trap was home for lunch and went running next door. As he entered the house, smoke was everywhere. He was afraid that his vengeance had hurt someone. He saw both his neighbors standing in the kitchen with clothes blackened by soot, but unhurt by the explosion.

The flue was blown off the wood cook stove and the oven door was blown open, but there was no fire. Evidently the explosion had extinguished the fire. The man felt bad about blowing up the stove so he never mentioned the stolen fire wood. Word got around the neighborhood about what really happened and most people said they got what they deserved. It was understood in the mill neighborhood that you had to work for what you got.

One chore that I could accomplish with the speed of the man of steel himself was collecting eggs from the hen house. The nests were in ten little boxes in a row. I could start at one end and run to the other, reaching in each box without breaking stride. Most of the time there would be an egg in each box. Occasionally an old hen would still be on the nest and I would reach under her and grab her egg. Sometimes when a hen became stubborn and refused to contribute to breakfast, Mama would put an old porcelain door knob in the nest. This tricked the hen into thinking she had an egg in the nest so she would lay another one to go with it.

Now even gathering eggs had its risks. There were two things you had to look out for. One was the ill tempered "setting hen". The setting hen was one who had decided to set on her eggs until they hatched. If she was determined to set, you had better not disturb her. She would jump all over you, flogging you with her wings and scratching you with her feet.

Another danger of egg gathering was the dominant rooster. He too was very skilled at flogging, but he had another weapon, the dreaded spur, and he knew how to use it. He had whipped all the other roosters in the chicken yard so he had no qualms about attacking a three-and -a-half-foot boy.

I am not sure which kind of attack caused Charlie Bill's phobia about chickens, but they were his Achilles' Heel. Charlie Bill and I were third or forth cousins on the Maitland side of the family, but we were more like brothers. His Father, Louis, was a Maitland and his mother, Opal, was a Little. He was a chunk of a boy who could whip most every kid in the neighborhood, but he and chickens did not mix. Now when a Cotton Mill Boy showed a weakness, others would surely exploit it. We tormented Charlie Bill with chickens.

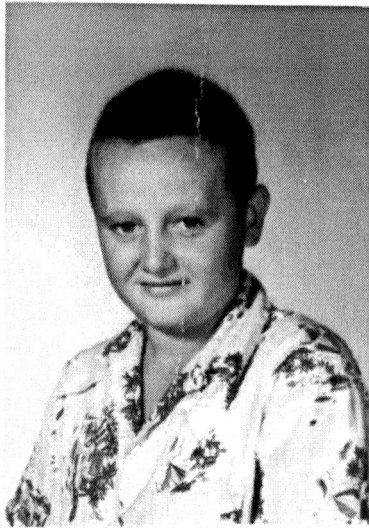

SCHOOL DAYS 1951-52
HUMBOLDT ELEM.

Charlie Bill was a chunk of a boy who could whip most every kid in the neighborhood, but he and chickens didn't mix.

26

Skeezer had an old rooster that would attack anyone and anything. It whipped most of the dogs in the neighborhood, even the brave and noble Snowball. Skeezer had a basketball goal at his house and one day we were all there playing basketball. It was hot and we took a break by drinking dippers of water from the water bucket on the back porch. He then suggested that we go in the chicken pen and get some plums off the plum tree. At first Charlie Bill balked, but his love of eating out-weighted his fear of chickens. We entered the pen and started around the hen house, then everyone made a mad dash for the gate leaving Charlie Bill in the pen. Skeezer slammed the gate to and locked it. Charlie Bill begged, but we wouldn't let him out. Then out of the hen house came the dreaded monster, Big Red, the Rhode Island rooster. He stood on his tip-toes and looked four feet tall. His feathers fluffed out around his neck in anger. His beady eyes focused on the creature that dared to enter his kingdom. Charlie Bill pushed frantically at the gate and cried and begged louder as Big Red approached to launch his attack with flapping wings and slashing spurs.

Just when he was in striking distance, Skeezer opened the gate and Charlie Bill fell to safety on the other side. Charlie Bill might have been safe but we certainly weren't. Leenova and I took off running for our lives. We knew we were dead men if Charlie Bill ever caught us. Even Skeezer, who was four years older than Charlie Bill, ran for his life. He was like a mad rampaging bull as he charged toward us. I am not sure, but I may have even seen some smoke coming out of his nostrils. Fortunately for us Charlie Bill's extra weight slowed him down enough that he couldn't catch us and after a day or two he cooled off.

There were other chores associated with the chickens. They had to be fed, but most of the time Mama did that and later when Gail was old enough, she fed them. Like David the shepherd in the Bible, we often had to defend our flock from the wild beast that prowled the neighborhood. We kept an eye on the sky for the dreaded Chicken Hawk. He had a reputation for swooping down and taking a young chick or even a grown hen, but of course he was no match for Big Red.

When we saw the villain soaring on the breeze near the chicken pen it was an exciting event. We would run in the house and get daddy to bring his gun and shoot the evil thing. Later as we got older we could run in and grab our own shotgun and shoot the varmint and be a hero.

There were other chores associated with the chickens. They had to be fed, but most of the time Mama did that and later when Gail was old enough, she fed them.

Next to the hawk, the worst varmint was the sneaky old chicken snake. He was renown for his ability to slip into a hen's nest and devour the eggs. He then would wrap around a post and break the eggs in his belly. The chicken snake, if spotted, received the wrath of Mama. In fact, any snake, good or bad that Mama saw received her wrath. Her wrath was dished out in the form of her garden hoe that was razor sharp to dispatch snakes and Johnson Grass with one chop. Mama believed the Bible and when God told the serpent that man would crush his head, she took it as a personal call to arms.

There were a few other wild beast that attacked our flock, but they were only a pest once in a coon's age. Speaking of coons, we did have one that tried to steal a chicken now and then, but Snowball kept him and the 'possum, and even an occasional fox, run off. No wild beast would dare to stand up against Snowball, the half Spitz and half, uh, half something else.

There was one other danger to the chickens, but it didn't come from a wild beast. The greatest threat to our chickens came from the mysterious neighborhood chicken thief. He always struck at night. He carried two burlap gunny sacks, wore a dark coat and hat, and may have even worn a mask much like the Lone Ranger's mask. There were sightings all over the neighborhood. Since almost everyone had chickens, I guess the chicken thief wanted to spread his business around. The mystery man could become invisible if cornered. Buckshot didn't phase him. He was able to leap tall fences in a single bound. Why if I hadn't read my comic books and knew Superman was a good guy, I might have thought the chicken thief was Superman.

There was a lot of speculation and talk on the bench in front of Zeb Barrett's store after each raid on someone's chicken house. Some believed it was being done by hobo's who were camping out under the trestle. Others believed it was someone right in the neighborhood. There was one guy in particular who kept to himself. No one knew much about him and he became a prime suspect. As far as I know no one ever called the law. The Humboldt police wouldn't come because it was out of the city limits and the Gibson County sheriff was in Trenton, some twelve miles away. Therefore the neighbors formed their own vigilante group, determined to catch the thief. This mystery also became a top priority with us. We put our detective skills to the test. Dick Tracy would have been proud of us.

After a crime we would go to the scene and look for clues. We would look for footprints in the mud, articles that might have been dropped by the perpetrator or other clues. At one site we found an empty Prince Albert tobacco can. If only we had a Dick Tracy finger print kit, we could have solved the mystery right then. At another site, we found a burlap sack with some feathers in it. We concluded that when we found a man that smoked Prince Albert tobacco and carried a burlap gunny sack, we had our man.

The chicken thief was having great success in spite of our detective work and the neighborhood vigilantes. But like all criminals he was about to meet his match, proving that crime doesn't pay. His fatal mistake came when he chose Mamaw Halley's chickens as his next victims. Mamaw was awakened by a great commotion in the chicken pen. She immediately awoke Skeezer and Uncle Whit. Uncle Whit grabbed his old double-barreled Stevens shot gun and dropped a couple of twelve gauge, number six's in the chamber. As they rushed to the back door a blood curdling scream came from the chicken house. In the moonlight was the figure of a man frantically fighting for his life. As he stumbled around, stepping in the watering pan and falling to the chicken manure covered ground, something was flailing away at him. It was on his face, in his hair and on his chest flogging and spurring away. Big Red had caught the chicken thief. The only thing that kept Uncle

Whit from letting him have it with both barrels was his fear of hitting Big Red. The thief finally struggled to his feet and managed to flip over the fence and disappear into the darkness. Big Red fluffed up his feathers, shook off the dust and marched right back to his perch in the hen house.

That was the last raid of the chicken thief. No one ever knew for sure who the mystery man was, but for about two weeks a certain neighbor was not seen by anyone. When he finally did make a public appearance, he looked like he had been dragged through a briar patch by a mule. I'm not saying he was the thief, but a lot of those scars looked like they could have been made by Big Red's spurs.

Another disgusting chore that I had was collecting slop from the neighbors. Slop was anything that the neighbors had left over, from table scraps to dirty dish water. Neighbors who didn't have a pig to feed, would put their scraps in a bucket on the back porch. I would ride my bike around the neighborhood and empty their buckets into a five gallon bucket I had hanging on my handle bars. Once I made my rounds I would take the big bucket and dump it in the pig trough in the chicken pen. The chicken pen was also the home of a Durock pig. He loved the slop and would come running when I rode up on my bike.

Bringing slop to our four legged garbage disposal brought me in contact with the only mad dog I have ever seen. I had heard numerous stories about mad dogs terrorizing the neighborhood years before I was born. Little Mama even told of a man who had been bitten by a mad dog and went mad and attacked some people until they threw a bucket of water on him. A mad dog had hydrophobia or rabies, as it is known today. If a person was bitten by a mad dog, the only cure was a series of shots with a long needle that was stuck in the person's stomach. By all accounts, it was one of the most feared diseases in existence. Dogs that were mad were characterized by foaming at the mouth, staggering, and being fearful of water.

There was a dog that roamed the neighborhood, living at first one house and then another. We named him King. He had a huge knot on his head that gave the appearance of a crown, therefore he was named King. He seemed gentle enough, however everyone avoided petting him on the knot on his head. It might be catching. One day he went mad. I was coming back from my rounds with five gallons of top grade slop when King charged at me from the side ditch. He was snarling with his teeth showing as slobber poured out of his jaws. He had a look in his eye that was like nothing I had ever seen. He made Cujo look like a Chihuahua. As fear set in, the adrenaline reached my legs. They moved so fast Lance Armstrong wouldn't have had a chance with me. I screamed "mad dog" at the top of my lungs. People came onto their porches to cheer me on in my race with death. As I raced down the big hill with King on my heels, I passed Miss Mary's. I think I heard her say "Lord help him" as I sped by. I know between screams of "mad dog" I was thinking Lord help me.

As I crossed the bridge in front of Leenova's house, Girdie was on the porch with her apron pulled over her face in fear. I looked on down the road to my house wondering how I could jump off my bike and beat King to the door. Even if I did beat him inside, he probably would come right through the screen door. Then I saw my salvation. There was Dad running out to the road with his old twelve gauge, J. C. Higgins pump. As I got even with him I heard a blast and then another. When I came to a stop and looked back, King was lying dead ten yards behind me. I felt a little sad for King, but the sadness soon went away as the neighbors started to gather to congratulate my dad, the hero who killed the mad dog of the Cotton Mill. Oh! Did I mention? I didn't spill a drop of slop in the whole ordeal.

King was the only mad dog I ever saw, but I did have a

close encounter of another kind with mad dogs. I was climbing the old Elm tree in deep centerfield one day. Sleeping lazily under the lowest branch was Bozo. Bozo was Bobo's dog. I wouldn't even attempt to assign him a blood line, but he was a good old dog. While descending from the tree I fell on the sleeping Bozo. The poor frightened dog reacted by snapping at the object that fell on him. I received a rather nasty gash on my thigh. I ran home to tell Mama. Her first words were "Lordy mercy, you'll go mad." Those words stuck with me for nine days as I was sure I would go mad or have to take shots from a foot long needle in the stomach. Nine days were significant. If Bozo didn't show any sign of going mad for nine days, I would be okay, but if he began to stagger, slobber, or avoid water, it was to Dr. Barker's and stomach shots for me.

I made it through the eighth day and everything was looking good but that night turned into a nightmare, literally. Some time in the early morning hours Mama awoke to see her darling son standing over her with his teeth bared, snarling and growling, with his fingers curled like claws. He was poised to strike. Mama nearly broke Daddy's ribs as she jabbed him violently with her bony elbow. She screamed, "Lord God Herbert, wake up, he's gone mad!" Dad was startled and half awake when I leaped over Mama and onto his chest. He was no weakling, but not wanting to hurt me, he was holding me by my arms, trying not to get bitten by his boy who had gone mad. After a struggle, I broke free and ran into the kitchen. After an extended chase around the table, they finally caught me and I woke up.

I came to myself not knowing how I had gotten in the kitchen, or why Mama and Daddy were up. Mama later told me the details of what happened. They felt of my forehead and I was burning up with fever. "Run call Dr. Barker!" Mama ordered Daddy. It was four a.m. but Dr. Barker came as he always did when he got a call from the Cotton Mill neighborhood. He was everyone's favorite doctor, but I sure was dreading that needle in my stomach.

When Dr. Barker arrived in his brand new 1952 Ford, he got out and hurried inside. (By coincidence, Dad later bought that car in 1956. It still had the smell of medications in it.) Dr. Barker stuck a pop sickle stick in my mouth and said, "Say ah . . ." He then took my temperature. "One hundred and two," he announced. He then pulled up my pajama shirt and stuck his cold stethoscope to my back. He looked at my back, my arms, and even had me pull down by bottoms and looked at my behind. He looked at my worried Mama and smiled, "Measles, just measles." Evidently the fever had me out of my head and all the talk of going mad had my subconscious mind in a turmoil, which led to my nightmare. Only measles! Neither Bozo nor I would go mad.

There were other minor chores that got in the way of a good game of football or baseball and even saved the life of a rabbit or squirrel or two, but there was still time for the Cotton Mill Boys to continue their informal education.

Chapter III: Summer Games

As soon as school let out in May it was "let the games begin." There was always some kind of activity in which to be involved. One of the summer sports that gained participation from neighbors of all ages was marbles. Marbles had a language of its own. Terms like "knucks down" and "no fudging" merely meant you couldn't raise your hand off the ground and use a forward motion when shooting your "big toy." Now the big toy was the marble, usually larger than the marbles in the "buck," that was used to strike the marbles in the buck to knock them out. Everyone knows that the buck is the square or circle drawn in the dirt that contained the players "dates." Of course dates were the required number of marbles each player had to put in the buck to play. Sometimes the dates were as few as two or as many as twenty-five. Marbles sold at the game sight for five for a penny, so if the dates were five, one could get in the game by sticking up a penny in the dirt inside the buck. The penny was a prize when you knocked it out of the buck, or if you knocked out the last marble in the buck you got any coins that had been inserted into the game.

There were basically two types of marble games. The most popular was "fats." Fats was played in a square buck and there was a "lag line" drawn in the dirt to see in what order each participant would shoot. The game started with each player standing at the buck lagging. The lag line was about twelve feet away and the person's marble that went closest to the line went first and so on. The first shot at the buck came from the lag line and from there the shot was taken from wherever the big toy stopped after each shot. The one place you didn't want to end up was in the buck. In fats, if you went "fat," that is in the buck, you were out of the game. The object was to hit the marbles in the buck, but bounce your big toy outside of the buck. The shooter got to shoot as long as he knocked out at least one marble each shot. The shooter got to keep all he knocked out, that is unless all had agreed to play for funzies, which was rare.

The other marble game was "bull's eye." It was played in a large circular buck about eight feet in diameter. The lag line was the far side of the circle and the person whose marble rolled closest to the line shot first. The first shot was from outside the circle, but after that you could "go fat" or "lay up" in the circle. The object was to knock the marbles in the buck outside the circle, while keeping your big toy in the circle. The shooter got to keep all that he knocked out. There was a danger to the shooter if he got near another player's big toy. When it was that player's turn, he could kill your toy if he knocked it out of the buck.

There were a variety of big toys and marbles. Some big toys were stoneys, bright red and tough. About the only thing that would break a stoney was a steely. Now a steely was a metal ball bearing. In most games they were banned because they broke too many marbles and big toys. Most of the marbles were glass, but some peewee's were made of what appeared to be hardened clay.

Marbles were a passion with all the Cotton Mill Boys. I don't think the town boys really had the fire for marbles that we had. Some did bring their marbles to school to play on the playground, but they were easy pickings for the Cotton Mill Boys. We played almost every day, but on Saturday and Sunday the games drew huge crowds. Sometimes there would be as many as three or four games going on at the same time with ten to fifteen spectators watching the games.

On Saturday and Sunday afternoon the boys weren't the only ones playing. Uncle Whit probably was the oldest participant. Zeb Barrett often played with us and Bobby Crocker and other high school boys participated at times. Bobby was almost grown, but he still played marbles and occasionally helped us in a construction project. He lived with his sister, Nellie, his grandmother, Miss Posey, and his mother, Sister Barrett. They had an elderly man, Carl Scott, who lived with them as a boarder.

Uncle Whit only carried his big toy. He always put his dates in the buck in the form of a penny or nickel. These coins were the objective for most everyone's big toy, but Bobo Butler usually wound up with the coins and most of the marbles. He had five cigar boxes full of marbles at his house and that was just his reserve. He had several Bull Durham sacks that were his "tote'n around marbles." He sold a lot of marbles, five for a penny or twenty-five for a nickel. He always had money during marble shooting time.

Occasionally an argument would break out during a game of marbles, but we learned to give and take and get along with one another. Usually one of the older boys would step in and give each boy an honorable way out of the situation and the games would resume. We had no officials or umpires in any of our games. I believe that is where our lessons on how to get along with others were taught.

There was one incident that happened that caused a rule change in the marble games. Vanny Dee was another Maitland. He lived up the lane past Leenova's house. He had two sisters, Margaret and Sharon. His father was D. F. and his mother was Lillie. Vanny Dee was always pretty slick. One day he came down to the big tree and didn't have any marbles or money to play. No one would loan him any marbles to play with so he started to swing on the cable to pass the time. After gliding across the ditch a few times he walked over to the buck and asked to borrow five marbles for his dates. Still no one responded. He stood around a minute and walked across the buck then back to the swing. Again he walked across the buck and back. When that game was over and we were putting in our dates for the next game, Vanny Dee produced five marbles for his dates. From those five marbles he managed to win enough to stay in the game.

On the way home he told me his secret. He had holes in the bottom of his shoes and every time he walked through the buck, he would step on a marble and roll it into the hole in his shoe. I don't know how long he had been getting his dates by that method, but I knew it wasn't right. I spread the word and that caused the origin of the new rule; no stepping in the buck.

Swimming was another one of the summer sports. We didn't exactly have an olympic pool to swim in, but I'll bet Johnny Wiesmuller couldn't have done any better under the circumstances. Our favorite place was Stallin's pond. It was about a half-acre pond with one deep corner over our heads. Only a few of us could actually swim. Bobo of course was an excellent swimmer and so was Skeezer. They had taught me to swim in Dover's little pond. Vanny Dee was a fair swimmer but most of the rest would not venture out into the deep water.

There was actually a swimming pool in Humboldt. It was affectionately called "Plu's Slough." It was owned by Pluto Lanier and it became a more popular place when we reached our teens and realized girls were okay. Before I learned to swim, my cousin, Billy Wages, took me to Plu's Slough. My Aunt Ethel and Uncle Joe Wages moved next door to us after the Smith's moved. Ethel was my mother's sister. Billy was the oldest of four children. Shirley was about four years older than I and Corkey was one year older. They had a little brother, Johnny, who was a toddler. They only stayed for a couple of years. I think the haunted house got to them.

I enjoyed being with Billy, even though he did shoot my eye out with a BB gun. I was especially grateful he had taken me to the swimming pool. I was to stay in the shallow end while he talked to some girls on the deep end. There were two army surplus rubber rafts in the pool. I was up to my neck when I climbed onto the raft. Before I knew it we were headed for the deep end. The big kids on the raft were fighting like pirates boarding a Spanish Galleon. Somewhere in the fray I was knocked overboard. My toes searched for the concrete bottom, but there was no bottom. I swallowed a big gulp of water and tried to come up. I looked up and all I could see was the bottom of the raft. I was trapped and would surely drown. Just when I thought the end was near I felt a tug at my swim trunks. Suddenly I was hurled toward the top and precious air. It was Billy. He had seen me go off the raft and left his girl to come to my rescue. I coughed up some water but I was alright. I believe Billy was so sorry that he had shot my eye out with a BB gun that he felt he should somehow make it up to me. As far as I was concerned, the debt was squared the day he saved my life.

That incident made me a little fearful of the water, but Skeezer and Bobo were determined to help me overcome it and learn to swim. They took me to Dover's pond, which was about four feet deep and worked with me until I could swim. It was lucky for Vanny Dee that I did because I was able to save him. Well, maybe it was my fault that he almost drowned, but I did pull him out, sort of.

It was one of those August, West Tennessee days when it was ninety-eight in the shade. There were no air conditioners in the world, well at least in the Cotton Mill community. The only way to cool off was to take a dip in the eighty degree water of Stallin's pond. Charlie Bill, Leenova, Vanny Dee, David Pillow, and I decided to go swimming.

David Pillow was not a Cotton Mill Boy by residency, but he was an honorary member and just as much one of us as if he lived next door. Well, in a way he did. His father, Ezra's, farm was just across the ditch from our back yard. Their house was on the Trenton Highway, but we had a short-cut to it. There was a bridge behind my house that we had made out of two-by-tens, confiscated from the mill scrap pile. After crossing the ditch on the walk bridge, there was only a cotton field, a fence-row and a cornfield to cross to come out at the Pillow's barn. We had some good times playing in the barn on rainy days, well, all but one rainy day that I shall tell about later.

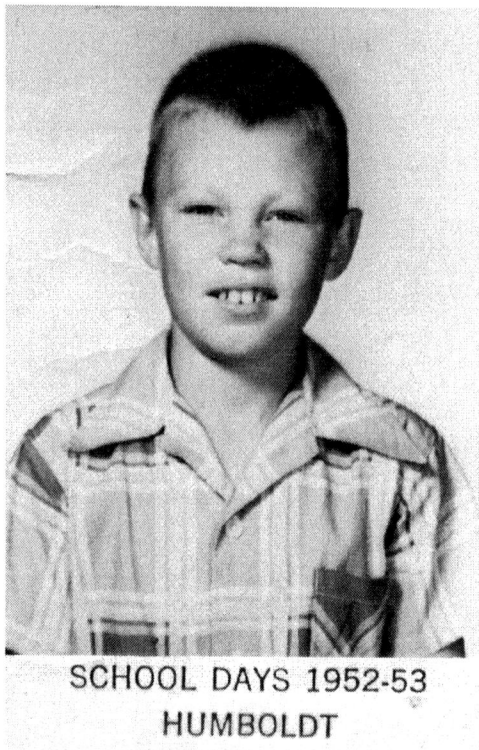

SCHOOL DAYS 1952-53
HUMBOLDT

David Pillow was not a Cotton Mill Boy by residency, but he was an honorary member and just as much one of us as if he lived next door.

40

David may not have lived right in the neighborhood but he was one of us. He couldn't swim and neither could Leenova or Charlie Bill, so that day only Vanny Dee and I could go to the deep end of Stallin's pond.

We were always watchful for snakes when we swam in the pond, but this year we were particularly vigil. This was due to a story that was told and retold that summer. The story related to an incident at Chickasaw State Park.

Supposedly a teenager had dived off the tower and when he came up he was covered with cotton mouth water moccasins. He had dived into a bed of mating snakes. We would prove our bravery by being the first to jump into the pond, but our cowardice showed when a crayfish or bream swam into our leg and we practically walked on water to get to the bank.

We arrived at the pond and surveyed the area for snakes. We then stripped down to our birthday suits and waded in. Vanny Dee and I were in the lead because we could swim. Compared to the warm air, the water felt cool, but it still was warm enough for a bath in the winter time.

In the deep end of the pond was an old wooden boat that was turned upside down. Only the bottom protruded out of the water. Charlie Bill wanted Vanny Dee and me to go get the boat and bring it over to them. We waded until the water was just under our noses and then we began to flail away at the water as we swam to the boat. When we reached the boat we both held on to it for a rest. I am not sure what happened next. I decided to crawl upon the boat that was kept afloat by a small air pocket underneath. As I got on the boat it began to sink. I looked around and didn't see Vanny Dee. I stood on the boat that was now about a foot under water. I strained to see into the muddy water. Suddenly Vanny Dee popped up spitting water and trying to say something, then he went under. He surfaced again with a look of terror on his face.

It was then that I knew he had gotten into a bed of mating cotton mouths. I was sure they were hanging all over him and pulling him down. What could I do? If I jumped in they would cover me too. He went under again and something Little Mama told me popped into my head. She always said if a person goes down for the third time, he is drowned. Vanny was down for the second time. When he surfaced this time I dived off the boat and headed toward him. By now he was in such a panic that when I reached him he grabbed my neck with a choke hold.

I couldn't breathe as we struggled in the six foot water. Finally I managed to slip out of the death grip and go under water. As my feet touched the muddy bottom I grabbed Vanny Dee's legs and pushed him toward shallow water. I repeated the process until we could both keep our heads above water. David, Charlie Bill, and Leenova watched the ordeal, unable to do anything to help until I got him to shallow water. They took him on to the bank and after a little coughing and spitting he was all right.

I kinda felt like a hero until Vanny Dee told me he was going under the boat to try to turn it over when I stepped up on it. The boat sank just enough to trap him under it. He managed to wiggle loose, but he had run out of air. So, maybe I wasn't a hero, but my friend was okay and all was well that ended well.

Fishing may have been our favorite summer sport. I started my angling career in the ditch between my house and Leenova's. A willow limb, a sewing thread line, and a safety pin hook was my first fishing tackle. It was no problem to dig earthworms for bait in the compost pile. That was a fancy name for the place all the decomposable garbage, that wasn't fed to the pig, was thrown. The decaying matter was added to the garden each year, but it made a great worm bed in the mean time.

Just down stream from the old wooden bridge was a hole that must have been five feet deep. We called it "the deep hole." Well, maybe it was only five feet deep when the ditch was swollen by rain and at the top of the bank, but it really was two or three feet deep. The deep hole was the home of some of the fightingest two inch green sunfish in existence. It would have even taken Bill Dance an hour to land one. My sewing thread line wasn't ten-pound-test, but I never had a fish to break my line at the deep hole but one time.

There were several fish attractors in the deep hole. There were a couple of broken bottles, and old cardboard box, assorted brick-bats and rocks, and an old lard stand that had a missing bottom. It was probably someone's old crawfish trap that had been thrown away.

The day the big one got away started like any other fishing trip. I caught four or five of the fighting sunfish and deposited them in my bucket. I had just put on a fresh worm and dropped the tasty morsel into the water. It slowly sank with a tantalizing wiggle. It had just disappeared in the murky water when the line began to move. I had not progressed to sophisticated tackle like bobbers and weights. With no bobber to warn me of the nibble on the worm, I waited. Suddenly the willow limb was nearly yanked out of my hand. There was a wake in the water like the Titanic had passed.

I held on, digging my heels in to keep from being dragged into the deep hole. Without warning the huge fish turned and headed for the old lard stand. When the line passed through the lard stand, it snapped. I don't know if I was pulling so hard that when the line broke I fell on my seat or if I just sat down in disgust. I just know I ended up on my backside.

I couldn't wait to tell everyone about the monster fish in the deep hole. The only problem I had was that there were no witnesses. Some of the Cotton Mill Boys were known for stretching the truth, but I knew what I had just experienced.

So I told and retold the fish tale. Some became believers, but others were skeptical.

There was much speculation about what kind of fish he was. Most everybody thought he must be a big old catfish. Charlie Bill said it was probably a grinnel. We never knew for sure, but after that day you had to elbow your way in to get a fishing spot at the deep hole.

Dad did a lot of trotline fishing in the Forked Deer River. Standing: L to R: Ham Henley, Bubbie Henley, Billy Wages. Front: Daddy and Blubber Henley with a stringer of catfish.

My dad was an avid fisherman and sometimes he would take me with him. He did a lot of trot-lining in the Forked Deer River. Well, on a part of the river. If you fished the Forked Deer, you had to go upstream from the Gasden Highway. The raw sewage from the city of Humboldt emptied into the river just north of the highway. Most people didn't like to fish below the sewage pipe. We did try it a time or two because we heard how fat the fish were below the pipe.

There were three or four factors that caused us to eliminate (no pun intended) the area below the pipe as a fishing ground. For one thing, it smelled very similar to the two-seater outhouse. Another problem was that Mama wouldn't let us bring the fish into the house if she knew we caught them below the pipe. There was an old man, Ben Ray, who would take all we caught, even if they came from below the pipe.

There were these objects that looked like a clear rubber balloon that floated down from the pipe. They would wash around your line and the current would wash your bait to the top, even when the line was weighted by a heavy sinker. Ben Ray told of cutting a fish open to gut it and it contained one of these balloons. I later learned what those balloons were in my sex education class.

We didn't fish below the sewage pipe much because there were just too many problems, but about three miles south of there, upstream, the South 17th bridge crossed the river. Fish that were caught out South 17th were okay to eat, so we concentrated our efforts on that stretch of the river.

It was on this stretch of the river that Daddy was bitten by a cotton mouth. The cotton mouth was considered to be one of the most deadly snakes in the world. In our arguments about which snake was the meanest, the cotton mouth usually came in second, right behind the cobra.

I spent most of the day that Friday wading around barefoot in the ditch. I carried my five gallon lard bucket and my tow-sack. My mission was to catch all the crayfish I could to bait the trot-lines that afternoon when Daddy got home. If I would catch him fifty crawfish, he would take me with him. I could even wade up the river with them to bait the lines. I worked tirelessly trapping and catching crawfish. My fingers were sore from encounters with the claw-endowed creatures, but I had fifty-four just for good measure.

When Dad got home we loaded the '48 Ford with trot-line boxes, a bait box (which made me beam proudly because I had contributed to the trip), and a stringer, just in case we caught some fish while we were baiting up.

We took off in a hurry so all the lines could be out and baited before dark. Across the railroad tracks, on 18th Street, he stopped to pick up Jimmy Ellis, a friend Dad worked with at Jones Manufacturing. Just around the curve on 19th Street, he stopped and picked up Billy Stanley. Billy was also an employee of the mill and a renowned bird hunter. As I got older he took me bird hunting several times, but this afternoon catfish were on everyone's mind.

When we headed out of town on South 17th, I knew it wouldn't be long before we crossed the river. As we passed over the old iron bridge, I could see the water lazily lapping at the trees that had fallen in the river. We turned left on a dirt road just past the bridge. The old Ford came to a stop and I hopped out. Billy Stanley crawled out on the other side. Daddy and Jimmy Ellis got out of the front and we all went to the trunk to get the gear.

One thing any good fisherman learns is to be careful not to scramble up the lines in the "jump box." The jump box was the box that was square and had little slots cut at one inch intervals all round the lip of the box. It had a bottom made of screen porch wire tacked on by roofing nails. Each "drop" on the line was slipped into the slots on the top and the hooks hung in perfect order around the sides of the box. The main line and the drop lines were neatly placed inside the box. All this preparation made it possible to put out a line quickly and easily, that is if it doesn't become tangled.

We had four jump boxes, a bait box and a stringer in the

trunk. I wanted to carry the stringer, that way if we caught any fish while baiting, I would get to carry them. I grabbed the stringer and started out of the trunk with it. I guess I was in too big of a hurry to claim the job of "stringer carrier". As the loop on the end of the stringer passed over the stack of jump-boxes one of the hooks on the top box just reached out and grabbed it. In my haste the box came out of the trunk and flipped over. Lines and hooks went everywhere. Now Daddy wasn't a "cussin' man", but I heard something like, "well she-it!" There wasn't time to re-box the line so we left it at the car.

Now Daddy wasn't a "cussin' man", but I heard something like, "well she-it!"

There was a short walk down the dusty road but it seemed far as the powdered dust burned at the bottom of my bare feet. It burned so badly I wanted to ask Daddy to carry me on his back, but I knew that wasn't a good idea, especially after I had dumped the jump-box. We finally reached the path to the water. The mud on the bank was a welcome relief to my barbequed feet. The water felt even better as we slid into the knee deep river.

Our destination was three or four deep holes upstream. When we came to the first hole, Daddy carefully took one end of the line out of the jump-box and tied it to a snag on the west bank. He then wadded upstream, carefully flipping hooks out of the box as he walked. He gradually angled across the river to the other side. The water on that bank was waist deep on him as he tied it to a tree.

Billy handed him his box and he continued to wade upstream in search of the next hole. Billy and I stayed behind to bait the line. I carried the bait bucket and Billy did the baiting. He baited with chunks of P&G Soap that had been cut into small squares. On about every forth hook, he would put on one of my prize crawfish.

By the time we baited sixty hooks and caught up with Daddy and Jimmy, they had the other two lines out. With all of us working together, it didn't take long to finish baiting and head back. The sun was nearly down and that brought all kinds of critters alive in the Forked Deer Bottom. I didn't say anything, but I thought to myself, "We couldn't have gotten the other line out before dark even if I hadn't dropped it." I guess that was a little rationalization to ease my guilty conscience.

As we waded back down to the first line we had baited, we could see the limb it was tied to just a-jumping.. This was a sure sign we had a fish. As Daddy waded over to the line, I anticipated a thirty-pound catfish, but since the largest one ever caught in the river was twelve pounds, I'd be happy with that. He lifted the line and a biggun was dancing on top of the water. He lifted the line a little and carefully positioned his hands around the razor sharp fins. When he brought him over it wasn't as large as I originally thought, but he was an "eater."

"Gimme the stringer," he said with his free hand outstretched. I reached in my right pocket and then my left. Where was that stringer? I tried both back pockets, but no stringer. I must have left it at the car after all the commotion with the spilled jump-box. Daddy carried it the rest of the way back to the car with it in the tight grip of his hand. The sad thing was that I had worked all day getting bait, burned my feet up, and got my butt wet, just so I could carry out a stringer of catfish.

The times for running the line varied. The work schedule for the next day usually dictated if the lines would be run the next day or later that night. Daddy had to go in at 7:00 a.m. the next day so the men would go back about 10:00 p.m. and run the lines. That was bad, because I couldn't go with them at night. To tell the truth, I didn't push the issue much. You know, all those creatures that came out after dark in the river bottom. Why, Bobby Crocker told me he had heard a wolf howling down in the bottom one time. Tonight there just happened to be a full moon. That howling he heard could have even been a werewolf, or maybe even a wolfus.

That night Daddy cranked up the Ford and headed down the road to get the other men. I put on my pajamas and jumped into bed. Mama had already rocked Gail to sleep and put her down for the night. Mama didn't go right to bed. I wasn't sure what she was doing, but a delicious smell came from the kitchen every time I heard the squeak of the oven door on the old coal-oil cook stove. She was baking something. I drifted off to sleep with the aroma tickling my olfactory nerve.

Sometime after midnight I was awakened by one of Mama's

loud "Lordy mercies." She repeated it again, "Lordy mercy Herbert!" There was a certain panic in her voice that told me something was wrong. I got up half asleep and headed in the direction of the "Lordy mercies!" They were on the back porch and Daddy was sitting on the door step "calling for Earl." "Calling for Earl" was a nice way to say "throwing up." After depositing two cans of beer and supper on the ground he said, "I'm okay." I wanted to ask him how many they had caught, but somehow it didn't seem to be the right time.

Dad asked Mama to go to the ice box and chip off a piece of ice. The ice box was right there on the back porch, so she quickly filled the order. Dad took the ice and put it on his hand. That's when everything I always knew about cotton mouth water-moccasins was confirmed. They definitely were mean, maybe even worse than a cobra. His hand was swollen as big as a cantaloupe and was blood red. Without even asking him he held his hand out for me to see and said, "A snake bit me."

Naturally I was concerned about Dad's health and even the possibility of his dying, but I just had to know how it happened, so I asked. He was in some pain and still feeling sick at his stomach, but he told me the details of what happened that night.

He, Billy, and Jimmy got to the river about 11:00 p.m. Now I knew that they left about 10:00 and it only took about twenty minutes to get to the river. I concluded they must have stopped off at C. C. 's poolroom for a couple of beers. I think Mama had already drawn that conclusion and wasn't happy about it. I heard her telling him the next day, "If you'd a stayed away from that poolroom, the Lord wouldn't have sent that snake to bite you."

Daddy continued the story. They waded up the river to the first line. I asked impatiently, "How many did it have on it?" "There were eight or ten on it," he answered with a scolding look. I then stopped jumping the gun and listened to his account of the events.

The second line was tied to an old root that was underwater. Daddy approached the line shining his Carbide head light along the bank looking for a stick he stuck up to mark the whereabouts of the line. He spotted the stick and there was a small drift of sticks and leaves that were caught against the line and was stacking up. He reached into the drift to pick up the line. When his hand went out of sight under water, something grabbed his forefinger. He instinctively jerked his hand back. When his hand came out of the water there was a very large cotton mouth hanging onto his finger.

It had Dad's finger swallowed past the knuckle. In desperation he popped his arm like Lash Larue popping a whip. The snake went sailing out on the bank. There was a mad scramble to get to the other side of the bank. Billy ran over Jimmy and knocked him down causing him to lose his Ray-o-vac flashlight. When they got to the other side of the river, the men went right to work on Dad. Jimmy pulled off his tee shirt and made a tourniquet. Fortunately the fang wounds didn't have to be cut. When Dad popped the snake it cut two big gashes that bled well.

The men brought him out and they rushed to Dr. Barker's house. Dr. Barker looked at the bite and told the men they had already done all that could be done and sent Dad home. As Dad recounted the events of the night, I couldn't help but think what a tale I would have to tell the boys the next day. Besides it just proved one of my arguments about snakes. Leenova was of the school of naturalist who believed that snakes couldn't bite under water or they'd drown. I believed all along that they could bite underwater, how else could the teenager at Chickasaw have dived into a bed of mating snakes and been bitten?

As my angling career progressed, I was allowed to venture

out to some of the ponds that were in walking distance of the Cotton Mill. The ponds we most often frequented were Stallin's Ponds. There were four ponds clustered together. Each one had a specialty. The big pond doubled as the swimming hole and the bass pond. The big pond was the second in the row of four ponds. The island pond was the first in the chain of ponds and was famous for huge black bream. The third pond in the series of ponds was the willow pond. In the willow pond small bream and crawfish could be caught. The fourth pond was so insignificant it was never named. Each year it would go dry so it did not support a population of fish. It was however a pretty good frog gigging pond when it did have water in it.

There were two main routes from the cotton mill to Stallin's ponds. Each held its own brand of danger. The most traveled path was up Avondale to the dirt road that ran by the Collinsworth plantation house and dead ended about a half-mile back at old Black Archie's house. The only danger on Avondale was an occasional dog that would run out and bark and growl, but once you left the main road and headed through the Collingsworth farm, there was a virtual maze of animals to avoid.

****

The most difficult animal to avoid was Billy. Billy was a goat with laser eyes and steel horns. Even when he lay sleeping in the soft dirt in the shade, he would some how sense that boys were near. Just about the time you thought you had tip-toed past him undetected, his ears would come up, his head would turn, and his eyes would flash fire. He would jump to his feet and raise his head, exposing his long urine stained chin whiskers. Mama always said they peed on their beard and that was what made goats stink. I certainly would have never disputed Mama's word, but I did think that would require a great deal of dexterity for a goat to do that.

Usually we could escape the savage attack of Billy if we ran for our lives and beat him to the wooden gate and safety in the cow pasture. Well, most of the time the cow pasture was safe. There was the time the bull was waiting on the other side, but that's another story.

On one particular day Leenova, Charlie Bill, and I were cutting through the Collinsworth place to go fishing at Stallin's pond. Each of us had a cane pole, a can of worms, and a band-aid can tackle box. We had progressed in our fishing to the point we carried extra hooks, sinkers, a single bobber and extra line. We also each had a homemade rope string on which to carry the catch of the day.

We looked uneasily for Billy as we rounded the curve by the big black gum tree. He was nowhere in sight. We might have hit it lucky so we speeded up our pace to get to the wooden gate. As we walked faster and faster, our heads were on a swivel searching from side to side for Billy. Thirty more yards and we would be ready to scale the wood gate to safety. Ten more yards and safety. About that time Billy appeared to pop out of the ground right in front of the gate. His piercing, fire brand eyes seemed to be focusing in on his target. He dropped his head and exposed the steel scimitars that shined in the sun. We turned to retreat, but there was no place to go. No tree was climbable. There was nothing to hide under and we could never beat him across the open ground to Andy Collinsworth's house.

I was sure we were dead, but I thought that there might be a chance for at least one of us to survive if we split up. "Every man for himself!", I screamed as I headed to the right. I knew Charlie Bill was the slowest and he would probably be Billy's first victim. Leenova peeled off to the left as he muttered something that sounded like "Oh she-it." Now the slowest moving target was Charlie Bill. Billy headed straight for him, head down and closing ground. I stopped behind a big White Oak to peep around and watch. Billy was right on him when suddenly he veered to the right. Oh no! He was heading my way! I ducked back behind the tree hoping he hadn't seen me. I had scarcely pulled my head behind the tree when I felt an excruciating pain in the butt. The next thing I knew I was airborne. My cane pole went flying like a javelin, my whole can of captive worms were liberated as the can rolled over and over, and my band-aid tackle box was scattered every where.

I seemed to be in slow motion as I plummeted back to earth. Who knew where I might touch down. Then beneath me I saw a blur of hair and horns. I landed right smack dab on Billy's back. He took off like a bucking bronco with me holding on for dear life. I know at the rodeo you have to stay on a bucking horse for eight seconds to win a prize. I didn't know what the time limit was for bucking Billies, but it seemed like I rode him for at least a full minute.

When I fell off, Billy turned and ran the other way and disappeared around the Collinsworth house. Charlie Bill and Leenova were both rolling on the ground laughing. I dusted off my jeans and gathered up my gear, that I could find, and then proceeded to search for the escaped worms. Actually I got the last laugh. From that day on, every time Billy saw me, he tucked his tail and headed around behind the house. I guess I must have broken his spirit with my now famous ride.

****

Another animal we often encountered on the Collinsworth farm was a large turkey called Tom. Tom wasn't as dangerous as Billy for most of us, but for Charlie Bill he was a walking nightmare. His phobia of chickens extended to all birds, even a sparrow. To Charlie Bill, Tom was six feet tall, weighed two-hundred pounds, had a wing span of twelve feet, and his spurs were at least a foot long. He wasn't quite that imposing to me, but I must admit, I didn't relish tangling with him.

As much as Charlie Bill liked to fish, if Tom was anywhere to be seen, he would take the alternate route. That route was longer and you had to wade some high weeds that usually harbored snakes. There were always red wasp nests and a bee hive you had to squeeze by, before you got to the ponds. Charlie Bill would risk an encounter with any of these creatures to avoid Tom. Now I, on the other hand, would rather face a sack full of wild cats than come in contact with creatures with stingers. I guess I am confessing my phobia.

It was an adventure just walking to Stallin's ponds, but it was worth it when you finally got your hook in the water. The Island Pond was my favorite pond. It was maybe one-third acre with a small island in the middle that had two sassafras trees growing on it. We had a path worn out down to the dirt that circled the pond from the levee and back. Poles with bait could easily be dropped into the water anywhere around the bank. We were limited in how far out we could fish by the length of our cane poles. We always felt we could "mop up" if we could fish the middle. We finally got our chance when we built a boat, but in our first few years we were confined to the bank.

There were two angling techniques that could be used to catch the big bluegill that inhabited the Island Pond. One was the float, sinker, and hook method. Our bait usually was worms in this method. This method was usually used in the deeper water along the levee. The key was to keep your eye on your bobber and yank when it went under.

Actually I liked the tight-lining method better. This method was used in the shallow water where the bream made their spawning beds. It was simple and death to the bream. It consist of a line tied to the cane pole with a hook at the end. The hook was loaded with a worm or cricket and flipped into the bed. A bait rarely sank all the way to the bottom before it was in the mouth of a big bream.

I'll have to credit Bobo Butler for coming up with one of the most unique techniques ever developed by anglers. It involved wading, tight-lining, pole floating, and snuff dipping. It was this technique minus the snuff dipping that won me first place at the Humboldt Lake Fishing Rodeo.

Bobo accidentally developed the pole floating method while we were on a swim outing. Well, actually it was a fishing trip turned swim outing. We were fishing the Island Pond in July. It was hot, the bream were off the beds, and the fish were just not biting. Everyone agreed we might as well go swimming. As we waded out into the big pond, a big tadpole sloshed out on dry ground. Bobo reached down and scooped it up. Not wanting it to go to waste he hooked it on his hook. What happened after that brought about the birth of the pole floating method of fishing.

Bobo waded out into about waist deep water and pulled the wiggling bull frog tadpole close to his mouth and proceeded to marinate it in snuff spit. Now Bobo didn't have many vises, but snuff was his weakness. One day I saw him without a dip of snuff in his mouth and I almost didn't recognize him. Every time I saw him he had a protruding bottom lip with brown lines coming out of the corners of his mouth. No one seemed to see anything wrong with a twelve-year-old boy dipping snuff. Why should they? Almost everyone dipped snuff or chewed tobacco. If they didn't chew or dip, they smoked Camels, Lucky Strikes, or Phillip Morris.

Even my darling Little Mama dipped. Bruton snuff was her brand. She bought it in a container that became a drinking glass when the contents had been consumed. I think a lot of the women in the neighborhood dipped just to get a set of glasses. Little Mama would take a little wooden dipper and reach it into the snuff glass and put it under her lip without spilling a grain. That was quite a feat for a woman who usually shook just drinking a glass of water.

Bobo had plenty of role models in the neighborhood to influence him concerning the use of tobacco. It turned out that snuff juice was a natural bass attractant. He flipped the tadpole, now gagging and spitting snuff juice, into the water and laid his pole down in the water. Immediately the floating cane took off. Bobo looked like Tarzan breast-stroking after it. He caught up with it and pulled in a two pound bass. It was quite a fight but Bobo prevailed by clamping his thumb in the bass' mouth and wading ashore.

Bobo tied his big bass on his home-made rope stringer and started kicking the water along the bank to try to strand another tadpole on dry ground. After three or four splashes, a fat tadpole flopped around helplessly on the mud bank. Bobo snatched him up and impelled his body on the hook. We watched with anticipation as Bobo waded out to waist deep water. Was it just a freak accident or had Bobo unlocked the secret of the ages.

He grabbed the line, pulled the tadpole within an inch of his mouth and let go with the juice that would revolutionize bass angling in America. After the tadpole was fully drenched, he flipped the line as far as it would go and lay the pole down on the surface of the water. The ripples from the pole had barely subsided when the pole took off leaving a wake.

We all cheered as Bobo raced after the run-away pole, "Get it! Get it! Don't let it get away!" He was about to the pole when a huge bass jumped clean out of the water. Then the bass submerged the pole, changed directions, and headed for the deep end. Bobo caught up with it just before he got to water that was over his head.

He stood neck deep in the water and fought the big bass to a standstill. The bass finally rolled over on his side and gave up. Bobo dragged him back to the shallow water and clamped his thumb in his mouth and waded ashore. He was bound to have weighed two and a half or maybe even three pounds.

Bobo wasn't on the bank a second until everyone of us was wading along the bank kicking water in search of a tadpole. Some were removing sinker and floats from their line. By the time Bobo had finished stringing the bass, everyone had his tackle converted and a tadpole on a hook ready to try the pole floating method. It was the most sure fire method known to man and we had witnessed it with our own eyes. We were missing only one ingredient and Bobo had it, Rooster snuff. He was reluctant to give up any of the secret ingredient, but after much begging and a promise that we would all pitch in and buy him a new can, he agreed to divvy up with us.

Now most of us younger kids had never had a dip of snuff, but it couldn't be too bad could it? After all old men and women dipped it and it didn't bother them. One after another we took the little tin can, pulled out our bottom lip, and gently tapped on the side of the can as the powdery substance in the can slid out and stuck to the moist area between our lips and gums.

I had pretended to dip snuff when I was a kid, four or five years old. I always wanted to know what Little Mama's Burton snuff tasted like, so one day Mama fixed me some pretend snuff. It was a mixture of cocoa and sugar. It tasted pretty good and several times I would get her to make me some snuff.

I guess I kinda expected snuff to taste like cocoa and sugar, but it didn't. As I flicked my tongue into the lump of brown powder in my lower lip, it tasted like anything but cocoa and sugar. I wanted to gag or spit it out, but I looked around and

David and Charlie Bill seemed to be doing just fine. I later learned they wanted to spit it out too, but they thought I was doing fine. Besides I had to keep it in to make the secret ingredient that was a fisherman's dream. The powder had to be mixed with slobber to activate the ingredient.

We spit some of the brown juice out to relieve the feeling that someone had turned a faucet on in our mouth, but Bobo warned us he didn't have any snuff left, so no more spitting. As we waded out to waist deep water, I kept getting the urge to swallow. I fought the urge by trying to extend the size of my cheeks that were swelling from the production of the secret ingredient. I felt some of the ingredient trickling down my throat. My throat began to tickle, and then, almost as if it were an involuntary response, I swallowed.

Almost immediately my stomach responded with a series of low growls. I could feel my stomach beginning to churn. It reminded me of Mama's old ringer washer as it churned clothes back and forth. After the growls and churning, came a buzzing in my head. Then I began to feel dizzy and hot. Sweat popped out on me like dew on an August morning. I felt like I was smothering, then there was a rumbling deep in my gut. The rumbling started up and kept coming. Before I could take one step to get out of the water, I heard Charlie Bill calling for Earl. I looked in his direction and he had a greenish glow about him. Floating in the water around him were chunks of potatoes, peas, carrots, and some other stuff digested beyond recognition. About that time the volcano reached my throat and my peas and carrots erupted and spread like lava on the water.

David made a break for dry land, but just as he got to the water's edge, he dropped to his all-fours and gave up his lunch too. He finally crawled out on the bank as white as if he had seen a ghost. In fact the only time I ever saw him whiter was the time he did see a ghost.

When Bobo finished laughing he gathered all the sick Cotton Mill Boys and his two big bass and headed for home. We stopped at old black Archie's and used his old hand pump to wash up a little and get a drink of the best water in the country. I was a little better by the time I got home. I must have still been a little green around the gills, because Mama asked me if I felt all right. I certainly never told her about the snuff.

* * * * * * * * * *

"Most people rise above others because they are standing on someone's shoulders." This was one of Mama's famous quotes. It must have been original. When I was younger I thought it was a quote from the Bible but I've never been able to find the chapter or verse that has the quote. I would rise above others by standing on Bobo's shoulders. I used his floating pole technique, minus the secret ingredient of course, in several exotic waters. It worked at Croom's pond, Dover's pond and even in the mysterious green pond, but the defining moment of my angling career came at the newly created Humboldt Lake.

Humboldt Lake was a huge lake by pond standards. It was constructed by the Tennessee Game and Fish Commission on a site about three miles outside of Humboldt. The water covered over ninety acres.

Once the lake was opened to the public, all our other fishing holes were neglected. It had big bass, catfish and bream. It was a five mile ride by bicycle, but riding our bikes five miles was fun. We peddled and chattered, but we didn't miss a thing from a mocking bird to a snapping turtle in the process of changing his residence from one side of the road to the other.

We even got to ride across the Forked Deer River Bridge on 152 Highway. Sometimes we would even stop and wet a line in the old river, but the lure of Humboldt Lake wouldn't let us stay long.

Humboldt Lake opened in June of my tenth year. The very first event that kicked off the opening was a kid's fishing rodeo. It was on a Saturday and Dad was going to take a whole car load of the Cotton Mill Boys. My cousins, Doug and Jeep, went with us.

They had moved into the house next door to me after the Wages moved out. My great Uncle Blubber and Aunt Linnie Mae Henley brought my cousins who became like brothers. There were two older girls, Sara and Betty Faye. Bubbie was an older brother, who was a senior in high school and a star end for the Humboldt Rams. After Bubbie was Bobby who was two years older than I. Then came Doug who was one year older and Jeep who was one year younger. We all grew up together. Doug, Jeep and I were going to show those city boys how to fish.

I was so excited about fishing and the prospect of putting the floating pole technique to the test against competition. Daddy had some pole racks mounted on the old Ford and we had the poles stacked up on them. With everything loaded, we headed toward Humboldt Lake. Every window had a boy hanging out of it yelling and waving at everyone we passed. It was a happy time.

When we got to the lake we signed up and we were told the rules. Prizes would be given in different age classes for first limit of ten, heaviest fish, and heaviest limit. Everyone was to go to their chosen spot on the bank. The announcer came on the loud speaker, "Boys and girls, begin fishing."

I had prepared for this day all my life, from fishing sewing thread lines in the ditch up until I had learned the floating pole technique. I was ready. I slipped off my loafers, rolled my jeans up to my knees and waded out. Daddy had gotten me a store bought bamboo pole that was fourteen feet long. I had a line as long as the pole with no weight or bobber, just a hook. I quickly reached into my coffee can and pulled out a juicy worm. I threaded him onto the hook and flipped him out as far as I could. I lay the pole down and waited with my hand poised above the pole ready to strike at the slightest movement. I didn't have to wait long. The pole started a forward motion and I grabbed it. On the end of the line was a nice black bream. I waded back to the bank and swung it out on the bank. I quickly hooked him on my new, store-bought, wire stringer and rebaited. A few steps back in the water and I had the pole ready again. The pole quivered and I grabbed it again. This time it was about a ten inch bass. I repeated the process until I had nine fish on my stringer. I had not heard the man on the speaker announce the first limit, just one more fish and I would win.

Now Mama always told me that the devil takes on many forms, but I would have never believed he would take on the form of my cousin Doug. As I waited for that all important one-more-bite, Doug pulled in his first fish. He said, "Here take this one and put it on your stringer and run to the judges." I wanted to win pretty bad and I considered the proposition I admitted, but something inside kept saying, "Don't You Do It!" It sounded an awful lot like Mama. The good Lord took away the temptation when my pole took off. I made a lunge and barely caught it before it went into the deep. It was a fight, but in the end the fish wound up on my stringer.

I slipped my muddy bare feet into my loafers and sprinted like an Olympian to the judges stand. It was confirmed, I had the first limit in the rodeo. My prize was a gallon water jug and a whole box of giant Baby Ruth's. Twenty-four of those chocolate beauties at ten cents apiece. Wow! What a prize. Besides the prize, I got my *picture taken and it was on the front page of the *Humboldt Courier Chronicle*. Well, maybe it wasn't on the front page, but it was in the paper. (*as seen on cover)

From the time the lake opened until I started college, I spent many a fun day at Humboldt Lake. Many fishermen were converted to the Bobo Butler floating pole method as my fame as an angler spread. The legend spread as more people began to use the technique. Even Uncle Whit could be seen on a Saturday afternoon, knee deep in water with his bamboo pole floating on top.

There was a man who was my friend and that helped to spread the legend. Joe Freeman was the manager of the lake. I spent some good times talking to Joe and his assistant, Leroy Curtis. When I caught my thirty fish limit, I would go to the store and talk with Joe and Leroy as they counted and weighed my fish. Joe would tell grown men with his low southern drawl, "If you'uns want to catch some fish, go with O'Neal." Even after I was grown, every now and then some older man would come up to me and ask, "Ain't you that boy that used to wade out there and catch all them fish at Humboldt Lake?" I'd smile and say, "Yes sir, and I did it all standing on Bobo Butler's shoulders."

It is amazing how life goes full circle. The old lake is now over fifty-years-old. It still provides pleasant outings for boys, girls and adults as well. Even today as I stand on the fishing pier and look down the right fork of the lake the memories flood into me. There's an old snag about knee-deep out in the water that bears a resemblance to Uncle Whit standing in the water with his pole floating on top.

Oh yeah! Did I tell you my son, Hunter, is now the TWRA manager of the lake? And he has my picture from the newspaper hanging on his office wall.

****

Baseball wasn't exactly a passion with me, but I could never admit it. I would have been excommunicated by both the Henley and the Maitland sides of the family. Heck, I probably would have been excommunicated from the Cotton Mill. Every Cotton Mill Boy dreamed of playing for the St. Louis Cardinals. If you went to Barrett's Grocery, or visited someone in the neighborhood, the Cardinals were playing. You could hear the play-by-play on the radio because it certainly would be on. Old Harry Cary could be heard all over the neighborhood.

The Cardinals had such greats as Dizzy and Daffy Dean, Red Schoendienst, and Stan-the-man Musial. I didn't keep up with them all that closely, but Charlie Bill knew everyone's current batting average, won-loss record, and all the team stats. He lived and breathed baseball.

Charlie Bill had two unique training techniques that, I believe, were his keys to success as a batter. The first hand-and-eye coordination exercise only required a sawed-off broom handle. He would stand at the edge of the gravel road, broom-stick bat in a ready position and crouched in the classic Stan Musial stance. He would then spit a large drop of saliva between his teeth. While the sticky drop was till in the strike zone, he would swing and hit it.

He would then move out in the gravel road for his next batting practice. He progressed from spit to chert rocks. Not just any rock would do. He would look through his selection and pick just the right rock. He then assumed the Stan-the-man stance, and pitched the rock in the air. The broom-stick would make contact with a crack as the rock entered the strike zone and would disappear in the hedge apple tree across the road.

Charlie Bill's power hitting would have made him the first

one chosen in the neighborhood baseball game if he had any speed, but his excess weight made it hard for him to stretch a home run into a base hit. There was that one time, that one shot at glory, when he out-sprinted every boy at the Cotton Mill, including me. That was the time he saw a ghost.

L to R: Betty Faye Henley, Shirley Wages, and Becky Butler in the driveway of my house. The boys were not the only ones who could play ball at the Cotton Mill. (In the background you can see Jones Mfg. Co. and the water tank. In the right foreground - the plum tree.)

Choosing sides for a baseball game was fairly methodical. It was an accepted fact that Bobo and Skeezer were the captains of the two teams. The make-up of the teams from that point on depended on who got to choose first. There were a number of ways to pick who got to choose first. One of the simplest ways was to have two guys get a number between one and ten. Each captain would pick a number and the closest to the number would get first pick.

Another method for deciding who went first was flipping a coin, that is if anyone had a coin. Bobo usually did during marble season. Sometimes the coin was a heads or tails call, but if both parties possessed a coin, the "alike" or "dislike" method was used. In this method, one captain would call either "alike" or "dislike." If he called "alike" and both coins come up heads or both coins come up tails, he was the winner.

****

Fortunately for me, most parents knew that almost any game was started by choosing sides with the coin-toss method. That knowledge once saved me and the plum tree. The plum tree conveniently grew right beside the front porch. It was Mama's switch factory. It grew new switches almost as fast as she could break them off, but in the summer it usually got behind.

One thing Mama couldn't abide was gambling. "Gambling can send you to hell just as quick as drinking," she'd say. Knowing her wrath against gambling, I was very careful not to be seen matching. Matching was flipping a penny up in the air and letting chance determine if it were heads or tails. The one who correctly called out "alike" or "dislike" got to keep the two pennies. One day during one of these gambling sprees we got careless. We were matching on the cinder road across from Miss Booker's house.

Mrs. Booker was one lady in the neighborhood who was

notorious for her gossip. The saying was "don't telephone, don't telegraph, tell Mrs. Booker and everyone will know." One of her tales caused Charlie Bill to get one of the worst whippings he ever got. She couldn't wait to tell Mama that she had seen Leenova and me gambling.

Mama was waiting just inside the screen door with her hands on her apron-clad hips with her dark, Cherokee eyes staring a hole in me.

When I came home she was waiting just inside the screen door with her hands on her apron-clad hips with her dark, Cherokee eyes staring a hole in me. "Well, what have you got to say for yourself," she demanded. Not knowing which crime of the day caused the interrogation, I remained silent. "Young man, I asked you a question!" she continued as her forehead wrinkled. I knew I had to confess to something, so I said, "Leenova and I ate the last piece of pie." "I'm not talking about pie! Miss Booker told me you and Leenova were gambling!" she fired back. Then in a stroke of genius, I told her we weren't matching we were tossing coins to see which would get to ride the scooter first. She muttered something that sounded like, "That old witch," or something similar, and I was off the hook.

Now I know the devil will get you for lying, but I believe the plum tree would have died that summer if it had one more switch broken off.

Besides the coin-toss, there was the "one-potato, two-potato, three-potato, four, five-potato, six-potato, seven taters more" method of choosing sides. I liked that technique because it was more random and I wasn't always the last one chosen. Being chosen last to play a game of baseball could hurt a boy's self-esteem, but we lived through it.

There was the standard bat toss-and-catch method for seeing who chose first and which team got to bat first. If given the choice, the captain always choose to bat first. That way, if the game ended before the final inning, that team would receive an extra bat. Many times a game was called before it ended because several key players were called to come home.

Most families had an approximate time for supper, but none of us were late. Each family had a unique call to come home. Leenova's daddy, Cecil, had about the best. He could be heard anywhere within the confines of the neighborhood. He would let out a shrill whistle that accentuated every syllable in Leenova's name. Daddy used the whistle method of calling me home also. It was one long whistle that he let out between his two fingers in the corners of his mouth.

Most of the women just screeched out their child's name. Opal probably had the loudest scream as she screeched out "Charlie Bill!" Mamaw Hallie had a unique yell when she called for Skeezer. She sang out like an opera singer, "Cor-ne-le-us." Floyd Corneleus was his real name, but he preferred Skeezer. If Opal screeched out, "Charlie Bill!", he'd drop his bat or glove and head home. If Mamaw Hallie sang out, "Cor-ne-lee-us!", he'd jump on Hadacol, his bike, and head up the hill. Sometimes a game was called because of rain or darkness, but most of the time it was called for supper.

We always played hard in our baseball games against each other, but we stepped our game up a notch when we played the town boys. We usually had a home and home arrangement with David Trimmer's Dairy Queen bunch. We always played Honey Williams' team at home because they didn't have much of a field. Next to the little league field downtown, we had the best field in Humboldt. We had a back stop and a home-run fence. Just around the corner of the mill was a water faucet for a drink of water. Across the street, at my house, there was the two-seater if someone just had to go, and poplar tree and maple tree on either side of the back-stop provided a home and visitors dug-out. Our field was the envy of every boy in Humboldt. Now I don't have the stat books to back me up on this, but I don't think we ever lost a game on our home field.

****

Bicycling was a large part of our life. Our bikes not only provided a means of transportation, they were transformed into all kinds of vehicles and animals. The latest movie or serial we had seen dictated what our bicycles would be that day. If it was a western, chances were our bike would be Champ or Trigger. If we had seen the "Blackhawks" serial, it would become an airplane. It was a motorcycle, complete with sound effects when we clipped a strip of cardboard to the frame with a clothes pin. The faster we peddled, the louder the motor as each spoke in the wheel hit the cardboard. It was a cop car in a "cops-and-robbers" chase. Occasionally it even became an elephant after a Tarzan movie.

Our bikes all had names, just as our dogs all had names. Skeezer's bike was named Hadacol. I, in my originality, named my bike Hadacol Jr. Hadacol was a then popular elixir that promised to give renewed energy and made old people able to dance around. Mama took a spoonful or two everyday. Sometimes, when she took more than the prescribed dosage, she did begin to dance around a little. If I hadn't known how opposed Mama was to Satan's old demon, liquor, I might have thought she was a little tipsy.

When it came to bike riding Skeezer was my hero. He could do every trick in the book. He could ride all the way to town and never once touch a handle bar. He could sit on the handle bars facing backwards and peddle his bike forward. He could jump over a row of four-55 gallon oil drums. Wheelies were nothing for Skeezer. He could keep the front wheel off the ground for a good half-mile. He could have easily been as famous as Evil Kenivel if he hadn't gotten interested in girls and joined the Navy to serve his country.

Most of my bike riding skills I owe to Skeezer. I, and many other of the Cotton Mill Boys, followed him all over town playing follow-the-leader. If he jumped, we jumped. If he did a wheelie, we did a wheelie. If he rode with no hands, we rode with no hands. If he stood up on the seat and balanced with no hands on the handle bars, we stood up—no actually we kept our seats because that was one trick we wouldn't try even on a double-dog-dare.

When it came to bike riding Skeezer was my hero.

Bicycles were used to transport us and our equipment from one place to another. Boys, and sometimes girls, could be seen riding from Barrett's Grocery with a loaf of bread or a sack of flour in their basket or under their arm, if they had no basket. It wasn't uncommon to see a fishing pole or a BB gun lying across the handlebars as one of us sped to a rendezvous with the rest of the boys. And then there was that infernal five-gallon slop bucket on my bike.

Yes, bicycles served as multi-purpose vehicles, but mostly they were just for plain old "ridin." We would start out early on a Saturday morning and ride until supper time that night. On trips that took us far from the neighborhood we would take a jug of water and a sandwich. There were all kinds of sandwiches brought along on an all-day trip. The snack could vary from bologna to peanut butter and jelly. Sometimes souse and crackers hit the spot. Hoop cheese and crackers weren't bad. I believe my all-time favorite was middlin meat on a biscuit garnished with mustard. No matter who brought what, if someone didn't bring a lunch for the ride, we all shared with him. The motto was "share and share alike." I can't remember if that was one of Mama's sayings from the Bible or if some of the boys came up with it, but I think it might have been Charlie Bill, because he always got his share and then some.

On our long Saturday rides, we would drink in all our surroundings. The chatter would stop and the bikes would become still when we stopped to observe a squirrel barking at the wandering band that disturbed his meal of hickory nuts. Down the gravel road that bisected Duffey's Bottom, eyes looked with anticipation for the shaking of a limb as frightened squirrels ran for their dens. Around the curve, in the sorghum field, a quail could be heard calling to his mate, "Bob White! Old Bob White!" There was always something to see or hear on our bicycle safaris.

After about an hour or so we'd all stop and Skeezer would break out the gallon jug that hung from his handle bars. Everyone would take a big slug and Charlie Bill would take out one of his sandwiches and gulp it down in about three bites. We never knew what made Charlie Bill have such a voracious appetite, but I suspected it had something to do with his accident.

****

When Charlie Bill was six, we were playing cowboys. I had a Hop-A-Long Cassidy gun and hoister set and Leenova had his Red Ryder BB gun. Charlie Bill didn't have a gun, but he knew where to get one. He headed across the street to his Grandpa France's house. Grandma Matt was at work at the mill and only Aunt Pauline was there. He slipped in the back door and into France's bedroom. Very quietly he slipped his hand under the pillow and felt for cold steel. It was there. Grandpa France's 38 Smith and Wesson.

Happy to be a full blown participant in our cowboy adventure, he ran outside with the gun. Proudly he showed us his prize. We looked at it in awe. It looked just like a real gun. We mounted our broom-stick horses, slapped leather, sunk spur and headed for home-on-the-range. Several times we encountered bad men and even some bad Indians. Each time we would pull the trigger, the bad guys would fall.

We noticed Charlie Bill wasn't pulling the trigger on his gun. "What's the Matter? Your gun broke?" asked Leenova. "Naw!" he snapped back. "Pull it," I said in a sarcastic tone. "I dare you."

Not being one to take a dare lightly, he pointed the gun in our direction and his finger began to squeeze. He strained harder and the hammer started to creep back. Then, in near exhaustion, he gave up and the hammer eased back down.

"I knew you couldn't pull it," I taunted. That did it. He had to prove he could pull the trigger. To get better leverage, he hooked both thumbs through the trigger with his fingers wrapped around the butt of the pistol and the barrel pointed right at his gut. He began to squeeze and there was a loud bang like a fire-cracker had gone off. Charlie Bill slumped to the ground. We ran into the house to get Opal. When she came out she started to screaming, "He's shot! Oh Lord he's shot!"

The neighbors from all around heard the screaming and came running. One of the men grabbed him and put him in their car and rushed him to St. Mary's Hospital. When it was all over I cried. I couldn't help but believe it was all my fault. If only I hadn't dared him.

Charlie Bill had a close call, but he made it. The bullet missed his liver by half an inch. There was some damage to his stomach. That's why I think he ate all the time, and because I felt responsible, I usually ended up giving him my sandwich out of shear guilt.

****

After everyone had his thirst quenched and Charlie Bill satisfied his tapeworm, we would continue on our journey. About halfway through our ride we entered a place we called "Cactus Canyon." The gravel road had been cut right through a big hill. The road bank exhibited layers of sediment from years gone by. We suspected we could find some dinosaur bones in the bank if we dug around in it. Cactus Canyon was our stop and play point on the Tour de Cotton Mill. It offered a mountain on which to act out the latest scenes of the cliff-hanger serial. It presented an up-hill course that tested who could climb the highest on his bike before the law of gravity yanked him back down, but most of all it provided the site for "King of the Hill."

Things to do today:

- [ ] Learn how Regions can help me build a better banking experience.
- [ ] Sign up for simple and safe banking with free Regions Online Banking with Bill Pay.
- [ ] Enroll in Mobile Banking to bank anywhere, anytime from my mobile phone.
- [ ] Use my Regions Visa® CheckCard to buy things like groceries, clothes or practically anything else.
- [ ] Get retirement planning info at regions.com/retirement.
- [ ] Ask Regions' lending experts to help me find the right loan to meet my goals.

- [ ] _____
- [ ] _____
- [ ] _____
- [ ] _____
- [ ] _____
- [ ] _____
- [ ] _____
- [ ] _____

REGIONS

It's time to expect more.

▼▼ REGIONS

- TO ENSURE SPEEDY DRIVE-UP
  SERVICE, WE SUGGEST THAT
  YOU BRING COMPLICATED OR
  LENGTHY TRANSACTIONS
  TO AN INSIDE TELLER.

- KEEP THIS DRIVE-UP ENVELOPE
  AND USE FOR YOUR NEXT
  DEPOSIT

- USE DEPOSIT TICKETS WITH
  YOUR PRINTED NAME AND
  NUMBER

- FILL OUT YOUR DEPOSIT
  SLIP BEFORE APPROACHING
  WINDOW

INSERT
CURRENCY
CHECKS &
DEPOSIT
SLIPS
HERE
➡

CONVENIENT
SPEEDY DRIVE-IN
SERVICE

Skeezer and me. Cactus Canyon was our stop-and-play point on the Tour de Cotton Mill.

Skeezer. King of the Hill was one of those games that tested a boy's courage and manhood.

King of the Hill was one of those games that tested a boy's courage and manhood. The object of the game was to be the lone occupant of the crest of the hill after a knock-down, drag-out battle to throw everyone off the mountain. Cactus Canyon seemed to be at least fifty feet high with a sheer drop-off of ten feet before the banks started their gradual slope toward the road. The clay banks were usually moist from a recent rain. This caused the banks to become very slick after a boy or two slid over the clay on the seat of his pants.

Now to the casual observer this may have seemed a simple and chaotic game, but there was as much strategy and negotiation as went on in the United Nation. The largest and oldest was sure to win such a simple game, right? Wrong! To the contrary, brains usually triumphed over brawn. Secret deals were made between different parties. Treaties were made and truces were called. By the time everyone assembled on top to begin, no one knew for sure who was really their secret ally or who would betray his partner with a double-cross. Skeezer and Bobo, being the oldest, usually were double-crossed by one of us younger kids. We would pretend to help them then, when we got our chance and their back was turned, we'd push with all our might. A ten-year-old felt pretty big if he could push Bobo or Skeezer down the muddy hill. The only problem with the double-cross was that you never knew when the big kids had anticipated the double-cross. They would turn their backs as if oblivious to the mite behind them. Then, as the double-crosser charged to make the deadly push, they would step aside and the double-crosser would plunge to his death. Well, it was a pretend death. The rules stated if you fall off the mountain, you're dead until the next game.

After an exhilarating game of King of the Hill it was time to have another slug of water from Skeezer's jug and eat our sandwich. By then all of Charlie Bill's sandwiches were gone. He would look longingly at each sandwich as part of it disappeared into someone's mouth. I would usually take my sandwich in my muddy hands and tear it exactly in half. Mama always said it was selfish to take the biggest part when you shared something.

****

After everyone finished we would continue our ride on the loop toward home. We crossed the railroad tracks at Hobo Grade. Mama said it got that name because during the depression hobos often jumped the train there as the engine slowed down and strained up the steep hill. During the depression hobos could be seen daily riding or walking up the tracks, but in the early fifty's they were becoming extinct. They were a rare sight at the Cotton Mill, but occasionally the ashes of a hobo's campfire could be found under the railroad trestle.

Hobos were often unjustly accused of things that happened in the neighborhood. Like when a pie came up missing from someone's window sill, it was always a hobo that stole it. I know they were falsely accused in one particular case of a missing pie.

Mama had just baked an apple pie that she made from some apples Sister Barrett had given her. She put it in an old pillow case to keep the flies off of it and put it on the window sill to cool. I couldn't wait until supper to bite into the thick lard-laden crust and taste the sugar and cinnamon interspersed with Sister Barrett's Red Delicious Apples. The aroma tempted me as I stood close and sniffed the air. As much as I wanted to taste that nectar of the gods, I knew I had to wait for supper. As I turned the corner of the house I leaned back for one more look. Yeah, it was still there.

I busied myself with a chore Daddy had assigned me. I

pulled nails out of old boards he had brought home from the mill. I worked for about an hour. When I went back around the house to take another look at the much anticipated pie, it was gone! My hope was that Mama had decided to bring it in and cut it, but I looked and it was no where to be found in the kitchen. I asked Mama if she had taken up the pie. With a surprised look, she said, "No!" and hurried to the kitchen window. It was indeed missing. "One of those darn Hobo's must've stole it!" was her very first accusation.

I ran outside and looked down the road toward the railroad tracks. No one was stirring. Then I ran out to the ditch behind the house. No one was out there. Then I discovered the horrible truth. Laying in the garden between the two rows of pole beans was Snowball licking the pan clean. If Mama caught him she would beat him to within an inch of his life with her broom. I couldn't let her find out, so I took the pan and sailed it across the ditch. To this day I feel bad that I didn't stand up for the hobos when they were falsely accused, but Snowball was my best friend.

We crossed the railroad tracks and continued our ride parallel with the tracks, until we came to "Sherwood Forest." Sherwood Forest was a half-acre woods that was called the thicket by the adults. Sherwood Forest was the site of untold adventures and misadventures. Leaving Sherwood, it was a short ride to our final destination, our baseball field in front of my house.

Bike riding provided hours of pleasure and took us to far away places, but like any man-made machines, they could cause a world of hurt and trouble. To keep a bike in tip-top condition for the grueling trips required a good bit of service and maintenance. Not only was Skeezer the best bike rider in Humboldt, he was also the best bicycle mechanic. He could fix a broken chain, patch a leaky inner-tube, tighten spokes in the wheel with his spoke wrench, and even customize bikes.

Hadacol was a stripped down, jazzed up Western Flyer. He took good care of Hadacol. He never left him out in the rain. Hadacol had a place reserved on the front porch. Skeezer kept Hadacol's chain well oiled with Uncle Whit's oil can. The spokes were always tight and the handle bars straight. Hadacol was always poised for action. Skeezer had his own special way of mounting Hadacol. He would run alongside Hadacol pushing, then when he had up a head of steam, he would leap on the seat. It was much the same technique that Wild Bill Elliott used to mount his horse, Coco.

**SCHOOL DAYS 1952-53
HUMBOLDT**

As Skeezer got a year or two older, he lost interest in his bicycle repair business and started spending his time with Becky Butler, Margaret Maitland and other girls.

79

I wasn't as picky with Hadacol Jr. as Skeezer was with Hadacol, but when I saw rust building up on the chain or the chain started to slip, I'd head to Skeezer's and get an overhaul job. I later wished I had paid attention and learned how to repair and service my bike because as Skeezer got a year or two older, he lost interest in his bicycle repair business and started spending his time with Becky Butler, Margaret Maitland and other girls. My bike was often out of commission and in disrepair after he became interested in girls.

There were a few simple things about bike riding and bike repair that even I knew. Some I learned from first hand experience and some I learned from others. One of the first things I learned was, if you didn't have a chain guard, roll up your pants leg on the chain side. I learned this as Charlie Bill and I were in a dead heat going down the big hill. We were in a race to the big tree. I might have been leading by a fender when it happened. The chain yanked my brand-new Levi blue jeans right into the sprocket. There was so much denim in the sprocket that it caused the bike to come to a screeching halt.

My momentum carried me over the handle bars head first. Now I had been thrown over the handle bars before, but I had never been attached to the bike by my pants leg. I hit hard on the cinder road and rolled. Everywhere I rolled the bike rolled with me, whipping me with handle bars and fenders. When we finally came to a stop, Hadacol Jr. and I lay in a heap. It was hard to discern the arms and legs from the handle bars and fenders. Luckily, neither Hadacol Jr. nor I had to be taken to the doctor. That day I learned to roll up the leg of my jeans on the chain side.

* * * * * * * * *

The gymnastics games took on many forms, some of which were not exactly those that could be seen in a coliseum. Sometimes certain rules applied, but many of the contests would go as far as someone would go on a double-dog-dare. Equipment for the gymnastic competition were ropes, cables, grape vines, roof tops, riding trees, the tank, the reservoir, quick sand and any other item that was worthy of a risk or dare.

The main training center for the Cotton Mill gymnastics was the big tree. Almost any time during the summer boys could be observed swinging on the cable and yodeling the Tarzan yell. The cable was accessed from the top of the ditch bank across the ditch from the cinder road. Just a slight push with the legs and one could glide all the way across the ditch and drop at the edge of the road. The gymnast had the option to stay on the cable and glide back across the ditch and land perched on the big root where he started. It would appear this was not a very complicated feat and certainly did not merit a nine or ten from the judges. There was a condition that increased the level of difficulty assigned to the task, thus increasing the judges points. The difficulty factor was added to the maneuver when the ditch was flooded and the water was at the top of the banks.

It was one of those days when the ditch was at flood stage, that Charlie Bill and I decided to display our skill and daring by swinging over the rain swollen ditch on the cable. We had to approach the big tree by going through his Grandma Matt's backyard, because the ditch was so deep there was no way to get across from the cinder road. Charlie Bill's Grandma Matt and Granddaddy France lived across Avondale from Charlie Bill. His Aunt Pauline lived with them. Their yard backed up to the ditch and the big tree.

When we got to the big tree the cable was flopping around as the rapids hit it and swept it from side to side. I found a stick and leaned out over the rushing water and slid the cable over close enough to grab it with my other hand. Pulling it out of the churning muddy water, I said, "You go first." "No, you go first," was his reply. "I asked you first," I shot back. "I dare you," he said. I countered with, "I double-dare you." You'd think I would have learned my lesson about daring Charlie Bill. He came back with the grandaddy of dares, "I double-dog-dare you."

I then had no choice but to go first. Bravely (on the outside), I grabbed the cable as high as I could and holding my feet up to keep them out of the water I glided across and dropped at the edge of the cinder road. The momentum of the swing carried it back across to Charlie Bill. He leaned out and pulled it in.

Charlie Bill stood on the opposite bank and stared across with a far away look in his blue eyes. He stood there, cable in hand, trying to get up enough courage to lift his feet off the big tree root that jutted out over the terrible torrent of water. "You can do it, just be sure to hold your legs up," I encouraged. Still he lacked the confidence to push off on this adventure. I then said the words that gave him the courage he needed. "You're chicken!" And with that, he pushed off.

I could see it coming from his take-off. His form was off. His legs were too straight. There was no bend in the knees to lift the feet above the water. He'd be lucky if the judges even gave him a one. As his feet touched water his smooth glide toward land and safety was stopped in mid-stream. He was below water from the waist down. The current tugged at him like a fish pulling on a bobber, but his hands stayed clamped on the cable like a vice.

Panic began to rush over me like the water that rushed over Charlie Bill, for I knew he couldn't swim. If the swirling water broke his hold on the cable, he was a goner. There was no time to go for help, I had to do something. I looked around for something, anything that could help. I saw about a twelve-foot piece of conduit propped up against the mill. I sprinted the fifty feet in two seconds. I then got to the edge of the water and stuck the pipe right next to Charlie Bill's hand. "Grab it!" "I can't let go," he replied with a voice that shook with fear. "If you don't let go, you're going to die," I shouted back.

He let go and with all the grace of a trapeze artist, he made the transition from cable to pipe. As I felt his weight on the pipe, I tugged toward myself with the strength of Sampson. The next thing I knew, Charlie Bill was on the bank with me. I don't know what kind of score the judges would have given us for the dismount from the swing to the parallel bar, but I gave it a ten.

****

Swinging on the cable was always fun, but to really get in the mood for Tarzan or just to prove that you were a resourceful outdoorsman, the best swing was a grapevine. Finding just the right grapevine was part of the fun. It had to be growing high up in the tree with no limbs to obstruct a smooth glide from point A to point B. The vine needed to be on the side of a hill or ditch. This added to the height of the glide and increased the danger. One of the most important things to check when selecting just the right grapevine was the limbs in the tree to which the vine was attached.

One day we found the perfect grapevine in Duffey's Bottom. I never knew who Duffey was, but the adults called the ten acre woods Duffey's Bottom, thus the name. The bottom started behind the levee of the Island Pond and sprawled out all the way across the gravel road that went through Cactus Canyon. There were some giant oak, hickory and beech trees that were the home to some fox squirrels that were as big as dogs. In fact Snowball had a fight with one that was as big as he was. I thought I would surely loose Snowball that day.

Duffey's Bottom had a deep gorge in the section of woods across the road. It was known to posses holes that contained quicksand. We were somewhat leery of quicksand, because in almost every Tarzan movie, someone got swallowed up by the watery muck. It was on the side of this gorge that we found the perfect grapevine. The branching vines were high up in the tree, there was not a single limb on the tree below the vine, and the main vine was hanging straight down over the gorge. The trunk of the vine curved upward and the root was attached at the base of the tree. It was perfect to glide out over the gorge in a circular motion and return to the point of take-off.

We all looked at the vine as if we had discovered a gold mine. Before anyone could say a word, Skeezer had his scout knife out of the scabbard and whacking away at the vine. The vine had to be separated from the root to free it to glide out over the gorge. Soon the chore was finished and we were ready for a test run. The bottom of the gorge looked a bit menacing with the half-liquid, half-solid appearance of the sand. "You know, that might be quicksand down there," Jeep suggested. "Naw, that's just some water in the gorge," argued Skeezer. "Who's going first?" was the next question. Though it may not have appeared to be so, most everything we did had a certain order and protocol. There had been established by our forefathers, a procedure for testing grapevines. Well, maybe it wasn't our forefathers, but the kids that were even older than Skeezer and Bobo developed the recommended testing method when Skeezer was my age. It had been handed down to the next generation of grapevine swingers.

First, the lightest kid would swing on the vine, and if the vine didn't break and kill him, the next lightest kid would become the test pilot. Jeep was the lightest so he got to go first. In a magnificent sweep, he circled out over the gorge. His brown locks of hair rippled in the breeze as he sailed back to the top of the gorge.

"It was great!" he announced with a smile. Now it was my turn. I pushed off and sailed out over the gorge. What a great feeling! This must be how it would feel to be in a hot air balloon, I thought. I touched down without a hitch. Next was Bobby's, then Doug's and then Charlie Bill's turns. Usually, if a vine held up to Charlie Bill, it was good for the rest of us for two or three weeks. He reached high on the vine and took off. The limbs in the top bent slightly, but he returned safely to the bank.

Now Skeezer was the only one left to take the death defying plunge out into the space above the gorge. His orbit started just fine. A smooth blast off and approach to orbit, but then a cracking sound filled mission control. The limbs! We forgot to check the limbs! All eyes shot to the canopy of the tree where the vine was attached. The vine was already on the way down and bringing a huge dead limb with it. Skeezer yelled something. I didn't understand (it was probably a prayer, or it could have been something my young ears didn't need to hear), as he and the top of the tree fell toward earth. He hit in the bottom of the gorge and must have been praying because the big rotten limb only missed him by inches. He also received the good fortune of landing in soft sand on the bottom.

He was unhurt, a miracle for sure. Mama always said God takes care of the ignorant. Or was that the helpless? Anyway Skeezer was lucky, that is until he stood up. When he put pressure on his right foot in an attempt to step, it began to sink in the muck. He tried to move his other foot and it went deeper. Before we could do anything to help, he was over his knees in quicksand.

His struggle turned to desperation as he went even deeper. By the time we climbed down to the bottom of the gorge he was up to his thighs. Quickly we made a human chain and, locked arm-in-arm, we pulled Skeezer free. He was all right, but there was one casualty. As he came out of the sand and water, he was barefoot. The quicksand had sucked off the gum boots he was wearing. The boots belonged to Uncle Whit and Skeezer had borrowed them without asking. It took some active imaginations, but we came up with a logical explanation. We told Uncle Whit that Skeezer lost his boots in some quicksand.

****

Vines were not the only gymnastic equipment that nature provided. There was the thrill of victory and the agony of defeat on the "riding tree." The riding tree varied in size, height, species, and performance technique, but there were certain unwritten rules. Rule number one was never use a willow, cottonwood, elm, sweet gum or sycamore for a riding tree. By the process of elimination and personal experience, these trees were determined to have no elasticity when they were put under pressure. To put it bluntly for all rookies and city boys, they will break with you. On the other hand sassafras, hickory, oak, or even a maple made good riding trees.

The object of tree riding was to find a proper species of tree that could hold the climber's weight until he reached the tip-top. When the climber reached the top he would lean all his weight to one side and as the tree began to bend to that side, he would swing out suspended only by his hands. The tree would bend and usually slowly float the rider to the ground. It gave the rider the sensation of parachuting to the ground. This was a lot of fun unless the rider chose an off-brand tree. Rookies were often directed to the off-brand trees for their first ride. The result was a parachute that didn't open and sometimes the need for a Johnson and Johnson band-aid.

Some of the larger, more stubborn riding trees were double-teamed or even triple-teamed. The stronger trees gave an added dimension to tree riding. Two or three of the larger boys would hold the tree in the ready position with the top bent to the ground and the trunk bent like Orion's bow. Then one of the smaller boys would climb onto the catapult and grab a branch or bear-hug the trunk and hold on for dear life. Not many rides at the Strawberry Festival could give a boy the adrenaline rush of a sixteen-foot sassafras sapling rocketing skyward. Long before Sputnik or NASA, the Cotton Mill Boys experienced weightlessness.

****

The balance beam took on many forms, and we were in training year-round. When we crossed the ditch behind the Little's house, we practiced the balance beam as we crossed the foot log. When we walked to town on one rail on the track, we balanced. These were just warm-ups and practice for the real contest. Slipping off the log or rail wasn't a danger to life and limb, but some of our balancing acts could get the gymnast injured or dead.

Probably the most dangerous balancing feat was the blindfolded walk around the ledge of the reservoir. This feat could only be provoked by a double-dog-dare by at least two people. The reservoir was a circular fish pond that at one time held the water supply for the mill. It was twenty feet to the water and five more feet of water to the bottom. There was a brick lip that stuck up two feet above the ground and encircled the reservoir. This lip, or ledge, as it was called, was one brick wide. It was pretty scary to walk the ledge and look down into the twenty foot drop to water, but to put on a blindfold and do it was the height of courage, or maybe stupidity.

The object of this gymnastic contest was to walk all the way around the reservoir without falling off the ledge. The ledge walker usually leaned to the right as he walked. That was the side that had a two foot drop. If the ledge walker fell off that side he lost the game, but if he fell to the left, he lost his life. If the gymnast dismounted to the left he could expect a twenty-foot fall into five feet of water. If he survived the fall, he would most likely be devoured by the alligator that inhabited the brackish water; the one the CCC boys put in there in '37. I never saw it, but I just knew he was lurking under the murky water with only his eyes and nostrils exposed. I don't recall anyone making it all the way around the reservoir. Neither do I recall anyone falling in. I guess most of the contestants just stepped off on the two-foot side and ended the game.

****

Roof tops were the sight of all sorts of acrobatics. We climbed on roofs of houses, sheds, smoke houses, wash houses and chicken houses, and many times, ended up hurt or in trouble. Like the time Leenova and I were climbing on the roof top next door to test our parachute. It was actually Mama's old black umbrella, but we just knew we would float to the ground if we jumped with it open.

I was so sure it would work that I didn't even try to get Leenova to go first. I stepped to the edge, bent my knees and jumped with every anticipation of floating to the ground. The ground rushed up at me and my eye-teeth vibrated when I hit the ground. I was able to get to my feet. Nothing seemed to be broken, and then I saw it. Yes, something was broken. It was Mama's black umbrella turned wrong-side-out and upside-down. I tried hard to straighten it back up, but a couple of bent spokes wouldn't let me. I would have to take it back to Mama inside-out and the poor puny plum tree would be minus another branch. So much for paragliding.

There was one other theory of flight that I developed. It was so brilliant I should have been an aeronautical engineer. My theory was that, if man could attain enough speed, he could run off a solid object into thin air and continue forward, walking on air at that speed until he touched down.

I had my capable and able scientific assistant, Leenova, to help me test this theory. We climbed up on Uncle Joe's house next door. It was vacant at the time. They had moved to another house, the ghost and all, you know. We got backed up to the top eave of the house. There was quite a slope and we held onto the chimney to keep from sliding down the roof. When the roof met the back porch the roof flattened out into a perfect runway.

We were all set to prove the O'Nealian Theory of Aeronautics. Wind south—Check. Runway clear—check. Pilot ready? No! My able assistant was about to chicken out. "I ain't gonna do it!" he said. "Aw, come on, it won't hurt," I coached. "You do it and I'll be right behind you after I observe the flight," I reassured him.

He leaned forward like a sprinter in the blocks and took off down the runway. As soon as he cleared the porch I could see he was loosing altitude. The next thing I heard was the thud as he crashed. I let go of the chimney and ran down the roof. I peered over the edge of the roof. Yep! He had crashed all right. Even with legs churning and arms flailing away, he'd crashed. I started to climb down the old drain pipe to get down and check on my assistant when I heard, "No you don't! You said you would if I would, so do it."

Now normally I had some pretty strong convictions about my theories, but after all the experiment was a failure. I had seen it with my own eyes. I started on down again and again Leenova said no, and he meant it because he reached down and picked up a half of a brick-bat and hoisted it above his head. Well maybe I would try it. After all Leenova might have just messed up on the experiment.

I backed up to the chimney and sprinted to the edge of the roof and right out into space with my legs never breaking stride. I was walking on air. Then the ground rushed up and hit me and everything went black. When I began to see some light, Leenova was standing over me saying, "You okay, you okay?" I was okay, but I was going to have to go back to the drawing board on my walking-on-air theory.

****

One of the summer sports that I believe was a Cotton Mill original, because I haven't seen it in the Olympics or Pan Am Games, was bumble bee ball. The required equipment to participate in a bumble bee ball game was a fishing pole. Normally the cane pole had to be at least twelve feet long, but a fourteen or sixteen footer was even better. The good thing about bumble bee ball was that the adults in the neighborhood loved for us to play it. Folks all over the neighborhood would invite us over to play. Sometimes they would bring us out a big glass of water when we were hot and sweaty from giving our all in the contest. Miss Mary even gave us a whole pitcher of grape penny-drink one time.

Mary Morrison was a widow who, in her later years married Peg Morrison. Peg's wife had died and they married for companionship. Peg had a wooden leg. Mama said he lost the leg trying to hop a train.

The rules of the game were simple, the boy who hit the most homeruns won the game. Everyone had to start at the same time and end at the same time. Each person was responsible for keeping his own scores, sort of like golf. Anyone who cheated or lied about his score was ostracized from BBBA. That stands for Bumble Bee Baseball Association. Once you lost your membership, you were out for life. Needless to say, we didn't cheat. Anyway our motto was "Cheaters never win", and we lived by it.

The game began with every player picking a spot around the house of the person who hosted the game. An official starter would yell "Go", and the game was on. Most players announced their running score verbally. "I got one, I got five", and so on. You could usually hear the swish of the cane pole and the crack of contact just before a new score was announced.

Charlie Bill probably was the Bumble Bee Ball champion. His practice of batting spit really helped his coordination. He would line up on a bee and just swing with his wrist and send the bee crashing to the earth.

We would circle a house swinging and swatting at the big black carpenter bees that bored holes in the eaves of every house in the Cotton Mill neighborhood. Out buildings were good places to swing a few strikes at the illusive targets. Just when one of the black blurs would give the batter a decent shot, he would buzz away, but enough of the creatures bit the dust, that by the end of the game, every one would have fifteen or twenty homeruns, and the homeowner would momentarily save his house from the wood-boring demons.

The next day we would be invited to a match at someone else's house. We never seemed to run out of balls to swat in our games.

Chapter IV: Winter Games

The start of September signaled three things. One was bad, one was not so bad, and one was good. They were the start of school, cotton picking, and the Winter Olympics. It wasn't that we disliked school all that much, but it took up so much of our time. Valuable time that could have been used making money picking cotton, or time playing was wasted sitting in a classroom.

We all attended Main Street Elementary School, which was about a mile walk from the Cotton Mill. The walks to and from school weren't so bad. We usually walked in a group and played along the way. We had the routine down pretty good. Walk down Avondale to the railroad crossing, then hit the rails and cross the trestle. The railroad would carry us to 18th Street and a straight shot to school. We usually had to hurry in the mornings to beat the late bell, but the trail home was a different story.

I knew I had an hour after school before Mama began to worry about my whereabouts so I usually got involved in some form of entertainment. By third grade I had made several friends that were town boys. If I returned home via 18th Street, I would usually take time to stop and pick up some pecans that had fallen on the side walk in front of Susan Smith's house. My next stop would be at Mack Hayes' house. Mack and I became good friends in later years. From Mack's, I would go by the Humboldt Ram's football field and watch them practice for a while. Then at the end of 18th Street, I would get on the railroad tracks and go home.

If I took the 17th Street route home my first stop was Thomas Oakley's house. Thomas had a swing that would rival the cable on the big tree. He, like I, was an avid Tarzan fan. He also could yodel the Tarzan yell better than anyone I ever heard, except maybe Skeezer. That Tarzan yell helped Thomas to develop his voice so well that later when we were in college he became a rock-and-roll singer with the Marvels. We would swing and yodel until I had to head home. I usually saved enough time to watch football practice before I had to go home.

Actually school wasn't all that bad. We had teachers who really cared about the students, but they were no pushovers. Every teacher had a paddle and wasn't shy about using it. If the paddling from the teacher didn't change a student's behavior, there was always Mr. McCarley. Mr. McCarley was the principal and it was his job to see that no one had too much fun at school. He had two basic pieces of equipment to insure that no student could go home and tell his parents he had a fun day.

Mr. McCarley wore a coaches whistle around his neck and anytime there was a shrill blast on the whistle everything would come to a halt. If you were running down the hall, there was that annoying whistle, tweeting away to stop you, or on the playground, if someone got the merry-go-round going too fast there was the "Tweet! Tweet!" to stop you. We always figured he slept with that whistle around his neck at night. He and his whistle were inseparable.

Besides the whistle, Mr. McCarley had another constant companion, his paddle. He could give you three licks so hard your great grand-daddy would feel it. But even at his best, he couldn't compare with one of Daddy's whippings. I only received one paddling from Mr. McCarley and I am sure he thought that was what straightened me up, but it was the whipping Daddy gave when I got home that kept me straight through the rest of elementary school.

Besides school, September brought cotton picking. Some schools let out for a month for cotton picking, but Humboldt didn't. That made Saturday or a holiday the only time a boy could make some of the good money. Most farmers paid three cents a pound for picking cotton. Some farmers would furnish a ride to the field free of charge. Others would debit a quarter from the days wages to pay for transportation. I was lucky. All I had to do was walk the footbridge behind the house and I was at the field. I picked for Ezra Pillow. He usually had several hands picking, but he never refused any of the Cotton Mill Boys who wanted to work.

Picking didn't start until the dew was off and lasted until about an hour before dark. In the morning, with dew on, the cotton weighed heavier and the farmer lost money on wet cotton, so it was usually around 9:00 a.m. before picking began. I would get there about an hour early and David Pillow and I would play until starting time. Each picker was issued a cotton sack if they didn't have their own personal sack. The sacks were eight to ten feet long and had a strap to hook over the shoulder. Most were made out of heavy domestic material and some had the under side smeared with tar to cut down on the wear and tear on the sack.

The picker was given a row to pick from one end of the field to the other. Some more experienced and skilled pickers would take two rows at a time. David Pillow and his brother Bobby were two of the best I had ever seen. They could out pick me two or three to one. I was slow and picked one-handed, but in good cotton I could get one hundred pounds a day and that equaled out to three dollars.

Three dollars a day wasn't bad considering a coke or candy bar was only a nickel and a box of 410 shotgun shells was fifty cents. About five days picking set me up for the winter.

* * * * * * * *

The good thing about September was that it brought on a whole new world of things to do and games to play. The first of September was the beginning of squirrel season. There was no big-game at all in West Tennessee in the fifties. Deer and turkey were hunted to extinction during the twenties and thirties by market hunters. The squirrel was the most sought after game animal in the state. There were two species, the gray squirrel and the fox squirrel. The fox squirrel was almost twice the size of the gray and its bright red tail was a trophy to be displayed from handle bars and antennae. Both species were highly prized for their meat.

Squirrel could be cooked in a variety of ways. My favorite was fried with thickening gravy. Little Mama could fry a young squirrel so tender it would melt in your mouth. Along with one of her thick buttermilk biscuits, sopped in gravy, the squirrel was fit for a king. I also liked the squirrel boiled, deboned, and cooked with dumplings. Little Mama also had a taste for squirrel and sometimes the consumption of the little rodent would prompt her to tell a story from her early years.

She told me about when my grandfather was a market hunter and sold squirrels for ten cents apiece. He would buy a box of twenty-two shot for ten cents and make two dollars a box on the squirrels he killed. He never missed and he never hit the squirrel anywhere but in the head. I was impressed, because sometimes I missed with a shot gun.

One story led to another as she leaned back in her rocker and almost closed her eyes as the memories flooded her mind. She told about the time Poppa was hunting in Black Bottom in Arkansas and was treed by a pack of wolves, but finally ran them off after killing three with his single shot twenty-two.

Then she turned to the time when they lived in a log cabin in Black Bottom and a panther came to the oxen pen, then tried to get in the cabin where she and the baby were alone. She was only about five feet tall, but she was as tough as a pine knot. I could listen to her all day long.

Squirrel hunting, like most everything the Cotton Mill Boys did, was competitive. We kept score on each squirrel we killed and at the end of squirrel season the one who had the highest kills was considered the best squirrel hunter at the Cotton Mill.

We had three or four techniques we used for hunting squirrels. Still hunting was the most popular method and required a great deal of woodsmanship. I always thought my Cherokee blood gave me a slight advantage in still hunting. To still hunt, the hunter needed to be in the woods by the time the eastern sky began to streak with a yellow and pink glow. The hunter would stand still and listen and look for some sign that would give away a squirrel's position. A clump of leaves shaking, a hickory nut falling to the ground, or the scrapping of sharp teeth on the hard shell of a nut were good signs that a squirrel was near. Once a squirrel was located, the real skill was being able to sneak over dry leaves and twigs quietly without alerting the squirrel of danger. Once in range of the 410, it was the hunters responsibility to make a quick, painless kill.

Hunting with a squirrel dog was the favorite method of squirrel hunting after the leaves fell off. Hunting with a dog did not require the hunter to be in the woods at daylight. After the sun came up squirrels would often be on the ground searching for fallen acorns. The squirrels left a scent that a good dog could smell and follow to the tree they ascended. The dog would rear up on the tree and bark until we got there. We took turns getting the first shot. The shooter would stand quietly on one side of the tree while the others would walk around the tree making noise. The squirrel would run to the opposite side of the tree to avoid the noise-makers and would become an easy target.

Dog hunting required a good squirrel dog. We had the best. A dog named Spot. He was Andy Collingsworth's dog, but he was our hunting buddy and anytime we cut through the Collinsworth place with a gun, he was right with us. Andy later became our hunting buddy, too.

Another method we used was unorthodox, but it worked. We called it den hunting. We would take turns climbing the beech trees that had holes in them that provided a home for the squirrels. With a long limber stick we would probe the hole until the occupants of the squirrel hotel vacated the premises. As the squirrels exited the tree to another locality, the shooters would pick them off. It may seem that we were unethical sportsmen, but there were certain practices, that if used, could give a hunter a bad name.

One of the worst things a boy could be called was a "nest shooter." A nest shooter was someone who shot into the leaf nest that the squirrels built in the branches. The thing that made this such a crime was the fact that in the early fall, many squirrels still had their young in the nest. A whole family could be wiped out in a single shot. We were conservationist. We never killed over the limit and we never killed anything we didn't eat or give to someone else to eat.

There were two main places where we squirrel hunted. One was Spangler's Woods and the other was Duffey's Bottom. Both were in easy walking distance of the Cotton Mill and both were at the edge of the wilderness.

Spangler's Woods seemed a lot larger then than it does now. It was the closest woods to the Cotton Mill where a hunter could find a squirrel and it also was the place we built a tree house that would have been the envy of Tarzan or Bomba the jungle boy. Spangler's woods, at one time, was the home of wild boars. Savage hogs roamed the fenced-in woods lot and presented a danger to anyone who dared to climb the hog-wire fence. Fortunately there were tree tops dispersed throughout the woods to provide a means of escape from the man-eaters.

After the wild hogs disappeared, there was a herd of wild horses that took up residence in the woods. All the live-stock just added to the challenge of killing a squirrel.

We knew every hickory tree and black gum tree in the woods. We even knew which trees the squirrels would cut first. Cutting was eating the nuts or fruit that grew on the trees. We would search under the trees for the tell-tale sign of chewed-up nut shells. If they were fresh, we would be sitting under the tree the next morning or afternoon with our gun across our lap.

Duffey's Bottom was a little bit more sinister than Spangler's Woods. A fellow could get lost in Duffey's Bottom. Well, maybe turned around would be a better description. But the fact that the far side of the bottom stretched into the unknown world made Duffey's somewhat frightening to a ten-year-old. A boy standing in the tall trees as day was breaking could hear all kinds of sounds. Off in the distance the scream of a wild cat could be heard. It might have even been a panther screaming or a wolfus. Daylight was always a welcome sight in Duffey's Bottom.

****

Next to squirrel, rabbit hunting was our favorite. Squirrel hunting was more of a solitary sport, but a rabbit hunt was a social event. A rabbit hunt usually started with one or two boys and a dog and ended up with a half-dozen boys and even more dogs. If Doug, Jeep and I took our single-barrel shot guns and headed up the hill with Snowball, the first person we would pick up would be Charlie Bill. He would come out with his old Mossburg bolt-action and ask if someone had a couple of shells he could borrow. The next to join our merry band would be Tippy, the half Border Collie and half something else. Next would be Zookie, Bobby Crocker's half feist and half something else. Across the road Colin Barrett would be putting on his daddy's hunting vest and heading to the road. Minnie, his full blooded beagle would be at his heels. Unless Skeezer decided to go with us, that was the party for the day.

We usually headed down the fence-row that separated Barrett's Grocery from the cotton patch across the road from Skeezer's house. Snowball and Tippy would bounce up and down on the piles of brush and honeysuckle. While they bounced on the piles in an attempt to flush a hiding rabbit, Minnie and Zookie would work the tunnels underneath the vines. It usually wasn't long before an old cottontail couldn't stand the pressure and would break for the cotton field. If someone didn't roll the rabbit before it hit the cotton field the race was on. Snowball and Tippie would run the rabbit as long as they could see it, then Minnie would take over. She would stay on the rabbit's trail bawling every breath until one of us killed the rabbit or until darkness fell. Like squirrels, rabbits provided meat, recreation and competition. Charlie Bill usually ended up with more rabbits than the rest of us and he never let us forget it.

There was one method of catching rabbits that didn't tear the rabbit up or ruin a good meal by breaking a tooth on buck-shot. There was no lead shot and no hair poked in the holes the buck-shot entered. For a lead-free rabbit, the best method was the rabbit gum.

The gum was made out of one-by-eight boards nailed together to form a rectangle. The gum was about two-feet long with an eight-by-eight board closing off the end. The opening to the gum had a door that would slide up and down inside grooves that stabilized the door so it could not be pushed forward or backward. In the middle, on top of the gum, was a forked stick that stuck up about a foot. The door had a string attached to the top that was tied to a balance stick about twenty inches long. The balance stick had a string attached that was tied to the trigger. The trigger was a slender stick that had a notch facing upward. The trigger was inserted into a hole about four to six inches from the back of the box and part of the trigger extended down inside the box. The notch hooked over the small hole and faced the opening to the box. The balance stick was held in place by the trigger and the door hung above the opening to the box.

Everyone had at least one rabbit gum. They were kept set between the rows in the garden or along rabbit paths in the honeysuckles. With the trigger set and the door hanging like a guillotine the box was then baited with apple peals or some other enticing food. The rabbit would smell the food and go into the box to investigate. As he hopped to the back of the box, he would hit the trigger stick, dislodging the notch, and the weight of the door would cause it to come crashing down. The rabbit was trapped and could only await his fate.

Mama said if it hadn't been for rabbits people would have starved during the depression. They were called "Hoover hogs", because most people blamed President Herbert Hoover for the poor economy that nearly destroyed this country. I read in the history books that it wasn't really his fault, but Mama would never believe it.

Occasionally the gum trapper would get a bonus. A 'possum would sometimes find his way into the rabbit gum. When I found a 'possum in my rabbit gum, I felt that I had struck gold. I would pull him out by his hairless tail, which made him "sull up." If you whack a 'possum, he will play dead. He is easier to carry by his tail if he is hanging limp as if dead. I would head to Uncle Whit's with my prize. He always gave me fifty cents for each 'possum I brought to him.

He would then put it in his 'possum coop and feed him sweet-taters for seven days. On the eighth day, the 'possum was cleaned and roasted. I never liked 'possum that much. I guess it was because I once saw a 'possum crawl out of the carcass of a dead mule.

When I found a 'possum in my rabbit gum, I felt that I had struck gold.

****

Football was my favorite of all the team sports. I played it anytime we could gather together at least two people. I even devised games I could play by myself. I would throw the football on the roof at such angles the return of the football could not be predicted. As it rolled down the roof I would catch it before it could hit the ground. If I caught it, it was a touchdown for my imaginary team. If it hit the ground it was a touchdown for the other team. I would play by myself for hours. It's no wonder Dad was always having to patch the roof.

If I could get one more person to play, we could play pass and catch. This game involved one person throwing a pass to the receiver. If the receiver caught the ball, he got a touchdown. If he touched the ball with any part of his body and dropped it, it was a touchdown for the passer. Naturally the passer never threw an easy catchable ball, but if the ball was too high or too short, the receiver could let it go and if he didn't touch the ball, it didn't count as an attempt.

Two people also could play set-back. This was a punting game in which the players tried to keep backing each other up until one was forced into the end zone to catch the kick. The player who kicked the ball in the end zone won.

These games were good practice and taught fundamentals, but on Saturday and Sunday afternoons, the real games were played. Choosing sides was similar to the methods used in baseball. The older boys were usually captains. Some of them were pretty old too. Red Walls must have been near twenty because he was already out of high school. Others who were already out working and some who were high school players for the Humboldt Rams joined in our games. Sometimes there were so many we fielded two full teams and had two or three subs.

Most of the time we started out playing two hand touch below the belt, but after an argument or two about touching or not touching a runner, the game turned into tackle.

There were always bloody noses and busted lips, but

occasionally there would be a broken bone. It was pretty rough, and since the field was right across the street from my house, Mama would embarrass me by yelling across the road, "You boys are getting too rough!"

Every Cotton Mill Boy wanted to play for the Humboldt Rams and wear the red and gray. All my uncles and cousins played and I knew I would someday play. The youngest boys enjoyed going to the Ram's games on Friday night. The Henley's were well represented with Bubbie and Doodler. They were in high school when I was in elementary. As a matter of fact, there was at least one Henley on the Rams football team from 1949 until 1962. My Uncle Bo Jack played in 1949 and went on to play for Memphis State and coach at Humboldt High. He was my coach in high school. Jeep was the last Henley. He graduated in 1962.

On Friday night three or four of us would go to the game. The worst part of the trip was crossing the dreaded trestle. It was usually still a little light when we headed to the field, but it was pitch black on the way home. Our parents would usually give us a quarter to get in, if we didn't have any cotton-picking money left. Having a quarter in our pockets lead us down the road to temptation and caused us to sin against God and the Humboldt Rams.

Charlie Bill, Leenova, Vanny Dee, David and I walked to the game that night. The bright glow of the stadium lights could be seen all the way at the Cotton Mill. We were anxious to get to the game. The opponent was Trenton Peabody, the cross-country rivals. We couldn't wait to cheer the team on to victory.

The stadium was surrounded by a tall fence with two stands of barbed wire around the top. Charlie Bill carried a scar on his right arm from the barbed wire that protected the security of the field. He caught his arm while jumping over the fence to slip into the game.

There were two or three dark areas where a good quick climber could slip in. The subject of slipping in came up in our conversation on the way to the game. "If we slip in, we can spend the whole quarter on popcorn and coke," Vanny Dee suggested.

"I don't know about slipping in, we might get caught by the police," I said hesitantly.

Charlie Bill said, "I'm not going to climb that fence again. The last time I tore my new shirt and cut my arm."

"We don't have to climb," replied Vanny Dee. "I know where there is a drain pipe we can crawl through."

With reluctance we followed Vanny Dee around to the Campbell Street side of the field. About half way down the block we located the pipe. We crawled up to the opening to the pipe and looked in. Light shown through from the other side. The opening on the other side of the fence looked small and far away.

"What if there's a snake in there?" I asked.

"There ain't no snake in there! I'll go first and show you," said Vanny Dee.

He wiggled into the pipe and all that could be seen was an occasional ray of light as he scooted from side to side uphill in the pipe. In a minute or two a voice came through the pipe, "I made it!"

Vanny Dee was a little taller than the rest of us, but he was pretty thin. I let Leenova go next and then David. My conscience was beginning to shame me about slipping in. "It was the same as stealing", it told me. Leenova whispered through the pipe, "All clear."

I was still fighting with my conscience when Charlie Bill

jumped ahead of me and entered the pipe. I was sitting there staring in the pipe thinking, "They'll call me a chicken if I don't go." Then I heard a muffled voice saying something. I looked into the pipe and absolutely no light penetrated the darkness. Again I heard the garbled words coming from the pipe. "What did you say?" I asked into the pipe. The words were garbled again, but I could sense panic in the voice. I heard someone at the fence above and looked up to see Vanny Dee.

"He says he's stuck," he interpreted the garbled words.

I crawled up in the pipe and tried to push forward on the chunky boy in the pipe. It only accomplished a grunt out of him.

At this point my imagination took over. I could see it all. The fire department, the police department and rescue workers drilling a shaft to save the trapped kid. Newspaper reporters swarming all over the place taking pictures. Then shear terror set in as I realized Mama and Daddy were going to find out I was slipping into the ball game. What would the coaches and players think? Why, I didn't even care enough about the Rams to pay to see them.

I was slapped back to reality by a scream for help. The claustrophobia was getting to Charlie Bill. Vanny Dee was on the other side of the pipe trying to shut him up before he drew attention to Leenova and himself inside the fence. We were on the visitor side, but such yells were sure to bring the police.

I scrambled up the bank to the fence and had a quick huddle with Vanny Dee to get our game plan together. With our plan intact we went to work. I crawled up into the pipe and grabbed Charlie Bill around the ankles. Vanny Dee crawled down the pipe and grabbed Charlie Bill by the wrist. We both held tight and pulled. His elbows straightened and his arms came free. I scooted down to the entrance of the pipe pulling Charlie Bill along with me. When he cleared the pipe he breathed a sigh of relief.

"Well, You want to try it again?" I asked.

"Heck no! Let's go pay," was his answer.

Football was more than just a game to me. It was a miniature snap shot of life itself. Nothing prepares a person to face the adversities of life any better than the game of football. If you get knocked down, you don't just lie there, you get back up and pursue the ball. Nowhere but in football, and life itself, is a person required to sacrifice self for the good of the whole. I believe the game of football has contributed greatly to the strength and might of this great country. Most soldiers who distinguished themselves on the battlefield were either athletes or outdoorsmen.

Some of my most memorable times were those spent on the football field with Charlie Bill, David, Jeep and Doug. All were Cotton Mill Boys, but football made me close to even some of the town boys. I guess I never got enough football, because I went on to coach football in high school and college.

****

When I was eight years old, I got a horse. He was a small horse and Daddy said he was an Indian pony. That suited me just fine, because I loved to play Indians. I would catch the old rooster with his back turned and yank out two or three feathers. I would then look through Mama's old quilting scraps until I found one just right to tie around my head. I stuck the feathers in the back and I was an Indian. The red juice from pokeberries was used to apply war paint to my face. Shirtless and with a strip of cloth hanging from the front and back of my belt, I was in costume.

Dressed as an Indian, I would jump on Lightning and take off. I named him Lightning because of his white blaze that zigzagged from side to side down his forehead. Sometimes I rode with a saddle and sometimes I went strictly bare back. I enjoyed riding Lightning fast and feeling the breeze on my face. Sometimes I would ride up to Colin Barrett's and he would get on his horse and ride along with me. Lightning was a gentle horse and I let all the Cotton Mill Boys ride him, but all the fun came to an end one day.

I kept Lightning in a pasture behind Uncle Bill's Store. It was only two or three acres, but it had good grass and an old shed that served as a barn. Toward the end of summer that year my cousin, William Maitland, from Texas, visited me. Of course everyone knows that Texans are about the best horsemen in the world, next to the Comanche's. William wanted to see my horse so we walked down to the pasture. Lightning came over to the fence the moment he saw us.

I was standing there rubbing him on the nose when William asked, "Can I ride him?"

I had never seen William ride, but I figured, "He's a Texan" and said "Okay."

He crawled under the barbed wire fence and took hold of the rope halter around Lightning's neck. He leaped on the horse's back like Rocky Lane mounting his horse Blackjack. When he touched down on Lightning's back the resemblance to Rocky Lane ended. Lightning took off as if he had been stung by a hornet. He ran and bucked across the pasture. William flipped head-over-heels backward off the little horse. As he turned the back-flip into a half-gainer, Lightning's hoof caught him just above the eye. He sprawled out on the ground and didn't move.

I crawled under the fence and rushed to him. No movement, he must be dead. I shook him and he groaned. Thank goodness, he was still alive.

William staggered to his feet with my help and we headed home. He had blood trickling out of his eyebrow and a reddish spot just the size and shape of a horse's hoof on his forehead. I was partially supporting him as we climbed the back steps. Mama came running out, "What in the name of the Lord has happened?" she asked.

I told her the story and she said, "We'll have to get rid of that horse!"

Now, in the movies when a horse went bad and they said they had to get rid of it, that meant the horse would be shot. I ran out the door screaming, "Don't shoot my horse!"

As I ran out screaming, who should I run into but Miss Booker. No doubt she was coming to give Mama a choice piece of gossip. She looked at me as I ran screaming and crying, then she peeped in the door and saw William with blood running down his face. She heard him say, "The horse kicked me," and didn't bother to get the details. She turned and headed to Miss Mary's house. Within half an hour neighbors from all over the Cotton Mill were gathering at our house to see what Mama was going to do about the killer horse.

Even Uncle Whit offered to get his old double-barrel and put him out of his misery. I cried even louder as I just knew Lightning would be destroyed.

Mama finally assured me no one would kill the horse, she meant we would have to sell the horse before it hurt someone else. I was glad Lightning would be spared, but I was sad that my trusty steed would be sold.

I guess I never really forgave William for causing me to

lose my horse. I always figured Lightning reacted that way because there were cockle burs in the halter and they stuck him when William jumped on. You would have thought a Texan would have known to check first.

****

There is an Olympic riding event called Three Day Eventing. The horsemen race around the obstacle course trying to beat the clock. Doug, Jeep and I once rode a horse in this event. The course was Spangler's Woods.

We were playing in the tree house when the old mare and her colt stopped to graze in some clumps of grass below us. We looked down at the broad back of the horse below us. We had never ridden on this horse but we thought she looked gentle enough so we looked at each other and said, "Let's ride."

We climbed down from the tree house and slowly approached the horse. She let us rub her on the face.

"Good horsey," I coaxed. I had owned a horse so I knew exactly what to do. We pulled up some grass and fed her. As she nibbled at the grass, we inched closer to a big stump. When we were even with the big stump, I stopped and dished out the long stemmed grass.

"Okay, Doug climb on the stump and get on her back," I instructed. He slid gently on her back as the horse nibbled at the hands-full of grass served up to her.

"Now Jeep, you get on," I said as I stroked the horse's forehead. Once Jeep was on behind Doug, I climbed on in front of Doug. I had no saddle nor reins, not even a halter to hang on to. I grabbed a handful of mane. An experienced horseman like me could guide a horse by its mane. The horse just stood there.

"Git up!" I demanded. Nothing happened.

"Gitty up!" I shouted. Still nothing happened.

I pulled my legs out and gave her a swift kick in the ribs. She took off like she had been shot out of a cannon. I grabbed mane with both hands, Doug locked his arms around my waist in a death grip and Jeep locked onto Doug. The horse headed into the woods at a full gallop.

The first obstacle in the course was a log that had fallen across the trail. We approached the log and the horse sailed over the log with the style and grace of a thoroughbred.

We then approached the water jump. It was a large mud puddle and the horse just plowed right through it. Next came a series of thorn bushes to slap our legs as the horse plunged through them.

The next obstacle was not seen by any of us, but we felt it. An overhanging limb caught me across the chest and broke my grip on the horse's mane. Like the Three Stooges, we slid off the rump of the horse with Doug hugging me and Jeep hugging Doug. All three of us landed smack on the seat of our pants.

Doug started crying and holding his arm. I told him it was only sprained and I would set it for him, but he refused. He said it was hurting awfully bad, so we carried him home. We couldn't tell Uncle Blubber and Aunt Linnie Mae we had fallen off a horse, so we said Doug fell out of the tree house. I felt bad about lying, but I would have felt worse if Daddy had taken his belt to me. If we had made the whole course that day we could have easily started a new equestrian event, Three-man, tackless obstacle course.

****

Bale climbing and jumping was an indoor sport. It was usually played on weekends when it rained. On rainy days we had a great place to play if the mill wasn't in operation. On most weekends the mill shut down at least by noon on Saturday. There was one night watchman to check the building, and he usually stayed in the break room most of the time. When the Cardinals were playing, he would have his old radio plugged in, listening to the game. We pretty much had the warehouse all to ourselves.

The warehouse had cotton bales stacked as high as three deep. There were carts or buggies that were used to transport the bales of mop yarn. There was also a tow-motor or forklift that was used to stack the bales of cotton. The warehouse was dimly lit and made a great place to play army, king-of-the-hill, touch in-and-out of jail, or just plain old follow-the-leader.

Follow the leader got us in big trouble on one rainy Sunday afternoon. There were five or six of us who became bored with sitting on the front porch swinging. We decided to go to the warehouse and play.

My cousins, Corky, Shirley and I headed up the switch-track in the light rain. Before long we were joined by Leenova and Charlie Bill. We ducked in the side door and slipped back to the warehouse. We peeped around the door and all was clear. We then began to argue about what game we would play.

Leenova and Charlie Bill headed over to the tow-motor and Leenova climbed in the driver's seat. Charlie Bill climbed on with him. Leenova pretended to drive the vehicle as he turned the steering wheel from side to side. I don't know which one hit the starter, but the thing took off and we all scattered as they came toward my cousins and me. We ran around behind a bale, but the powerful machine pushed our refuge toward another stack of bales. We jumped out of the way just in time to avoid becoming the meat in a cotton-bale sandwich. When the bale being pushed, hit the stack of bales, the forklift bounced off and headed toward the door to the part of the mill that contained long lines of machinery.

Charlie Bill was screaming, "Get your foot off the gas!"

Leenova followed instructions and the big machine came to a stop just before it entered the mill. They killed the motor with the switch and jumped off and ran. We all ran because we thought the night watchman would surely come to investigate. After hiding and watching for a few minutes, we knew we were in the clear.

We decided to play follow-the-leader and chose a leader by the one-potato, two-potato method. Leenova was the leader. He started by climbing up on a cotton bale. Everyone got to the top with no problem. The next feat was to jump off the bale onto the oily hardwood floor. The hard floor stung my feet through my PF Flyers but everyone made the jump. Next he climbed a stack of mop yarn balls. This was a dangerous feat because each ball weighed one-hundred pounds. The balls were stacked five high with each line of balls holding one less ball than the stack below it. This gave the balls at the end of the stack a stair step effect. To make climbing the stack even more difficult, the balls were loosely wrapped in burlap bagging. If any ball were to be dislodged from the stack, the whole stack could come down like an avalanche.

Leenova made it to the top. Then, Shirley, then Charlie Bill, then Corkey, and finally I stood on top. We walked back down the stair steps formed by the balls. We had escaped without anyone getting a scratch. Unfortunately our luck would not hold out.

The bit of daring involved climbing a stack of cotton bales that were two high. There was a gap between that stack of bales and the stack that paralleled these bales. The gap gave the appearance of a deep canyon. Gaps were left in the storage of the bales to allow space for the forklift to travel between the stacks. There was about a twelve foot drop to the floor from the top of the stacked bales.

Leenova stared down into the dark gulf between the stacks of bales. He then backed up and with a mighty leap, cleared the chasm. Shirley was next. She got to the far side of the bale to get a running start. She ran and leaped and disappeared into the darkness below. We heard her let out a scream.

We couldn't see her so we all scrambled down from the top of the bales and ran into the darkness between them. There was just enough light to see Shirley hanging on the side of the bale. Only one foot touched the floor and her right hand was stretched out above her head. She was crying but she managed to whimper out, "My ring is hung, my ring is hung."

We looked and the metal band that held the bale together had caught her ring as she slid down the side of the bale. I looked and it almost made me sick. Corkey almost fainted. Shirley's ring had cut into her finger so deep the bone was exposed. There wasn't a lot of blood, but the meat was peeled back to the bone. She was literally hanging by her ring finger.

"Get me down, get me down!" she cried.

We all got her around the legs and lifted her up to take the pressure off her hand. Her ring came off the metal strap and Shirley saw it for the first time. She fainted. We propped her feet up and began to fan her. I had seen Mama do that when Little Mama fainted.

She finally came to and I grabbed a handful of the white cotton and wrapped it around her hand so she could not see it.

We headed to Aunt Ethel's house as fast as we could. Corkey ran on ahead and screamed for Aunt Ethel. As soon as she saw us, her first words were, "Lordy Mercy." I guess those "Lordy Mercies" ran in the Maitland family, because that was usually Mama's first words, too.

She yelled at Mama next door, "Call Dr. Barker and tell him to meet us at the emergency room."

She had already awakened Uncle Joe from his Sunday nap, so they jumped in Joe's old car and headed out. Corkey came over to our house and waited to hear what would happen. We thought they might have to cut Shirley's finger off, but the only thing that got cut off was her ring.

When she came home she had twelve stitches in her ring finger. After some questioning we finally confessed that it happened in the mill warehouse. The poor old plum tree got two limbs broken off. One for me and one for Corkey. Shirley escaped with her stitches.

Chapter V: Acting Lessons

Much of our spare time was filled with our heroes of the silver screen. When we weren't watching our heroes in action, we were acting out the parts of the heroes we had seen. Most of our study of the art of acting was done on Saturday afternoon. Almost every Saturday Uncle Whitt would take Skeezer and me to the movies. We would usually go to the new show, The Plaza, first, and then go to the old show, The Ritz, next. Sometimes there would be a double feature at each movie and the whole afternoon would be devoted to our heroes.

Each theater had a serial that was continued from week to week. Each short episode ended with the good guy in a dangerous situation with no way out. We racked our brain from one week to the next trying to guess how the hero would be saved.

The serials featured an array of heroes from Jungle Jim to Rocket Man. There were others like Captain Marvel, Buck Rogers, Ramar of the Jungle, Zorro, and the Blackhawks. I liked them all, but one of our favorites was the Blackhawks. This was a serial about a group of airplane pilots who were out to save the world from evil. I don't remember but two of the character's names. One was Chuck. I remember his name because, when we all got together and did a remake of the episode we had seen that week, I played Chuck. I don't know what actor played Chuck, but I can see his face today like it was 1952.

The other character I remember was Chop-Chop. He was a small Chinese with a pig-tail and his weapon of choice was a meat cleaver.

Jon Hall played *Ramar of the Jungle*. He was a doctor who lived in the jungles of Africa. He was no ordinary doctor. He could out-shoot and out-fight a whole tribe of bad natives. He managed to escape all kinds of perils that seemed to be his doom as the episode ended each week. The week's offering might end with Ramar falling in quick sand. His head would go under the water and sand, and the announcer would ask, "Can Ramar escape death? Come back next week to this theater to see if he will survive."

We usually came back and we usually had his escape already figured out by the next Saturday. Johnny Wiesmuller played Jungle Jim. He had gotten a little too old and a little too fat to play Tarzan, but he could still whip a lion with only his knife. He didn't swing through trees, but he could still out-swim a crocodile and, if need be, he could wrestle it down and kill it with his knife. He was still running around holding hands with a chimp like he did as Tarzan.

We didn't act out the *Jungle Jim* serial because there was only one role and unless we were playing alone or someone would play the part of the chimp, there just wasn't any other parts!

Rocket Man wasn't a bad serial to act out but Skeezer always got to be rocket man and I had to be his sidekick. Rocket Man had this neat suit. He had a large metal helmet shaped like the nose cone of a rocket. He wore a leather jacket that had little dials on the chest to adjust for speed. On his back was a silver rocket that spewed smoke and fire out like a jet. When an emergency came up, he would slip on his helmet and backpack rocket, adjust the dials and leap into the air to fly to the rescue. The serial always left you holding on to your seat, but when the feature attraction came on every boy and girl in the theater cheered. Uncle Whit cheered right along with us.

The Saturday Matinees were usually westerns. Most of the westerns followed the same format. There was the cowboy hero, the pretty girl who liked the cowboy hero, the sidekick who was funny, and the mean old villain. The plot varied from the villain trying to take the girl's ranch, to rustling or trying to steal all the girl's cattle. The good guys always won.

We learned that good beats evil every time. The good guy, whether it be Hoppy, Roy, Gene, Rex, or Tex, would go in the saloon and order a glass of milk or sarsaparilla. The bad guys would laugh at them, and then the good guy would mop up the place with them. I never refused to drink my milk or eat my vegetables because my heroes ate theirs. If it was good enough for Rocky Lane, then it was good enough for me.

Kids today don't really have any good heroes and role models. Their time is spent watching fictional animals on the screen of their Game Boy or some cartoon with characters that are rude to their parents and everyone else. Today's characters leave the impression with kids that it isn't wrong to lie or steal.

Most families the kids see on T. V. are dysfunctional. It makes me glad that I grew up in a time when real men were heroes who were willing to sacrifice themselves to save the helpless widow or orphan. I don't know if the movies influenced society or if society influenced the movies back then, but there were real heroes who would risk their own safety to save others, just like the heroes in the movies.

There were men who proudly served their country in the military. Many of the men at the Cotton Mill were Veterans. Charlie Bill's dad, Louis, served in the army in World War II. My Uncle, Roy Henley, was in the campaign in North Africa and Italy. He even brought home a German rifle and helmet. My dad didn't go because he had a soft spot in his skull, but he tried to volunteer to be a bombardier. They wouldn't take him so he must have had a pretty bad handicap. There were some who had served in World War I in France. Carl Scott would tell us what it was like in the trenches of France. My Uncle Bud Maitland was in World War I and told horror stories of their crossing the Atlantic in a storm. The waves were so high the other ships would disappear as if they had submerged. They would then pop back up and be above the other ships. He said he was more afraid during the crossing than any time during the war.

The veterans, along with John Wayne, led us into many wars. Next to cowboys, army was our passion. We would listen to the war stories or see a movie, like *The Sands of Iwo Jima,* and we were good for a week of machine guns and hand grenades. We would choose sides and one side would go hide and the other would come looking. We usually used rifles made from a brown stick, but sometimes our BB guns became our M-16's.

Green walnuts made great hand grenades. The problem with our wars was that there was no sure-fire way to know if the enemy had been killed in the conflict. "Bang! You're dead!" would be a cry from one side.

"No! You missed," would be the reply.

There was one sure way to know if an enemy soldier had been killed. When the enemy was hit by a hedge apple or green walnut grenade, they usually didn't deny being killed. As a matter of fact, a whop up-side the head with one of these grenades made you think you were going to die.

We went all out on our pretend war. Some guys would wear an old World War II helmet, some even had an old army shirt. The sleeves had to be rolled up, but it was a real uniform. Some had old army canteens. I would sometimes sneak out the German bayonet that my Uncle Roy brought home from Italy.

Our wars would last almost all day. We would climb trees and become snipers. We would dig fox holes along the ditch bank. Each fox hole would have a supply of green walnuts or hedge apple grenades. There was only one rule that I remember about playing army. The rule was that you could not be shot if you were crawling on your belly, but if someone tossed a grenade on you, it killed you if it touched you.

Playing army gave the Cotton Mill Boys a sense of patriotism. We always stood at attention when the Star Spangled Banner was played. Caps were removed and placed over the heart, eyes focused on Old Glory, and we proudly sang along. Every day school was opened with The National Anthem, the pledge of allegiance, and a prayer.

No one objected when we had an assembly and a preacher came and read from the Bible and prayed. I had never heard of the ACLU, and anyone who wouldn't stand and say the pledge would have been considered a traitor.

I remember when the pledge had the words "under God" added. There certainly were no objections from any of the people at the Cotton Mill. Patriotism was high in this country or at least at the Cotton Mill. It was a good time to be an American. Growing up in that time had a great influence on the other Cotton Mill Boys and me. To this day I am proud to be an American.

The wars we fought were not always modern wars. Sometimes we were the Seventh Calvary fighting Indians. I always liked to be one of the Indians, I guess because of my Cherokee blood. I always thought the Indians got a bum deal in the movies. Except for Little Beaver and Tonto, most Indians were portrayed as blood thirsty savages looking to take a white scalp.

I later found out in the history books that the British were the ones who taught the Indians to scalp. They paid the Indians in trade goods for each French scalp the Indians took. So who were the savages?

Probably the oldest war we fought went back to the reign of King Richard. We liked to play Robin Hood and his merry men. There were enough parts for everyone when we played Robin Hood. If Bobo was there, he was Robin. If he wasn't, there was usually a squabble over who would be Robin Hood. We settled it in true Sherwood fashion by each shooting an arrow from our homemade bow. The closest to the target would get to be Robin Hood. I was a pretty good shot with a bow and about half the time I would win. Of course, no one could beat Bobo. I'm not sure Robin himself could have beaten Bobo.

Charlie Bill was the perfect Friar Tuck. Pee Wee or I usually would be Will Scarlet. Skeezer made a really good Little John, because he could use a quarter staff better than any of us. If someone didn't get a major role, he still would play and be one of Robin's men.

The only role that didn't cause a dispute over who would play it was the role of Maid Marian. No girls played in Sherwood Forest with us, so if someone complained about not getting to be Robin or Will Scarlet, or some other character, the standard answer was, "Okay, you can play Maid Marian." That always shut up the complainer.

We had the perfect place to play Robin Hood. It was a small woods lot we named Sherwood Forest. There were a few large trees that were perfect for Robins' men to climb. There were some smaller riding trees that would be ridden down and made into a catapult. One large oak had branches that spread out, side by side, and was perfect for our lookout platform. The locust trees were a nuisance with their long, sharp thorns, but on the other hand they were tough on the Sheriff of Nottingham's men.

We had the perfect place to play Robin Hood.
It was a small woods we named Sherwood Forest.

There was one place we tried to avoid in the forest. There was a spot about six feet long where the ground had sunk about a foot. At the end of the sunken place was a stone. It had no inscription, but we knew there was a grave there.

One of the unsolved mysteries took place there at that grave site. The site became the subject of some ghost stories and that sort of put a chill on Sherwood Forest, but until the ghost stories began, we had some great times there playing Robin Hood.

We were all in training to be in Robin's army. We had to be proficient with the bow, the sword, and the quarter staff. We practiced daily with each weapon. We had contests with the bow and arrow. Sometimes we had a target with a bull's eye drawn on an old newspaper, and sometimes we just shot at a stump. There was no doubt Bobo was the best archer in Sherwood Forest and the rest of us set our goal to be as good as Bobo.

Sword fighting could get a little bit rough. We would square off with a partner and yell out, "On guard!" Our wooden swords would rattle against each other as we dancedforward then backward. The thing that hurt the worst was a whack across the hand. Pee Wee was pretty good with a sword and everyone wanted to beat him.

Skeezer was king of the quarter staff. We each would cut an eight-foot hickory sapling for our staff. There was a fallen log that made the perfect practice area.

Two people would mount the log facing each other. The fight would begin and the one left standing on the log at the end was the winner. We got plenty of practice being Robin's merry men in our beloved Sherwood Forest.

In the 1950's there was something called the Cold War. The Cotton Mill Boys had their own version of the Cold War.

It didn't happen very often, but maybe two or three times a year we would have a snow that was two or three inches deep. Sometimes it was so deep school would be dismissed or it snowed on Christmas break. Those days were usually devoted to rabbit hunting in the snow. A rabbit could be tracked right up to its hiding place and shot. Mama said during the depression people would track rabbits in the snow and knock them in the head with a stick where they sat. They were mainstay for people who had no job and no money. We did it for sport, but the meat was always good, even when there was bologna in the house.

The days were devoted to hunting but in the late afternoon and evening we fought the cold wars. We usually spent most of the afternoon building a snow fort. Most of the time we would ward off attacks on the fort with a volley of snowballs. The snowballs could do considerable damage if they were tightly packed and allowed to crust over on the outside before they were fired. We usually made and stored a supply that would withstand charges by the enemy well into the night hours. Leenova and I had been working on ammunition for some time when Charlie Bill finally showed up.

We asked, "What took you so long?"

"Aw, I had to dig up the top of the new-fangled septic tank we got," was his reply.

Louis and Opal had one of the first indoor toilets in the neighborhood, but they were having problems with it filling up, especially after a heavy rain. The rain that preceded the snow had caused back-up problems. Charlie Bill had spent a good portion of his afternoon digging up the worrisome lid to the tank. He dug down to the lid and Louis removed it when he got in from work. It was almost dark so he left it for the next day.

Charlie Bill wasn't too happy about missing out on the fun

in the snow. He didn't get to go rabbit tracking or participate in the "cold war" snowball fight. Colin and Bobby had to go home for supper. There was no one left to have a battle with. Our fort was on a bank that overlooked Avondale Street. It was in the vacant lot between Charlie Bill's house and the lane that went back to Bobby Crocker's. It was across the ditch and up the hill from my house.

We were sitting in the fort with only our head exposed when we saw a figure coming down the road toward us. We thought it might be Skeezer. We ducked down and armed ourselves. He came closer and as we peeped over the top of our fort, we could see that it was Bad Eye Elam.

Bad Eye Elam was in his fifties and was a bachelor who lived with his mother. He often became the object of our torment. To give credit where credit is due, he was a pretty fair handy-man and did quite a bit of construction and repair in the neighborhood.

Charlie Bill whispered, "Let's get him." He had missed all the action and was ready to rumble.

As Bad Eye got closer, we whispered back and forth debating the consequences. "You know how he is! He'll try to kill us if we hit him," I argued.

Bad Eye usually carried a claw hammer in the loop on his overalls. He had been known to threaten men, kids, and even women with his hammer. He even threatened Mama with his hammer one time. I think he was sorry he did but that's another story.

While we discussed the pro and cons of an attack on "Bad Eye," Charlie Bill stood up and let him have it with one of our slushy snowballs. The missile exploded right in his face. He let out with his favorite curse words, "You yellow bellied sap-suckers!"

We all fired another volley and he started up the road bank after us. About halfway up the hill he slipped and slid down on his belly into the muddy side ditch. When he stood up he drew his trusty hammer. At that point we abandoned fort. We ran through the weeds in the vacant lot, making a bee-line for Charlie Bill's.

We looked back and he was running after us and gaining ground. We ran down the hill and around behind Charlie Bill's house with an angry Bad Eye in hot pursuit. We rounded the corner and Charlie Bill hit the clothes line and ripped it down without losing a step.

Our pursuer wasn't as lucky. The clothes line was now hanging about shin high. Bad Eye caught the wire clothes line right on the top of his shoe and did a long swan dive. We heard the splash and looked back just in time to see Bad Eye coming up out of the septic tank. He was covered from head to toe with the smelly thick brown water. Somehow he never dropped his hammer in the whole ordeal.

Charlie Bill ran around the house and in the front door. Leenova and I continued down the road and he ran inside. By the time I got to my house I could see Bad Eye coming down the road. If I went in my house, he would see where I went and know who I was. I continued on down the street until I got to the railroad. I hid and watched him from the railroad bank. The lights in the mill window gave off enough light to see him walking around in the fresh white snow, dripping the sewage water in his tracks.

He raised his hammer above his head and yelled, "I'll get you, you yellow bellied sap suckers! I'll get you!"

I almost froze to death lying in the snow waiting for him to go back up the hill so I could go home. He finally left and he didn't recognize us because the next day he was telling at Barrett's Grocery that someone set a trap for him and he fell in a mud puddle.

It may have looked like mud, but it didn't smell like mud.

****

To act out our war stories, whether World War II, cowboys and Indians, or Robin Hood, we had to come up with the proper weapons of war. Most of us had a BB gun and some had store bought cap pistols. However, most of our weapons were home made. We made our tomahawks from rocks we found along the railroad or in the ditch. Any time we found a flat rock shaped like an ax we would pick it up and save it for a tomahawk head. A tomahawk was easy to make. We would cut a sapling that would fit our hands. The sapling was cut off to just the right length. The handle was split at the top so the rock would fit inside the split. The handle above the split was then wrapped with string and tied to hold the tomahawk head in place. A rooster tail-feather tied to the handle put the finishing touches to the tomahawk.

We also made some pretty good spears. We usually used a cane as the shaft of the spear. Spear heads varied from an old knife blade to spindles. Spindles were perfect. They were metal rods about six to eight inches long. They were sharp on each end with a hump in the middle. We would find them around the mill. Daddy said they were used to spin cotton into thread when the mill made cloth.

They were great spear points because one end would fit into the hollow end of a cane. It would slide up to the hump and catch. The head could easily be secured to the shaft with a string or tape. The spindle was heavy enough to make the spear land on the point every time it was thrown.

Spears were great for playing Tarzan or Bomba the Jungle Boy, but they also had a practical purpose. We would wade down the creek with our spears ready to strike. If a frog was spotted, we would fling our spears at the creature. Sometimes we would even hit one. Snakes usually ran from us but if they didn't, they had to dodge spears. We also used the spears for fishing. When we were wading we would come to holes that were one or two feet deep and usually there would be bullhead catfish in these deeper holes.

Tarzen, Bomba, or an Indian could creep up to the holes and spot the catfish when the water was clear. Bobo Butler once threw his spear at a catfish and when he retrieved his spear, he had two catfish stacked together on the point. Two in one throw! That was really something. We had fun making and using the spears and we became pretty proficient with them.

The one weapon that everyone had was a bow and arrow. This is me with my bow and arrow in the front yard of my house when it had asbestos shingles. In the background, Leenova's house and Avondale Street.

We sometimes carved rifles, pistols or swords out of wood. They were important props as we acted out a movie or serial that we had seen. We used them to play army, cowboys, or Robin Hood, but the one weapon that everyone had was a bow and arrow. Not one of us had a store bought bow and arrow, but we could all shoot like Robin's merry men.

Making a bow required a lot of work and decision making. "What is the best wood for a bow?" someone would ask. That usually started an argument.

"Bodock! That's the best!" one would say.

"No! Hickory is the best!" would say another.

"Locust makes a good one," another would add.

It would usually be settled by, "Bobo always uses bodock."

Bobo did use bodock and he made great bows. He was a good shot, but his fame grew for the distance he could shoot. I've seen him stand at home plate at the ball field and shoot an arrow over the fence in center field. He even performed a feat we thought was impossible, he shot an arrow all the way over the tank.

Our arrows were pretty good for homemade. We sometimes used cane, but most of the time we used the stems of golden rods. Once the golden rods were dried, they became very hard and had a soft pith in the center of the stem. A slit could be cut in the stem and a chicken feather cut to fit and inserted into the cut to make a fletching. A notch cut on the end of the arrow served as a nock.

We were very innovative in making our arrowheads. Sometimes we put nails on the railroad tracks. The train flattened them out and, with a few strokes of a file, we had sharp arrowheads.

Another really good arrow head was the mattress needle. My Uncle Joe and Aunt Ethel made mattresses at their house when they lived next door. There were still a few needles laying around in the storage room. We stuck them in the end of a golden rod and had a long, very sharp, arrowhead.

We used the bows and arrows to shoot targets, but I must confess, we also shot at birds with them. There were two birds that we didn't shoot, the cardinal and the mocking bird. I was told by Mama never to shoot a mocking bird. I was always careful not to kill a mocking bird, but I did kill a few blue jays and sparrows.

There was another weapon that we made and used to shoot birds and even a squirrel now and then. It was the sling shot. Uncle Whit was about the best sling shot maker at the Cotton Mill. He made them for almost every boy out there, but he did his very best when he made one for Skeezer or me.

He started with a forked limb. He would cut off the limb below the fork, then top off each fork even with the other. The stock of the sling shot looked like a "Y". He then would cut two strips out of an old inner-tube. He always kept one or two old tubes around just for making sling shots. Red rubber made better sling shots than black rubber so he used the red. He would attach the two strips of rubber to the forks in the stock. They were tied with several wraps of string. The two rubber strips then had each loose end tied to a side of a leather pouch.

The shooter would hold the stock with one hand and the leather pouch by the other. He then would stretch the rubber as he pulled back on the leather pouch. He would then let go of the pouch and the rubber would snap back, sending the missile that was in the pouch flying. For many years I thought this was the weapon David used to kill Goliath, but it turns out they didn't have rubber during Bible times.

The missiles that we used, I believe, were somewhat similar to the ones David used. A smooth, round river rock made some great ammo for the sling shot. Pig iron was another much sought after ammunition. Pig iron could be found along the railroad track. It was a heavy, brittle metal. I'm not sure what it was or how it got mixed in the rocks on the track, but it was a magnum load when shot in a sling shot. We could slam the pig iron against a rail and it would shatter into smaller pieces that would fit into our sling shot pouch. The only thing better than pig iron was a steely. A steely was a metal ball-bearing. Steelies always shot straight and hard.

BB guns were an important part of our lives, until we got our shot guns. BB guns were our source of training to shoot and safely handle guns. I got my first BB gun when I was five years old. It was my Christmas wish. I told Mama I wanted Santa to bring me a Red Ryder BB Gun for Christmas. She warned me that I was too young for a BB gun and probably wouldn't get it. She asked me to choose something else, but I said all I wanted was a BB gun.

Christmas morning I rushed to the tree and there under it was a package just the right size to hold a Red Ryder BB Gun. I ripped into it like a possum dog digging a possum out of a hole. Sure 'nuff, a BB gun was in the box. I took it out and grabbed the lever to cock it. I could barely budge it.

"Don't load that thing in the house," Mama ordered.

"Yes ma'am," I replied as I ran out on the front porch.

I had shot both Skeezer's and Bobo's gun, so I knew how to do it. I put my foot on the stock, grabbed the barrel with my left hand and strained with my right hand until the lever cocked. I pointed it toward the tank and pulled the trigger. For a second I almost thought I heard a plink as the BB hit the metal tank.

No, it couldn't have been, the gun wasn't loaded. There were five boxes of BBs with the gun so I loaded it up. I pulled the top off the cardboard cylinder that held the BBs, turned it up to my mouth and filled it full of BB's. I then opened the magazine and spit BB's in like they were coming out of a machine gun. I was lucky I didn't cough or someone might have gotten hit by a stray BB.

Once I had the gun loaded, I again cocked it and aimed at the mailbox across the street. "Plink!" I hit it on the first shot. I ran in the house and asked if I could go show Charlie Bill my new Red Ryder BB Gun.

My first gun lasted me almost a year before it finally broke. I still used it in pretend games, but I missed hearing the "plink" of the tin cans. The next Christmas brought an even greater surprise. When I looked under the tree Christmas morning, I had a new BB gun. It was a pump like Skeezers.

Pumps were more powerful than lever action guns, so I couldn't wait to see if it would ring the water tank. I loaded it up and walked up to the big tree. I took aim at the "O" in Jones and pulled the trigger. "Plink!" Wow! There was only a second between the sound of air rushing out of the barrel and a loud plink.

I had the best BB gun made and I couldn't wait to show someone, so I headed to Charlie Bill's. He was outside riding a new bike Santa brought him. "Come on, let's go to the big tree," I said.

"I can't get out of the yard with my new bike," he said.

"Why not?" I asked.

"Because there is something wrong with the brakes and Daddy has to fix them," was his answer.

I didn't understand it at the time, but it seemed like Santa often brought toys that needed a little more work on them.

I finally pressured him to get off his bike and walk up to the big tree. It took a little bribe but when I told him he could shoot my new BB gun, he decided to go.

When we got to the big tree I pushed the safety off and aimed at the O. The "plink" was loud and Charlie Bill took the gun and let another BB fly. It "plinked" again just as loud. I now had a witness that my BB gun would ring the water tank from the big tree.

I enjoyed my new gun for about two months. All the other boys bragged on my gun. They thought it was the strangest gun they had ever seen. Then one day in February my cousin Billy and I were shooting cans in the back yard and my fun ended.

Billy dared me to hold the can in my hand while he shot it. Now I had done some dumb things, but for a six year old I wasn't stupid. I refused to hold the can for him. He told me if I didn't hold it he would shoot me. Billy was twelve and I looked up to him a lot, but I wasn't going to hold that can while he played Buffalo Bill.

As I said, I had done some dumb things and I usually paid for it. There was the time Skeezer was Lash Larue and I was dumb enough to hold a piece of paper and let him pop it out of my hand . His whip was an old ironing cord tacked to a sawed-off mop handle. He was pretty good with it. He could snap the whip and it would make a loud crack. He could side aim it and wrap it around the old cane bottom porch chair and yank it over. He was so good I trusted him to flick the rolled up newspaper out of my hand. He was a little off and I received a bloody whelp around my wrist that looked like a red bracelet.

No, this time I would be smart and refuse to hold the can. Billy told me to dance and shot at my feet. I jumped , then took off running around the house. He pumped the gun and fired at me as I ran. I made it around the back corner of the house just in time. I kept running as I heard him pump again. The nearest refuse from the hail of BB's was the old outdoor toilet. I sprinted to the door and as I closed it behind me, I heard the distinct sound of a BB bouncing off the wooden building. I latched the door so Billy couldn't get in.

I waited for what seemed like ten minutes and there was no sign of Billy. Maybe he went home, but if he did he had my new BB gun. I unlatched the door and slowly cracked it open. I peeped out and he was nowhere to be seen.

Then I heard the muffled sound of air leaving the barrel of an air rifle. At almost the same instance, I felt a stinging in my eye like a hornet had hit me. A big black spot blurred my vision and at that point I knew I had been shot. I let out a scream and slapped my hand over my eye.

The next thing I heard was Billy saying, "I didn't mean to, I didn't mean to."

I was crying and holding my eye as I came in the backdoor. Mama let out one of her, "Lordy mercies" and grabbed my hand and pulled it away from my eye. She pulled my eyelid up and said, "He's shot your eye out! We've got to get to the doctor!"

By now Billy had run next door and told Ethel. She came running in the house and Mama said, "We've got to get him to the doctor! The BB is stuck in his eye."

Uncle Joe worked the night shift so he was asleep. Ethel ran back to their house and woke him up. He put on his pants and cranked up their old Chevy and we headed to Dr. Barker's office.

Hazel was Dr. Barker's nurse and as soon as we came in

and she saw my eye she said, "Go on back to the examining room and I'll get the doctor."

Dr. Barker came in, but he didn't have his usual smile on his face. He pulled my eye lid back and said, "You need to take him to Jackson."

He called the hospital and told them I was on the way. He then called Dr. McIver, an eye, ear, nose and throat specialist, and sent me his way. It took about twenty minutes to get there. When we arrived at the emergency room, everyone was waiting for us. I was rushed to a back room and Dr. McIver went to work. He removed the BB but he could not save my sight. I was blind in my right eye.

Now I never really thought of being blind in one eye as much of a handicap. It did force me to change to the left hand to shoot a gun or bow, but I learned fast. It would feel funny to shoot right-handed today. I was never much at shooting pool left handed and I couldn't see well enough to find the hole at running back, but other than that, having one eye never bothered me.

I think it bothered Billy quite a bit. He was always very protective of me and he was pretty tough, so the older boys didn't try to bully me. I hated to see him move because I lost my protection.

Chapter VI: The Cotton Mill Animals

There were other residents at the Cotton Mill other than the people. There were assorted pets, domestic animals and wild animals, some of which could not be found in the zoology books. I had several dogs as I grew up, but two really stand out in my mind.

Trixie was about as near a full blooded dog as there was in the neighborhood. She was as white as uncluttered snow, with long slightly curly hair. She was not a big dog, but she wasn't small either. When she looked at you, she had smiling eyes and her pink tongue with black spots flicked in and out of her mouth as she panted.

I can't remember when I got Trixie. She must have been brought by the same stork that brought me. We grew up together and she was nine years old when she died. She was more like my sibling than my dog. Mama made me stay inside the picket fence until I was about six years old and I only got to play outside the fence once in a while at Leenova's, next door. Trixie was my playmate. She would have made a pretty good retriever, because I would throw a ball and she would fetch it for hours.

She saved me from some pretty close calls. I remember one time in particular when I tried to escape the prison bars of the picket fence. I found one of the slats in the fence loose at the bottom. I pushed on it and it gave. There appeared to be enough room to slip through the fence at this breech in the security, so I tried it.

Daddy and I in front of the picket fence with the mill in the background.

I stuck my head through the opening. Then I tried to twist my shoulders to slip through. I twisted the other way. I couldn't get through. I tried to pull my head back out but it wouldn't come out. I pulled and my ears caught on the slats on either side. I began to panic and the more I pulled, the more it hurt. I would be trapped in the fence for the rest of my life! As that realization hit me I started to cry. Trixie came running when she heard me crying. She surveyed the situation and ran to the screen door and started barking every breath.

It wasn't long until Mama left her chores in the kitchen and came to see what was wrong with that infernal dog. I heard the spring on the old screen door creak as she opened it. I couldn't see because I was facing the road, but I knew she was coming to my rescue.

"Over here Mama," I called. "I'm over here."

"What in the name of the Lord have you done?" was her question.

"I'm hung in the fence," I said in a pitiful voice.

She went right to work to free me. She grabbed me around the waist and pulled. I came plum off the ground and my neck stretched farther than a snapping turtle's neck catching a frog. I yelled and she stopped the tug-of-war with the fence. She went inside and came out with a claw hammer.

"You're not going to try to pry my head loose with that hammer, are you?" I asked with a sob. I could just see the claws on the hammer peeling my ears off as she pried away.

She didn't pry me out with the hammer, but she did vibrate my ear drums a little as she whacked the slat to knock it loose at the top. The slat came loose and my head popped out of the medieval stock that imprisoned me.

I was free and Trixie was a heroine. I would have probably been in that fence until I starved if it had not been for Trixie. Well, maybe not, because Mama checked on me every thirty minutes to an hour when I played outside alone.

Trixie really did perform a heroic act later on when I was about eight and Gail was four. We had a little peddle car that Daddy bought used from someone. He mounted a gasoline motor on the little car and, someway, rigged it so it was self-propelled. He may have used the same old motor he used when he built the gasoline lawn mower, but it was neat. I could get in the car and Daddy would pull the crank rope and off I would go. The motor eventually played out or something happened, plus I outgrew the little car.

The car still was a useful toy even after it was de-motored. We could still put Gail in the car and push her around. Mama let us go outside to play and Gail and I headed for the car. It was parked under the grape arbor. The grapes were not yet ripe. When they got ripe we spent a great deal of time under the arbor eating them. Besides being a place to shop for fresh grapes, the arbor doubled as a garage for the little peddle car.

As soon as we came out the front door, Trixie was with us. She followed us to the grape arbor. She then started acting strange. She stood between Gail and me and the car. She even growled at us. She had never done that before. I started around her and she stepped in front of me and bared her teeth. Something had to be wrong with her. I picked up Gail and tried to carry her around Trixie and put her in the car. She grabbed my Levi's at the cuff and wouldn't let go. I almost tripped and put Gail down to keep from dropping her.

"Run tell Mama to come here. Something is wrong with Trixie," I instructed Gail.

Now that was the wrong thing to do because Mama came running around the corner of the house with a look of horror on her face.

"Get back! She might be going mad!" were her orders.

I answered in defense of Trixie. Trixie turned and started barking under the car. She would stick her nose under the car and then jump back and bark. We could see some movement under the car each time she jumped back. We moved a little closer to get a better look and there it was. A huge copperhead.

Mama ran around back to the shed to get her hoe. I tried to call Trixie off so she wouldn't get bitten by the snake, but she wouldn't leave the car until Mama returned with the hoe. Following God's command, she bruised the head of the serpent. Heck! She not only bruised his head, she slap-dab cut it off. She was shaking like a leaf in a wind storm, but she leaned down and hugged Trixie's neck and whispered in her ear,

"Good dog, good dog."

And she was a good dog. She was a real heroine and I loved her very much. One of the saddest things I have ever had to do was crawl under our house and drag her body out when she died. It's been fifty years, but I can still see those smiling eyes as she looked at me with pure love and loyalty.

Trixie never completely left me, partly because she was so engrained in my memory and partly because she left me her son, Snowball.

I was never sure who Snowball's father was, but I suspected it might be Bozo. They always got along well together and Snowball did seem to be jealous when I petted Bozo. He was snow white like Trixie, but his hair wasn't quite as long and he stood a bit taller. He had her eyes, but his jaw was more square. He could run like the wind and swim like a dolphin.

Snowball was two when Trixie died and I had never given him the same kind of attention I had given her. I liked him alright and I played with him some, but it wasn't until Trixie died that we became close. When I got my first shot gun and started hunting, we became hunting buddies and we were buddies until he died in my mid-teens.

Snowball was the all-purpose hunting dog, but he could fish too. One time we were at Stalling's pond and the fishing was slow. We all set poles out and headed down in the woods to play. We found some riding trees and bounced around a while before we returned. When we did head back to the pond, Snowball ran on ahead of us. When we got to the top of the levee, I didn't see my pole that I left stuck in the bank by the butt end. I looked and saw it in the edge of the water. The pole started to move and Snowball saw it. He made a dive and grabbed the pole in his teeth. He then proceeded to back up the bank dragging the pole. When the line cleared the water there was a big black bream beached on the muddy bank,

Yes, Snowball caught a fish on my pole.

He was an all-purpose dog. He would flush quail, tree squirrels, and dig possums out of their holes. He had a rabbit hunting technique all his own. He would climb on a brush pile or honey suckle thicket and jump up and down until the rabbit ran out. He would then chase the rabbit by sight until the rabbit was gone or he caught it. He did catch several rabbits that tried to beat him across open ground.

His possum hunting made me a little spending money from time to time. Normally possum hunting was done at night, but Snowball had his own way of hunting during the day. He would go around smelling in holes in the ground or in hollow logs. If he detected the odor of his arch enemy, the possum, he would bark into the hole. If the hole was in the ground the possum was a goner. He would dig the hole out until he could reach his mouth in and pull the possum out.

If the possum was in a log or stump I had to assist. I would take a forked stick and poke it in the hole until I could feel the possum's soft fur. Then I would twist until I had his skin rolled up tightly around the stick. I would then pull the possum out and Snowball would grab it. When Snowball clamped his jaws on a possum it usually played dead and I would grab it by the tail and drop it in my toe sack. It was then off to Uncle Whit's to collect fifty cents.

Snowball was not a great squirrel dog like Spot, but if he saw a squirrel on the ground he would chase it up a tree. I saw him leap into the air one time and snatch a squirrel off the side of a tree. There was one time, however, that I thought a squirrel might kill him.

We were rabbit hunting in Duffey's bottom just behind the levee to Stallin's pond. I had killed a big fox squirrel in that area a week earlier. Spot treed him and when I shot him out with my 410, I must have just made him mad, because when

Spot grabbed him, they had an awful fight. He bit Spot several times before he finally killed the squirrel.

Right in the same area where this battle took place, I looked up in a leaning tree and in the fork I could see a huge bushy tail. It was a giant squirrel. It was nearly as big as Snowball. I shouldered my 410 and took aim. When I shot, the gargantuan squirrel leaped out of the tree onto the ground. Snowball grabbed him and there was the most awful squealing and growling I had ever heard.

Charlie Bill couldn't believe his eyes and he pointed his old bolt action at the behemoth.

"No, don't shoot! You might hit Snowball." I warned.

All the time I was thinking we had to do something or that squirrel would kill Snowball. I thought, if a squirrel the size of the one that fought Spot could do as much damage as he did, this Goliath would surely kill my dog. They fought for what seemed to be an hour and finally the fracas became quiet. When it was over, Snowball was standing over the dead squirrel.

I walked over and looked at the critter. It didn't look like a squirrel in the face. It had pointed ears and a long snout with sharp teeth. It had paws like a dog. It's color and bushy tail was like a squirrel, but it definitely was not a squirrel.

I grabbed it by the tail and threw it over my shoulder. It was heavy, but I carried it awhile, Charlie Bill carried it awhile, then David finished the last leg home. We were proud of the mystery animal and we couldn't wait to show it to everyone.

I carried it inside the house and Mama like to have had a hissy-fit because it did have an odor to it. Daddy took one look at it and said, "It's a gray fox."

I had never heard of a fox climbing a tree or I might have

guessed it. Daddy skinned him out and sold his hide along with some coon hides he had collected.

Snowball was a tough dog, but he was always gentle with kids. When my youngest sister, Booger, (Barbara Diane) was born, he was her personal baby sitter.

****

There were several dogs in the neighborhood and they were pretty much like the kids. Every now and then they would get into a fight with each other. But the next day they would be right back playing or hunting with each other. Tippie was my cousin Jeep's dog. He lived next door and was three or four years younger than Snowball. He pretty much was trained to hunt by Snowball and he used the same, "Jump on a brush pile," method for coaxing rabbits to leave their hiding place.

It was fun to see Snowball and Tippie working together. They would jump up and down on a brush pile like they were on a trampoline. Soon a rabbit would dart out and head for new cover. If he ran in high weeds, all that could be seen of the dogs were their heads bobbing up above the weeds, then back out of sight. They could keep up with the rabbit by jumping above the weeds to see his fleeing little white powder-puff tail in the weeds ahead. They would run the rabbit as long as they could see him.

Tippie was a black and white, part Border Collie. He had a white tip on his tail. You guessed it, that's how he got the name Tippie. Snowball and Tippie were pals. I can't remember their ever having a fight, not even when a good-looking female like Lady came by with several boy friends following her. They both had a hole dug out under the old plum tree where they lazed around until the front door opened, then they would jump up ready for the action of the day.

Snowball had a bad habit, fortunately he didn't teach it to Tippie, or he had better sense. He ran cars. There weren't all that many cars that passed our house, but when they did he thought he had an obligation to chase it away. He would run along-side the car biting at the wheels. As he got older he became less agile and one day the thing we dreaded, but knew was bound to happen, happened. Snowball didn't dodge the wheel and he was killed.

I can't be certain, but I believe animals establish bonds and friendships with other animals. After Snowball died, Tippie was never the same. He would still lay in his hole under the old plum tree, but he didn't jump up when the door opened at my house or Jeep's house. He moped around and wouldn't eat and finally one day, not long after Snowball died, we found him laying in his sunken hole with his face looking toward the empty hole where his buddy Snowball usually lay beside him. He was dead.

* * * * * * * * * *

We had one other rabbit dog that usually joined us on our rabbit hunts. Minnie was a full-blooded Beagle. She belonged to Colin Barrett, but she was everyone's rabbit dog. No matter who went by her house on the way to the fields to hunt, Minnie would fall in with them and be a part of the hunting party.

She was white with black spots with just a little bit of brown. She had long ears, and a nose that could follow a two-day-old trail. She was a pretty good jump dog and used the 'under the brush-pile and honeysuckle vine' technique.

Most of the time Snowball or Tippie would run the rabbit out and she would get on the trail. Once she got on the trail she would not quit barking on the rabbit until we either killed it or it got dark and we went home. I have even heard her running at night and I'm not sure that she wasn't still running the next morning.

When Minnie got on a rabbit she would usually run it in a circle and it would come back to about the same place it was jumped. We would line up at intervals and wait the return of the rabbit. We had an unwritten rule that a person could not move out front and cut the rabbit off before it got back to the place of its origin. Charlie Bill usually broke that rule. He would listen to Minnie's voice and as soon as she said, "He's turning left", or "He's turning right", Charlie Bill would inch out in front of the rest of us in that direction.

Minnie communicated with us as easily as if she spoke fluent English. If her barks were high pitched and close together, she was saying, "I just jumped one and he's high-tailing it away." If her barks were slow and spaced out she was saying, "I smell where he was this morning and I'm following him to his hideout." When her slow bawl got faster and turned to a chop she was saying, "The trail is getting hotter. Get ready, I'm about to jump him." We all loved Minnie and she put a lot of meat on the tables in the Cotton Mill.

* * * * * * * * *

Spot sometimes accompanied us on rabbit hunts, but he always ended up in the woods treeing squirrels. He belonged to Andy Collinsworth and his farm was always one of our first stops on the hunting circuit. Spot was white with a brown spot about like a saddle on his back. He was part hound and part bird dog. He didn't bark on the trail, but his tree voice would almost chop a tree down. He provided squirrel meat for our families, but he had one other attribute that endeared him to Mama.

Spot was just as good at killing snakes as he was at treeing squirrels. I was always fascinated by his snake killing technique, however, I was never tempted to try it. When he located a snake, the first thing he would do was circle it to make it coil up. He would then lunge at it and make it strike. He would jump back to avoid the fangs. He would circle and jump, circle and jump, until he got just the opening he was looking for. He would then lunge and grab the snake somewhere from the middle of it's body to it's tail. He then would shake his head from side to side so fast and violently, that he would pop the head off the snake. It was something to watch. He had to be the best snake dog in the world, or at least at the Cotton Mill.

****

Speaking of snakes, of all the animals at the Cotton Mill, the snake was probably one of the most talked about, yet misunderstood animals with which we came in contact. We spent countless hours listening to snake tales and then telling our own tales.

"Which is badder, a Cottonmouth or a Copperhead?" someone would start the scientific discussion.

"A Cottonmouth no doubt," someone would answer.

From there we would start our debate. "Did you know that a snake won't die until the sun goes down, even if you chop his head off," a learned herpetologist would offer.

"Yeah! But I bet you didn't know you can lay a dead snake over a fence belly-up and make it rain," another would add.

"Did you know that a mama snake will open her mouth and her babies will run into her mouth to escape danger?" someone else would ask.

The old wives tales would start to fly. Little Mama told me about a snake called a hoop snake. It would take its tail in its mouth and make a hoop. It would then roll down a hill like an old bike tire until it caught up with the person or thing running from it. When it hit the object it sought a stinger would come out of its body and sting its victim.

Now I never relished getting bit by a snake, but I hated stinging things even more. One of my greatest fears was that I would come face-to-face with a hoop snake and it would be up-hill from me. Fortunately I never saw a hoop snake, and now that I think about it, I don't know anyone who did.

The milk snake is another illusive snake that I never saw. They were notorious for sneaking up on cows or nanny goats and milking them dry. Anytime someone had a cow that decreased the output of milk, it was always because an old milk snake was stealing milk. Now we didn't have a cow and the milkman ran a route out by our house, but I still think we had milk snakes that stole milk.

Mama would always leave the empty glass milk bottle as an order for the milkman. He would come by and check and leave full bottles to replace the empty bottles. Mama always left the right amount of change in the bottles to pay the milkman.

The reason I think we had a milk snake was, once in a while a bottle of milk would come up missing. Mama thought it was those old Hobos or maybe a certain neighbor. I never really believed that because no money was ever missing from the bottles. If it were humans that stole the milk, surely sometime they would have stolen the money.

I had it all figured out and I told Mama it had to be a milk snake. "Well, Mr. Smarty Pants, how did the milk snake carry off the bottle? In his pockets?" she chimed. That kind of blew my theory out of the water, unless the milk snake was so big he swallowed the whole bottle.

And then there was the infamous black racer. If a person should happen upon a black racer, he should freeze in his tracks. Under no circumstances should a person run from a black racer. He was just too fast and he would catch you and wrap around your ankles and make you fall down. I fancied myself to be faster than the average kid, but I wasn't really confident that my speed would allow me to out distance a black racer. Then one day I got my chance to challenge a three foot long speed demon to the race of both our lives.

One afternoon I was walking the switch track coming home from a hard day of marbles on the cinder road. I was walking with my head down stepping from one cross tie to the next. Something between the rails caught my eye. It was two ties in front of me. I froze. A long, forked tongue flicked out, then in, as his head turned in my direction. "Uh oh! He's seen me," I whispered to myself. Still I froze. His head rose about four inches above the cross ties and turned in my direction. His whole body turned and his head was only one tie away.

"Be brave, don't move," I told myself. Eight years of seeing Mama flailing away at snakes with a hoe and calling them the devil's own creatures finally got to me. I moved.

I'm not sure but I may have turned from the waist down and then the rest of my body caught up. I was still brave from the waist up, but my darn legs turned chicken on me. The next thing I knew I was striding so long and fast I was skipping every other cross tie with my P F Flyers. I didn't look back, but I could feel the snake gaining ground. I opted to leave the ties.

I hit the well worn path between the switch track and the mill. When my feet touched dirt, I kicked up a cloud of dust behind me. He had to be right on my heels because no one could out-run a black racer. I was expecting any minute to feel his body wrap around my legs, tying them together and making me fall to the ground. I had never heard anyone say what they did to you when they got you on the ground, but I knew it had to be something horrible.

Just as these thoughts flooded my mind and made me run even harder, I felt something wrap around my leg. "It's got me!" I yelled in a loud voice, hoping there would be someone to save me from my horrible fate if I fell to the ground. No one was in sight. I ran harder and screamed louder as I turned the corner of the mill, running, kicking and jumping all at the same time. It still had me by only one leg. If I could run with my legs spread out wide enough, maybe he couldn't wrap around my other leg and throw me to the ground. I then saw my chance to be saved from this awful fate.

There was Uncle Whit coming out the back door of the warehouse after making his rounds. "Help! Get it off!" I cried in a panic. I must have been a sight charging at him as fast as I could run with the odd gait caused by my bowlegged attempt to keep the snake from grabbing my other leg. I almost knocked him down as I literally tried to climb up him.

He grabbed me and finally got out, "What in the world has happened?"

"Snake! Snake!" was all I could get out as I pointed to my right ankle. He looked down and laughed. I didn't think it was funny at all, until I looked down and saw that the black racer wrapped around my ankle was a piece of rope. I don't know how I got tangled in the rope, but about half way around the mill in my flight from the horrible fate, the rope jumped up and grabbed me.

There were some Cotton Mill Boys who had absolutely no fear of snakes, and then there were some who would run from a little green snake. I fell somewhere in the middle. If a snake had not been designated as dangerous, I could usually tolerate it. Evidently Mama's phobia for snakes was not genetic, or if it was, maybe it was a recessive gene.

There were two boys who had no fear of snakes, therefore, they terrorized those who did show fear. Bobo and Vanny Dee both loved snakes. They would catch them and rub them. They would even let them crawl around on their neck and arms. When they had a snake in their hands, they always invited everyone they met to pet their snake. The wise move was to accept their invitation and at least touch the snake. To show fear, and especially to walk or run away was a bad mistake. At the first show of fear, a person would become the target of all kinds of attempts to scare them to death. One day that almost happened. Up until that day I had never seen a half-grown boy faint.

Bobo caught a beautiful king snake. Well, at least he thought it was beautiful. He was showing it around to everyone. It was wrapped around his arm in three or four coils with its head sticking up to see each one who was invited to pet it. I knew not to show any fear so I stepped up and stroked a stroke on one of the coils of his back. Whew! I was safe. Bobo wouldn't chase me with the snake, but I could already see who his victim was going to be. Alton Morris was already backing up and showing signs that he would bolt and run at any second.

Alton (left) didn't live right in the Cotton Mill, but he came and played with us regularly.

Alton didn't live right in the Cotton Mill, but he came and played with us regularly. His grandfather lived on the lane between the end of Avondale and the Trenton Highway. Alton lived next door to him and for some time they were the only houses on the lane. Alton was two years older than me so we played junior high football together one year. He was pretty tough as non-Cotton Mill Boys go, but he did have a fear of snakes.

Bobo took a step toward Alton and asked, "Here, do you want to pet him?" For every step Bobo took forward, Alton took two backward. Bobo stepped faster and Alton stepped even faster. Alton was a little bit heavy, in fact his nickname was "Fats." He couldn't stand it any longer and turned and ran faster than I have ever seen him run. Bobo was fast, but he was having a hard time catching Fats. As the gap between them began to widen, Bobo unwrapped the big king snake from his arm and began to twirl it around and around over his head like David twirling his sling. When he let go of the snake Fats went down just like Goliath. He rolled and went limp. The king snake flew around and around through the air and caught him right at the neck. The momentum of the centrifugal force wrapped the snake around his neck like a scarf on a cold day. The second he felt the snake around his neck, the lights went out. By the time we all got there he was as white as a ghost and as limp as a dish rag. We had heard that a person could be scared to death and we were sure we had just witnessed it happen.

Bobo bent over him and slapped him on the cheeks a couple of times. His eyes opened and he tried to get up. Bobo held him down and told him to be calm. Fats felt of his neck and the snake was gone. Heck, I'm not sure the snake wasn't more afraid than Fats, for when he hit the ground around Fat's neck, he took off with speed that probably would have out-run a black racer.

****

You wouldn't think that a chicken could strike fear in anyone but Charlie Bill, but there was this one time that my cousin Corkey and I thought we were going to cash in our chips because of the chickens. The hen house wasn't the most desirable place to play, and I don't remember why we were climbing around in there. It must have been to steal a feather or two out of a chicken tail to play Indians. I was only around six or seven so that is not clear, but what happened stuck in my mind very well.

We found one of Mama's hens in the nest and it was dead. We went and got her and pointed out the casualty. She looked it over and pronounced her diagnosis, "Mites, it is covered with mites. I better dust them or they'll all die." Mama went back inside and we resumed our quest for feathers or whatever we were looking for.

Inside the hen house were rows of poles staggered like stair steps where the chickens roosted at night. We started to swing on the poles like the uneven bars in the Olympics. Of course we had never seen the Olympics, but we would swing on one and drop and catch the one below. We would climb to the top and swing and drop and catch on the next one all the way down. There was some black and white slippery stuff we had to avoid to keep from slipping and falling.

We played this new game for nearly an hour when we began to itch and scratch. I looked at Corkey and she had some kind of small black specks all over her. She had coarse, curly, brown hair and they were all in it. She looked at me at the same time and pointed in horror at the little black specks crawling all over me. In unison we both screamed, "Miiiiites!" We ran to the house screaming, "Mites! Mites! Mites!" We knew we would drop dead any minute, just like the old hen.

Fortunately Mama caught us at the back door before we could get inside and strow mites all over the house. When she looked at us she immediately saw the problem and headed us in the direction of the tub. There was a full tub of water setting out in the sun to warm for our bath that night. She promptly dunked us both, clothes and all, and ran inside to get some soap. She pitched the big square bar of P&G soap in the tub, along with a scrub brush, and demanded, "Scrub until the hide comes off."

Knowing that mites were fatal, what was a little hide, so we scrubbed. Corkey grabbed the soap and brush and scrubbed until her curly hair was just about straight. We dunked our heads under repeatedly. The tub was filled with soapy water when Mama came back with a two gallon water bucket and ordered us to stand up. We did and she poured the cold water on our heads and rinsed us down.

"Now get out and get those clothes off," she demanded. I was normally a modest person, but what would be worse, to have my girl cousin see me naked or die from mite bites. We both blushed a little, but we lived.

* * * * * * * * * *

There was one animal that was a resident of the Cotton Mill that could be a cute furry pet at times and at other times, he could terrorize the neighborhood. It had long, black fur with a white stripe down its back and tail, little beady eyes, and a sharp nose. It was brought to the neighborhood by Zeb Barrett when it was very small. He was fine as long as he was left alone and undisturbed, but get him angry or frightened and everyone in the neighborhood knew it.

The funny little critter looked very much like a kitten and at times would let Colin, Virginia Nell or Zeb hold it. It really made a good pet in the daytime, but at night the mild mannered kitty would turn into a hideous monster whose mission was to over stimulate the olfactory nerves of the whole mill village. This little creature would go about its own business around the neighborhood catching crickets, roaches, grasshoppers, or other insect pests. He did a great service ridding the Cotton Mill of insects, but sooner or later he would enter the wrong yard and the family dog would attack. At that point windows would slam shut, doors would close and all over the neighborhood there was the dreaded cry, "Skunk! Zeb's skunk is out again!"

Many a night in the summer I would lay in bed with the window open with only a screen between me and anemia from mosquito bites. I would listen to the crickets as they chirped away on their violins. In the old sycamore tree on the ditch bank a little screech owl called his eerie call as if he were shivering from the cold, but it was eighty degrees. Over across Ezra Pillow's field a chuck-will's-widow was calling in search of a mate and up the hill a dog was barking. Soon after the barking started an odor somewhat similar to burnt popcorn would drift through the window screen and begin to settle to the floor in my bedroom. The smell would get stronger and all the night sounds had to come to an end. Zeb Barrett's skunk was out once again.

As I closed my window one of the last sounds I would hear would be someone up there where the barking started, yelling at their dog, "Get out of here, get off that porch!"

****

There were other animals that lived in the wilderness beyond Duffey's bottom that ever so often would leave their lairs in the forbidden zone and actually come into the Cotton Mill area. Some could be classified by genus and species, but some were in a class all their own. They were so rarely seen and so unlike any known animal they had to be given a name by the Cotton Mill Wildlife Society. I knew of two such creatures, but I only actually saw one of them.

****

Besides the two mystery animals, there would be a panther sighting about every year or two. Panthers were large black cats. They were usually described by those who spotted them as larger than a coon hound with a long narrow tail. They were known to scream like a woman. Little Mama told me several tales about panthers she had encountered while living in a cabin in the Black Bottom in Arkansas.

She told how she had called one up one day while answering what she thought was a woman screaming because she was lost. The woman would scream and Little Mama would answer her with a like scream. The woman got closer and closer and Little Mama realized it was a panther and ran into the log cabin.

The cabin wasn't much protection because they had added on a room that was made of canvas. The sharp claws of the panther could rip right through the cloth and then come tearing in on her. She sat there holding her first born, Mama's oldest sister Cleo, in one arm and a single-shot 22 rifle in the other. The cat didn't come in, but when my grandfather got home there were tracks just outside the door.

Stories like Little Mama told made me a little leery of journeying out into the great unknown beyond Duffey's bottom. In fact, I got a little nervous if I was in Duffey's and it started to get dark. I never saw a panther but several older people in the neighborhood would spot them after they had been to Uncle Bill's Store and drank some of that homebrew stuff he kept in the back room.

* * * * * * * * *

I did see one creature that could not be identified and we had to go to the Cotton Mill Wildlife Society to try to get it named. The wildlife society consisted of two lifetime members and various others who served on the board, based on their availability. The two lifetime members were Carl Scott and Uncle Whit. They could be found almost any day sitting on the bench in front of Barrett's Grocery. In later years they moved their office to Henley's Grocery. They had seen or heard of almost any animal in existence. Usually a pretty good description of the critter would bring an immediate response as to its scientific name. Others who were sitting around talking with them would become members of the board and add their two-cents worth. If someone came up with a description of an animal that they had never seen or heard of, they would put it to a vote and come up with a name for the new species. After a frog hunting trip, Charlie Bill and I brought them their greatest challenge.

There was a pond that we sometimes fished that was across the highway from Ezra Pillow's farm. It was right on the fringe of the forbidden zone. We called it the green pond. The pond's color was green because of an aquatic plant that floated on top of the water. In the hot summertime it covered the pond. It was a mysterious pond, because it contained every species of fish that could be found in the Forked Deer River. We caught catfish, big grinnel, carp, gar, bass, bluegill, and even crappie. It was located in the middle of a grove of trees and one lone cypress grew at the water's edge.

There was much speculation and discussion about how all these species of fish could have gotten into this pond. Even the Cotton Mill Wildlife Society couldn't come up with a reasonable explanation. When we got a few years older and learned about Reelfoot Lake and how it was formed, we decided this pond must have been formed about the same time. Probably at one time it was big and deep. The Forked Deer River probably ran backward and filled up the deep hole formed by the same earthquake that caused the Mississippi river to flow backward to form Reelfoot Lake in 1811. This would explain all these species of fish. Well, it sounded as good as any other explanation. Not only did it have strange fish it also had huge bull frogs and that led to the discovery of the new creature.

We had debated for a couple of years about whether frog hunting in the pond would be worth the risk of going to green pond at night. It was a long walk to the Trenton Highway and about that much farther to the pond after crossing the highway. If we went, it would be the only pond we would have time to gig.

We knew there were several frogs in the pond, because they would jump in when we went fishing. We couldn't decide whether to go to the green pond or take our usual route and hit Andy Collinsworth's pond and the four Stallin's ponds. With that much indecision there was only one way to settle it. Charlie Bill took out a nickel and said, "Heads we go to green pond, tails we go to Stallings." With the toss of a coin, our fate was settled for the night. When the coin landed, we were staring at Thomas Jefferson's pony tail.

We got our two-cell flashlights, our gig and croaker sack and headed up the lane to the Trenton Highway. "Don't turn your light on while we're walking the road. Save the battery for the woods and pond," Charlie Bill advised me but he turned his on to inspect every shadow on the road. It was a half-moon and a clear night. We made it easily to the highway. When we crossed the paved road and entered the grove of tall trees, the darkness seemed to close in on us. It was very still and all we could hear was the occasional hum of tires on pavement as a few cars traveled the highway.

We each had on our black rubber knee boots which gave us some feeling of security. We always heard that snakes couldn't bite through rubber boots, so we weren't too worried about old cold jaws. As we neared the pond and heard the sounds, we threw all caution to the wind. There must have been twenty bullfrogs all competing to draw out the others. The rhythm of their singing gave the impression that one big frog was standing before them with a conductor's baton leading the music.

We smiled at each other and could already taste the delicious golden-fried frog legs. Charlie Bill took the croaker sack and I took the gig. I would gig the first frog and he would gig the second and so on. We kept our lights low and crept up close to the bank of the pond. We got almost to the edge of the water and raised our lights up and shined. Everywhere we shined, it looked like a set of headlights shining back. We had found a frog-leg gold mine. In all my years of frog gigging, I had never seen such a sight. All my years of frog gigging added together came to two. It was a sight though, I must admit.

We whispered, "Let's go get that one. No, let's get that one," pointing in one direction and then the other. While we quietly argued some ripples came on the water. We both shined in that direction. We thought it might be a cotton mouth. I would have gladly welcomed a cotton mouth instead of what we saw.

At the center of the rings of ripples that spread across the water was something round and dark. It appeared to be furry or hairy. It continued to rise above the surface of the water. It began to take shape as it gradually surfaced. It looked like a head of something. About six inches of it cleared the water and our lights were reflecting off two round luminous objects. They glowed a silver-blue in the light.

"Oh my gosh! Look at those eyes!" Charlie Bill whispered in a shaky voice.

Just as suddenly as it appeared, it went under and was gone.

I can't tell you how we made it back to the highway, but it had to be a record time. We ran across the highway and down the lane and didn't stop until we reached Avondale Street.

We stopped in front of Charlie Bill's house and discussed the situation as we glanced up the road to make sure the thing had not followed us. At first we made a pact not to tell anyone what we had seen, then we decided we owed it to the rest of the world to warn them about green pond.

At the center of the rings of ripples that spread across the water was something round and dark. It appeared to be furry or hairy. It continued to rise above the surface of the water. It began to take shape as it gradually surfaced. It looked like a head of something.

The next day we went to Barrett's Grocery to bring the events of the night before the Wildlife Society Board. Uncle Whit was in his place on the bench and Carl Scott was holding down his spot to the right of Uncle Whit. Across from them, in the old cane-bottom chair, was Dave Elam. Zeb was standing in the doorway. We had a quorum for a meeting, so we presented our discovery of this new species.

"Uncle Whit, we got something we want ya'll to help us with," I sort of stuttered.

"Sure, what is it?" he asked with a smile.

The board was always happy to be of help in identifying any animal so I said, "We saw this, this. . . well I don't really know what it was."

"What did it look like?" was their next question.

I went into detail about where we saw it, and then I described what we saw.

Carl said, "I'll bet it was a big old snapping turtle. Some of them get as big as a number-two washtub, you know."

"You say it had shiny eyes?" asked Uncle Whit.

"Yes, and they were far enough apart that you could have put your hand between then and not even touched them," I answered.

"Wasn't a turtle then," declared Uncle Whit.

"I'm pretty sure it had hair on it's head," I said.

"Couldn't have been a Wolfus, cause a Wolfus don't like water," Dave chimed in.

The discussion went on for at least an hour and the members of the board finally got their heads together to name the creature. They reached their final verdict, but when they announced, "We just don't know what it could have been." Charlie Bill and I were disappointed.

I never forgot that experience and as I grew older and received a degree in biology, I searched for an answer for what the creature we saw might have been. For some years I thought it might have been some sort of Big Foot, but it wasn't until I married and had children and moved to Springbrook, that I heard of a creature that lived in Blair Swamp, near our home, that closely resembled the nameless creature Charlie Bill and I saw. I still don't know what it was, but if the legend of Blair Swamp could be true, it is possible I saw a swamp monster when I was ten years old.

****

This menacing creature had come to be known as the Wolfus.

There was one mysterious creature that prowled the fringe of the forbidden world and occasionally entered our world at the Cotton Mill. He had long since been named by the Cotton Mill Wildlife Society and no one doubted his existence. He had been seen and heard by so many people, who could deny his existence. This menacing creature had come to be known as the Wolfus.

Descriptions of the creature varied, depending on the amount of light at the sighting, how fast it was running, how close it got, and how much of Uncle Bill's homebrew the Wolfus sighter had drank. Two distinguishing characteristics were always included in the description. It had eyes that glowed red, and it was furry. The size varied from large as a German Shepard to five feet tall standing on all fours. It had been observed running on all fours and once it stood on it's hind legs and ran. It could jump objects as tall as a four-rail fence or even across a car hood in one case. It rarely left foot prints, but if it did they were larger than any dog tracks in the neighborhood.

I never saw the Wolfus, but he ruled my life to some extent. It seemed that anytime I asked to do something that Mama didn't want me to do the Wolfus came into play. "No, you can not go wading down the ditch today," Mama would declare in a matter-or-fact way when I asked to wade down to the fork of the ditch.

"Why not?" I would ask.

"Cause last night I heard the Wolfus howling down the ditch behind the house," was her answer.

"Okay, I'll just play inside today," would usually be my response.

Most of the Cotton Mill Boys were respectful of their parents and out of pure respect they wouldn't do anything to upset their mamas if there had been a Wolfus sighting in the neighborhood. The Wolfus was an even better deterrent than the plum tree switch. That darn Wolfus prevented me from doing so many things that I wanted to do. I vowed that someday I would kill it as soon as I got a gun.

It was the same thing with other kids in the neighborhood. Many great plans were spoiled by the Wolfus. We would plan to go to Spangler's woods for a day of playing in the treehouse and swinging on grapevines, but some mama would bring up the Wolfus. "No you can't go. Zeb Barrett saw the Wolfus run across the road in front of his car last night. Stay here and work in the garden."

"Okay Mama," would usually be the dejected reply.

We were held hostage in our own neighborhood by this devilish creature with the glowing red eyes. For as long as I could remember, even back to when I was three or four-years-old, Mama would warn me not to get out of the yard or the Wolfus might get me.

Some of the older boys like Bobo and Skeezer became doubters about the existence of the Wolfus, but they too never missed a chance to scare us with the Wolfus.

One time we were playing in Sherwood Forest and for some stupid reason I let them tie me up with some mill rope. As soon as I was securely tied to a tree, they ran off yelling, "Wolfus bait! Wolfus bait!" They then let out the howl of the Wolfus. I'm not sure if it was the mating call or the feeding call, but I knew I was dead.

I struggled at the ropes frantically. I couldn't budge them. I begged the others to come back, but there was no response. Finally things got quiet and I began to think about the situation.

"It wasn't more than an hour until supper time and when

I didn't show up for supper or answer Daddy's whistle, they'd come looking for me," I reasoned out loud. My pessimistic side answered, "Yes, but it's only about three hours until dark and the Wolfus will be on the prowl." My optimistic side countered with, "They'll find me before dark."

It seemed like I had been tied up for an hour or two when I heard someone or something walking toward me. I started to yell out, but what if it's not someone, what if it is the Wolfus? It came closer and I shut my eyes as tight as I could. I didn't want to see those hideous red eyes looking at me. Closer, and I could hear breathing much like a dog after a long run. It had to be standing right in front of me. I squeezed my eyelids tighter. I could actually feel the hot breath of the horrible creature and then there was a smell. It was the smell of decayed meat. Maybe it'll think I am dead and go away I thought. I felt a wet tongue slide up my cheek. He's tasting to see if he wants to eat me, was my next thought. I heard other footsteps coming and I just had to open my eyes.

When I opened them, Bozo was standing face-to-face with me and Bobo and Skeezer had returned. They untied me and I started to cry. They knew that was a bad sign, because when I got really, really mad, I cried. As soon as I was free I grabbed a big stick of wood that was laying by me and took off after them. They out-ran me and after I lost them, I went home. I never again participated in a game that required me to be tied up.

The Wolfus kept us under control and terrorized us for several years, but we finally were freed from his grip by my Uncle Joe Collier. He was Mama's oldest sister's husband. They lived downtown, but they would come to visit and see Little Mama.

One night Mama was telling us that a man who had been down to Uncle Bill's store saw the Wolfus run across the road just down from our house.

Uncle Joe chimed in, "Now Alene, don't be scaring these kids with stories like that. You'll have them afraid to get out of the house."

I kinda liked his attitude about the whole situation. Joe was known to carry a pistol in his car and I was very pleased when he announced, "If I ever see that Wolfus, He's a dead Wolfus."

Maybe our prayers had been answered. No grown-up seemed to want to exterminate the Wolfus. The thing would live to plague us, our children, and our grandchildren, if someone didn't kill it. I added fuel to the fire, "Uncle Joe, do you think your pistol would kill that old Wolfus?"

"Why a 38 hollow point bullet would knock a hole in him big enough to stick your fist in," he answered.

That night everyone said their goodbyes and goodnights and we stood on the front porch as Joe and Cleo got into their car and headed home. As we watched, just as he got between my cousins house and Uncle Bill's Store, the car stopped. That is when Uncle Joe became every Cotton Mill Boy's hero. There was a flash of light and a loud bang. The car went in reverse and backed up in front of the house and stopped.

"I got him," he announced. "I got the Wolfus."

We never found the body, but Uncle Joe said he was mortally wounded and crawled off in the high weeds. Free at last! Free at last! Great God Almighty, free at last!

Occasionally a mother would claim she heard the Wolfus howl or one of uncle Bill's customers would claim to have seen him cross the road, but we knew the Wolfus was dead. Never again would he terrorize us or keep up from doing things we wanted to do. The only thing now that stood in the way of total bliss was the plum tree switch.

I never regretted the demise of the Wolfus nor did any of the other boys, but most of the mothers in the neighborhood seemed somewhat saddened by the death of the unknown creature. I guess it was sort of like the death of the last dinosaur.

Chapter VII: The Construction Projects

Most of the houses that were built at the Cotton Mill were built by their owners. The Cotton Mill Boys had ample opportunity to learn the building trades industry. Most of the houses used the "add on as needed" architecture style. Rooms were added on as the family grew.

Our house started with two rooms and grew to four when I was born. It later grew to six and a bath when my youngest sister was born. The siding on the houses progressed as the owners got promotions or raises. Our house, like most of the houses at the Cotton Mill started with brick-siding. Brick-siding was a tarpaper that had a brick design on it. It came in red, brown or gray. Next Dad covered the brick-siding with asbestos shingles. It was a mint green and I never really liked it. The final covering came when I was in college. It was real brick. We finally had a brick house.

In my early years, it was still four rooms with brick-siding, a front porch, and an outdoor toilet. I never felt deprived, because I had as much or more than any boy at the Cotton Mill. I helped Daddy build a hen house and a storage house we called the wash house. It was called the wash house because Mama washed clothes in there. My greatest contribution to the projects was the lumber.

Daddy would have all the old flooring that was torn out of the mill delivered to our house. My job was to pull out all the nails and stack the boards. I didn't really mind the hammering and nail pulling, but I always ended up getting splinters when I stacked the boards. Daddy always said I got in too big of a hurry. I guess I did, because I couldn't play until I was finished.

I wasn't the only Cotton Mill Boy to gain experience in the building trades industry. There were others who were better than me. We used our skill to build many projects. Some turned out really good and some turned out, well, not as well as we hoped.

One of the good projects we turned out was Hobo's Mansion. I think the mansion was Skeezer's brain child. There was a vacant lot between the lane to Sister Barrett's house and Charlie Bill's house. It was the scene of the cold war and the massacre of Bad Eye Elam. There was a field large enough to play catch and practice infield during baseball season. We spent quite a bit of time on the lot. I'm not sure who owned the lot, but no one ever objected to our playing there. In later years, Bobby Crocker built a house there, so it might have belonged to his mother.

We had several hideouts in ragweed patches, plum thickets, and holes we had dug, but none of these hideouts were much good when it rained. One day Skeezer suggested that we build a clubhouse. It was the thing to do. We were long overdue in having a place of our own. No girls, no adults, and no telling anyone about our secret place.

We went right to work scouring the neighborhood for lumber, nails, tar paper, shingles, windows, doors, anything that we could use on this construction project. I got into Daddy's wood pile and got all the boards I could carry. Charlie Bill found a bucket of nails at his house. Skeezer came dragging a Radio Flyer wagon full of Uncle Whit's tools. Leenova had a half of a roll of tar paper.

Boys could be seen all over the neighborhood, dragging lumber. Someone even came up with an old set of bed springs. We worked hard and there were no arguments or disputes among the workers. We had an excellent construction crew. Hammers were banging away at nails and saws were slicing through boards to cut them down to size. Not since Noah built the ark, had a group worked so diligently to finish a project. We would get up early and work until we got called to lunch. We would gulp down our food and as soon as we could be excused, we would head back to work. Doodler and Bobby Crocker jumped right into the project and, with the expertise of two older boys, the clubhouse began to really take shape. Doodler was out of school for a week. I'm not sure, but I think he was suspended for fighting. While he was out, he and Bobby made a lot of progress.

The project took two and a half weeks of steady work. The crew varied from time to time, depending on who had chores at home or who had to baby sit. Skeezer was the crew chief and he got the most out of the work force that showed up.

Finally the day came when he made his inspection and proudly announced, "She's finished."

We all went inside and set on the dirt floor and looked around at our spacious accommodations. It looked good, but the job still wasn't finished. We needed a door, a window and a whole lots of furnishings for this spacious mansion we built with our own hands. It was very sturdy and stood up to a big wind and a thunderstorm that very afternoon. It didn't leak a drop. There was a little water that ran in under the lower side and created a puddle, but it was nothing a little shovel work couldn't take care of.

But we still needed a door and window. Skeezer left for a while and when he returned he had a door and a window laying across the Radio Flyer. I never knew where he got the window, but I did find out where the door came from. The next day I was up at Skeezer's house and Mamaw Hallie came in from collecting the eggs. She looked a little puzzled. "That's the darndest thing I've ever seen," she said.

"What?" asked Uncle Whit.

"The door is gone off the hen house. I thought at first we had had a chicken thief, but none of the hens are missing," she explained.

I looked at Skeezer and he looked at me. We both grinned but didn't say a word. Such a nice mansion deserved to be furnished with the very best furniture and accessories. We went right to work collecting anything that wasn't tied down. We took the old set of springs and with the help of some imagination and concrete blocks, it became a bed. It was comfortable too. Well, at least it was more comfortable than the bed of nails we saw a man lie on at the carnival.

Four or five cane or string bottom chairs, with the bottoms missing, were given new life as we wove rope in the bottom to replace the missing material. Colin brought in some old wooden ammo boxes his father had hauled from the Milan Arsenal. Zeb even built a four room house out of lumber from his stack of ammo boxes. It was his rental house and it still stands after fifty years. Colin had sneaked a few of the boards when we were framing and siding the clubhouse, but these boxes were to be stacked and used as storage shelves. We kept precious items on the shelves. There was at least one of every kind of comic book stacked on the shelves. A baseball and bat graced one shelf and there was a Sears and Roebuck Catalogue on another shelf.

I always thought the Sears and Roebuck Catalogue was only good for two things, but I found out from some of the older boys it had another use. I knew we always had last years catalogue hanging on a string beside the throne in the outhouse. It was pretty coarse for the intended purpose, but it beat a corn cob. The other use for the catalogue gave it the nickname, "wish book." We looked at all the toys and hunting and fishing equipment and wished we had them. I found out in my sex education class that older boys actually looked at the girls in their underwear.

There were other items on the shelf from time to time. Mamaw Hallie's plum jelly or Mama's dewberry jam would not stay on the shelf for very long. That was especially true when we could scrape up fifteen cents to by a loaf of bread. When we could not put together the price of a loaf of bread, someone usually smuggled out some of their mama's biscuits. Sometimes someone would bring a can of vienna sausages and share until they ran out.

We kept collecting furnishings for the clubhouse and soon we had a coal oil lamp, quilts, two beds, a table and several chairs. We had all the comforts of home. We even spent the night several times. We would sit outside around a campfire and tell ghost stories until time to go to bed. For some reason most of us had a hard time going to sleep after we settled in.

It was one of those nights as we sat around the fire roasting hot dogs and telling tales, that the clubhouse got it's name. Skeezer was trying to scare us by telling us that some hobos were camped under the trestle. He told us they might come to the clubhouse after we went to sleep and get us and sell us to the gypsies. It had been well documented that gypsies bought and stole children. Our mothers began to warn us more and more about gypsies after Uncle Joe killed the Wolfus. When we wanted to go somewhere they didn't argue, they just said, "Go ahead, but if those gypsies catch you they'll kidnap you and we'll never see you again."

It wasn't as effective a deterrent as the Wolfus, but it worked sometimes. Skeezer continued his tale and then he said something that turned on his light bulb. "Compared to living under the trestle, our clubhouse would be a mansion for a hobo," he stated. From that day on our clubhouse was called "Hobos Mansion."

****

Another one of our successful building projects was the tree house. Almost everyone of us had a tree house in our back yard, or on a fence row or ditch bank, but one day we decided to build "The Tree House". Most of our tree houses were a few boards nailed between two limbs. It was just enough for one or at most two people to stand on. Like Hobo's Mansion, The Tree House, became a community project. I think Bobo came up with the idea. We would build it in Spangler's woods and we would use the same blueprint Tarzan used.

The first step in building the perfect tree house is to select the perfect tree. We covered the whole woods until we found a red oak that must have been here when Davy Crocket roamed Spangler's woods hunting bears. It had branches that spread out evenly and were level with each other. They were about twenty feet up in the tree. It was a good six feet to the limbs above them. As the two limbs spread out the distance between went from about three feet to twelve feet. The two limbs would make a perfect foundation for the tree house. Unlike Hobo's Mansion, we had nearly a mile to carry tools and materials, and there were two barbed-wire fences to cross. Getting everything on the site wouldn't be easy.

Bobo came up with the answer to the problem. He wasn't the first to invent the wheel or even the wheel barrow, but he rigged up some kind of push cart with bicycle wheels and handles to push from behind and handles to pull from the front. It resembled a miniature horse drawn wagon that had a place front and back to hitch a horse. Next to horse power, boy power was about as good a means of locomotion as there was. Four in front and four in back could move a pretty heavy load, if all did their share.

It took several trips, but we finally relocated enough lumber from the neighbor's and Jones Manufacturing Company's lumber piles to build our dream house. A pocket full of nails here and a hammer and saw there and we were ready to start. The first obstacle we had to overcome was the height at which we planned to build. We chopped down two really tall cedar trees and made a ladder that would reach the limbs. Bobo climbed up and nailed four or five boards between the two limbs at their narrowest point. This served as a walkway to the point we intended to build the floor. He then tied on some Jones Mfg. Co. rope and dropped it to the ground to hoist the boards to the work site. We worked diligently on the tree house and when we finished the floor, there was enough room for all of us to stand and look down at the ground. After several days of work the tree house began to take shape.

Some old two-by-fours were cut to six foot and they became the studs for the sides and top. We had the house nicely framed. It might have been a little off, but for a project built without the luxury of a level, it was pretty good.

The challenge and the danger came when we started to put up the walls. We had no ladder that could reach the sides, so we had to get inside the tree house and lean out and nail the boards on the outside of the frame. Bobo did most of that building and someone held him by his belt as he leaned over suspended in space. When the wall got so high he could no longer lean over, he climbed on top and had one boy hold each leg as he hung upside down and hammered away. He was some daredevil or he had a lot of faith in us as we held on to his ankles.

It took a lot of daring and a lot of acrobatics, but we eventually finished the Tree House. It was a work of architectural wonder. When we finished, it was large enough that five boys could lie down side-by-side and still have room for another to lay cross-ways at their feet and never touch each other. We added a few luxuries like a chair or two, some shelves, some candles, and Bobo even kept a spare can of Rooster snuff for anyone who wanted to try it.

The Tree House Hotel had such good accommodations, some of the older boys would spend the night. It was just a daytime hang-out for me. The Tree House was built after the death of the Wolfus, but there were still unknown creatures that lived in the world just beyond Spangler's woods. There were even some critters that lived in the woods that would eat you alive if they caught you.

The hogs that lived in Spangler's woods were trapped in the woods by a fence. We were never sure if they were wild hogs that had gotten inside the fence or if they were tame hogs someone put in the woods and they went wild. The one thing we were sure of was that they were vicious. Jeep and I were almost devoured one day. We were headed to The Tree House to play and instead of taking the long way around, we decided to climb over the fence. The Tree House was built on the edge of a field and the hogs could be avoided by going around the fence, but we had not seen the hogs in a while so we thought they may have become bacon.

We were walking a path through the woods and Tippie, Jeep's dog, ran along ahead of us. He had just gotten out of sight when we heard him bark. Then there was some squealing and grunting and it sounded like every tree and bush in the woods was falling down. We heard Tippie let out a yelp and it sounded like an earthquake was headed right toward us. Tippie scrambled through the underbrush right straight for us, and what we saw behind him struck as much fear in us as Frankenstein or Dracula ever could.

A whole heard of hogs were right on his tail and he was leading them straight to us. "Stampede!" I screamed, and we turned and ran. A glance over the shoulder revealed that Tippie and the hogs were gaining ground. We would never beat the rampaging beasts to the fence. We were doomed to be hog feed. At that point I would have given a dollar for my five gallon bucket full of slop to bribe them.

They were closing on us fast, when Jeep spied a tree top that might save us. He jumped on the fallen tree that lay at an angle and swiftly climbed up the large branch out of reach of the hogs. I was one step behind him all the way. Tippie tried to climb the tree with us, but he fell to the ground and the hogs closed in. Tippie leaped over another fallen tree and escaped, but the hogs now had discovered Jeep and me. They held their ugly snouts in the air and sniffed as if to say, "That meal up in the tree smells good."

We figured they would stay under the tree until we could no longer stay awake and fell on their dinner table or we would become so weak from lack of food and water we would lose our grip and become their snack. Tippie proved he was no coward, or maybe he proved he was a real dummy. He returned and started to bark at the hogs again. They seemed to loose interest in us and off they went chasing Tippie. As soon as they were out of sight we ran for The Tree House. We scrambled over the fence and up the ladder. We were out of breath when we reached the porch of the house, but we paused to listen and see what might be Tippie's fate.

We were expecting to hear the hogs squealing and grunting as they tore him apart. There were no sounds of mortal combat. Then we saw Tippie heading to The Tree House on the outside of the fence. He was no dummy after all. He had led the hogs away from us at great risk to himself. As soon as we were safe he jumped the fence to safety and returned. Tippie was our hero that day. Even Lassie or Rin-Tin-Tin couldn't have saved the day any better.

****

One construction project that didn't turn out very well was the raft we built. This project was inspired by a book that I checked out of the library at Main Street Elementary. The name of the book was *The Adventures of Tom Sawyer*. In reading the book, I thought how much the Cotton Mill Boy's were like Huck and Tom and their bunch. We loved to fish and we loved adventure. Charlie Bill was an avid reader and had already read the book. When I talked about building a raft and floating down the ditch to the Forked Deer River and then down the Forked Deer to the Mississippi River, he was all for it.

We could visualize ourselves laying on our backs looking up at the sky as we lazily floated down the 'big muddy'. Heck, Mark Twain might even write a book about us. We snapped out of our dream world with the realization that first we had to have a raft and we had to get it to the Mississippi River. This would have to be a secret project. We couldn't tell anyone or they might tell our parents and they wouldn't let us go on this great adventure.

Our first priority was to build our raft. Now, the only raft we had ever seen was a drawing in the book. It appeared Huck and Tom had used logs for their raft. We had no logs, but we could find some boards so we went right to work. Without the help of some of the older boys, we were kind of lost in this project, but we couldn't ask for help or our secret might be discovered. We did the best we could as we hammered as quietly as we could. We were lucky and no one caught us as we worked on the project. It might have been luckier if we had been caught.

When we completed the raft it was about six foot square. Well, maybe it wasn't square, but it was more square than triangular. In the absence of logs, we used two-by-fours on the underside of the raft to float it and one-by-sixes for the floor. Actually it didn't look all that bad, but how would it perform in the Mississippi River?

We formulated the plans for our adventure. The ditch was too shallow to float the raft so we would have everything ready and the first time the ditch came up after a big rain, we would launch the raft and drift down the ditch to the Forked Deer and then we would be on our way to the mighty Mississippi.

We had food packed to carry. Two cans of pork and beans, some crackers, and two apples would sustain us until we could catch some fish. Naturally we had our fishing poles, band-aid-can tackle boxes and pocket knives. We had a large pole to push and steer with, but we made no attempt to make a sail. We wouldn't need a sail anyway, because we would be drifting with the current.

We hadn't figured out how we would get back home after we reached the mouth of the Mississippi, but we would worry about that when the time came. All was ready. All we needed was a small flood and we would be on our way.

I don't know if we would have followed through with our plans if the opportunity had presented itself, but we never got the chance. Our secret was discovered. One of us made a big blunder. We decided to go ahead and launch our raft in the six inches of water that was in the ditch at low tide. We tied it off to a tree on the bank. That way, when the rain came and the ditch rose, we could jump on and be off.

We got the raft all set and it looked like it would float just fine when the water rose. We just had to do a dress rehearsal of how we would jump on the raft and take off down the ditch to the Mississippi River. Charlie Bill jumped off the bank and onto the raft. I jumped, and when I hit there was an excruciating pain in my right foot. I jerked my foot up and when I looked at the bottom of my tennis shoe, blood was coming out of a hole in the sole.

I ran in the house with my foot throbbing with every beat of my heart. By now I was crying and as soon as Mama saw me she let out one of her "Lordy mercies". I sat down in the kitchen floor and pulled off my shoe.

"You stuck a nail in it, didn't you?" she asked.

"I guess that's what happened," I said as I wiped tears from my cheeks.

"Was it a clean nail or a rusty nail?" she inquired.

"I don't know," was the only answer I could come up with.

"If it was rusty, you'll have to get a shot or you might have lock jaw," she stated.

"I think it was clean," I countered.

Then the dreaded question was asked, "Where was it?"

I couldn't tell her or our secret would be out. If I didn't I surely would be going to the doctor for a shot. It was a dilemma, but I had a fifty-fifty chance that the nail wasn't rusty and I wouldn't have to go to the doctor if I showed Mama the nail. She would just have to see the raft.

I hobbled along with Mama to the ditch to point out the nail on the raft. She climbed down the bank and inspected the raft. She rubbed her hand over the surface until she felt something. She got down on her hands and knees and looked closely at the nail. She shook her head, which I was sure meant, "Uh oh, we have to go to Dr. Barker's"

She climbed back up the bank and took me by the arm and led me to the house. All the time I know I am going to have to get a shot. Charlie Bill took off home just as soon as I headed to the house. I guess he knew I would spill my guts about the raft and he didn't want to be anywhere around when Mama found out. Unfortunately I had to face her alone.

"Where did those boards come from?" she asked.

She didn't even recognize them as a raft. I might could get out of this without letting her find out we were going to run away from home and float the Mississippi. I found out it doesn't pay to lie, but I tried. "I don't know where they came from," I answered with a pang of guilt.

"That's too bad because it looked like that was a new nail, but if we can't tell for sure, we'll have to go to Dr. Barker and get a shot," she stated with a frown on her stern Cherokee face.

I wilted and began to confess the whole story. I told how we had planned to leave home and float the Mississippi River like Tom and Huck. We had built the raft and we had used new nails that Charlie Bill had swiped from Louis' nail bucket. I added that we had planned to come back home when we reached the mouth of the Mississippi.

I got a lecture about how I would have drowned if I had gotten on the raft when the ditch was up. Mama couldn't swim and she was always afraid of water. She accepted my apology and hugged me, then she said, "Let's fix that foot."

She went and got the coal oil jug and dabbed some on a piece of white cloth. She then tied it around my foot with the coal oil over the puncture wound. I'm not sure I wouldn't have come out better by having the shot.

****

When we fished the Island Pond, we always felt we could really catch more fish if we could just get out in the middle of the pond. We would see big bass leap out of the water near the island in the middle. The pond was too deep to get out very far using the floating pole method, so we concluded we needed a boat. They say that need is the mother of invention. In our case, need was the mother of another of our construction projects.

Building a boat requires more planning and skill than building a clubhouse or tree house, so we went to an expert, Daddy. He had built several boats of varying materials. He had one boat that was made of canvas. The boat had wooden ribs and a wooden walkway in the bottom, but the outer skin was canvas, smeared with tar. It was a very light boat that he used for duck hunting. That light boat got me in big trouble when I was five or six years old.

Mama had done something to make me mad that day and I vowed to make her pay for it. I would run away from home and she would be sorry she had been mean to me. I told her I might run away and she said, "Go ahead and see if I care." She knew I couldn't get out of the fence so she played it cool.

I went outside and walked the perimeter of the fence, looking for an escape route. None could be found, but an idea popped in my mind. I now know that the devil put it there. I would find a place to hide and when she couldn't find me she would think I ran away.

I first started to crawl under the house, but she would look there, because that's where I hid to avoid whippings. I thought about the outhouse, but she might have to go and she would find me. I spotted the canvas boat turned upside down. I picked up one side and I could get it just high enough to crawl under. The perfect hiding place, even Trixie couldn't find me under there.

I had only been under the boat about half an hour when she called me to lunch. "O'Neal, come to dinner," she sang out. It was called lunch after I started to school, but at home there were three meals a day; breakfast, dinner and supper. I didn't respond to the call to dinner. A minute later it was, "Herbert O'Neal, come to dinner!"

To be called by my full name was a threat. It meant, "If you don't get here quick, I'll get a plum switch."

I still didn't answer. I heard the screen door on the back porch slam. "O'Neal, where are you?" she asked in a loud voice. "You'd better answer me," she demanded. I detected some fear in her voice. My plan was already working, she'd be sorry.

She took a quick look around the yard and I heard the gate on the picket fence slam shut. There was silence for a while and then I heard other voices calling my name. Miss Mary was calling, "O'Neal! O'Neal! Where are you?"

Others were walking along the ditch calling my name. I was in big trouble now, I had not thought she would call out the neighborhood search party.

I lay under the boat in sheer terror. Now I really would have to run away. I had two alternatives. I could run away or I could jump down the toilet hole and commit suicide. I had threatened Mama with just that a few times when she was going to whip me, but I certainly never intended to end it that way. Just when all hope was gone, I heard a familiar voice. It was Bobby Crocker calling my name. He had joined in the search and maybe he could save me. He was my older buddy and even though he was a teenager, he would often help me build a bow or even play with me. He called out again, "O'Neal, where are you?"

"Here I am," I answered. He heard the voice under the

boat. He lifted it up and I crawled out.

"Boy! Your mama is so upset she is gonna kill you!" were the first words out of his mouth. He grabbed me around the wrist and practically dragged me into the house. Mama was sitting on the couch with Girty on one side and Miss Mary on the other. They were trying to console her. I later learned that she had seen me in the deep hole of the ditch laying underwater drowned. Actually it was a paper sack the same color as the kaki shorts I had on, but she was sure her boy was dead.

"Here he is!" Bobby announced.

She looked up with the tears still in her eyes and when she saw me she stretched out her arms like the rich man welcoming his prodigal son home. I jumped in her arms with a feeling of remorse and guilt that I had caused her so much pain. Deep down, I thought I was home free and there would be no punishment. After all, she was so happy to see me alive she would not do anything that would hurt me. Wrong! She grabbed my hand, marched out to the front porch, broke a limb off the plum tree, and proceeded to tan my hide right in front of Bobby and all the neighbors.

Daddy had made other boats besides the canvas boat that got me in so much trouble. One was built out of two car hoods welded together end to end. This was long before aluminum bass boats became popular and I don't think fiberglass boats were even in existence. It was a neat boat, but we just wanted to build a plain old wooden john boat.

With Daddy's help, Bobby Henley, my cousin next door, and I built a boat that would actually float. It seeped a little bit of water, but the quarter inch plywood held up very well. We caulked it, painted it, carved out some paddles and we were ready to fish in our very own fishing boat. We couldn't wait to try it out.

The maiden voyage was at Stallin's pond. It was a successful voyage and the first of many trips that yielded the phantoms of the deep, that had eluded our hooks for years. The one thing we learned about the boat the hard way, was that snakes would take up residence under the boat if it sat on the bank for a time without being used.

Charlie Bill, Leenova, and I went to the pond one day. I don't remember having any poles, so we probably went to swim. We decided to take a boat ride while we were there. The pond was a little low and as the water receded, the boat was stranded on a mud flat. Only the transom was at the edge of the water. We slid the boat out about half-way into the water and Charlie Bill and Leenova got in and moved to the back. The back end was floating in the shallow water and I pushed hard to get the rest of the boat into the water.

The boat slid easily over the slick mud as I dug my feet into the mire. As the front of the boat cleared the mud, Leenova and Charlie Bill started to screaming and pointing at something. I looked around and less than ten inches from my bare foot, a big cotton mouth was striking at me. The only thing that kept him from sinking his fangs into my skin was the fact that the middle of his body was buried in the mud. I had actually stepped on the snake as I moved his wooden home off of him. My weight mashed his body into the mud, causing his strikes to fall short as the mud kept his body from uncoiling far enough to hit me.

I jumped four feet into the air and somewhere in the process I gave the boat such a push that Leenova and Charlie Bill skipped across the water. "Throw me the paddle!" I screamed. It was the only weapon we had. Leenova grabbed it and heaved it my way.

The paddle tumbled end over end and landed only inches from the snake. So much for that weapon. I looked for something else and about that time the snake made a lunge and pulled free of the mud. It headed straight toward the boat. Charlie Bill and Leenova couldn't swim nor paddle at this point. They were sure the snake would come right in the boat after them. They were both standing up yelling as the snake approached.

They screamed, "Throw us the paddle!" I did and it landed in the water between the snake and the boat. The snake reacted by turning around and heading back toward the bank where I stood at the edge of the water. I turned and ran back up the bank and Charlie Bill was able to grab the paddle and get the boat all the way across to the other side. They went so fast I could have sworn there was an outboard motor on the boat. I don't know what happened to the cotton mouth, but it probably died of a heart attack from all the commotion.

The old boat gave us three or four years of pleasure. We had to keep a coffee can in it to bail out the water as it began to leak with age. It was abandoned as we started to fish Humboldt Lake where, for a dollar, we could rent a fourteen foot aluminum boat. The old boat finally sunk and became the residence of some big black bream. It was kind of sad to see the plywood side barely sticking out of the water because it had been one of our really good construction projects.

Chapter VIII: The Conveniences

There were lots of conveniences that added to the quality of life at the Cotton Mill. Some were store bought and some were homemade. One such item was the outdoor toilet. The outdoor toilets were gradually replaced by commodes as residents put in indoor plumbing, but in the early fifties, almost everyone at the Cotton Mill still had the outdoor john.

The outdoor toilet usually came in a standard four foot by three foot building, but some of the more luxurious models could be as large as four by five. It was usually unpainted to give it that weathered look, but occasionally someone would paint them barn red. Some of the fancy ones would have a crescent shaped moon cut out at the top of the door. The inside was usually floored with a concrete slab with one or two holes in the concrete. Built over each hole would be a throne. It had a wooden seat with an oblong hole cut in it. Sometimes there would be a lid that was hinged to cover the hole when it was not in use.

I was involved in the building of one outdoor toilet when I was very young. As I remember it, the hardest part was digging the hole that served as the holding tank. I don't know if there was a standard depth, but I do remember it was over Daddy's head and looked like the Grand Canyon to me.

As was usually the case, other neighbors pitched in on the "toilet digging" and it didn't take long. It must have been pretty deep because Mama had the awful fear that I might fall in the toilet hole. I took advantage of that fear and played it for all it was worth, for a while.

I really wasn't a bad child, but it seemed like I got caught in everything I did. Other boys could sneak around their mothers with all kinds of things, but let me slip up and I was caught. For self preservation, I had to come up with ways to avoid the plum tree switch. I tried running when Mama came after me with a switch. She would catch me and whip me for my offence and then whip me some more for running. I tried crawling under the house, but she would wait me out and give me some extra stripes across the legs for crawling under the house. I would climb trees to avoid the dreaded plum switch, but as I found out, Mama could climb pretty well herself. None of my avoidance tactics seemed to work. Then one day, by accident, I discovered a way to avoid the plum tree switch.

I was shooting my sling shot at an old tin can and became bored with the "clank!" as the pig iron hit the metal. I looked around for some new target. I went into the wash house and there I found some quart fruit jars. "They would make a good target," I thought.

I lined them up in a row. I made a game out of it. There were ten jars. I assigned points to each jar. Ten out of ten would make me an expert. Eight out of ten would be a marksman and five out of ten would be average. I took aim as I looked through the yoke of the sling shot and stretched the rubber back as far as my strength would allow. I let go and the hurling missile hit it's mark. The jar shattered and I was one for one. I reloaded and eyed the second jar. I pulled and released and with another shattering crash I was two for two. "Man, I'm good!" I thought. I pulled back to make it three for three when I heard Mama scream, "Herbert O'Neal! What in the world do you think you are doing?"

I let off the pressure on the sling shot and turned to see Mama coming at me like an Indian on the warpath. I would never know if I could have gotten ten out of ten. I panicked and ran, and as I ran, I knew I was doing the wrong thing, but

I just couldn't stop.

She was as angry as I had ever seen her and I knew I was going to get a good one. I saw the outhouse and I ran in and hooked the hook that locked the door. She came up to the door and warned me to come out or get a whipping twice as hard. I refused to open the door. "You've got to come out sometime young man, and when you do!" she said in a very angry voice. It was the 'and when you do', that sent chills up my spine and forced me to make my next move.

I knew I had to come out sooner or later and I knew I had really messed up this time. That's when this little voice, no doubt it was the devil, told me to crawl down in the toilet hole and hang by my arms and Mama would go away. I followed instructions and called to her, "If you're going to whip me I'm gonna drop in the toilet hole." Mama looked through the crack in the door and saw me dangling in the hole from my waist down. Only my arms propped me up and kept me from going down.

It scared her so bad she started to beg me to please come out. "Are you going to whip me if I come out?" I asked.

"No, I won't," she said in a frightened voice.

"You promise?" I asked, knowing that Mama never broke a promise.

"I do. Come on out before you fall," she pleaded.

I came out and she kept her promise and didn't whip me. For some reason I just didn't feel good about my defeat of Mama in a war of wills. I felt like I had somehow cheated.

That feeling didn't keep me from using the toilet hole as sanctuary one other time. I remember it was a Saturday because Daddy was home. I was usually a pretty good boy when Daddy was around. Those plum tree switches that Mama used were nothing compared to Daddy's belt. If I was doing something he didn't like, he didn't have to say a word. He would just reach for the buckle on his belt and I would straighten up. The whippings he gave me would border on child abuse today, but I don't have any lasting emotional scars. I do, however, have a small scar on my behind.

I don't even remember the event that lead to Daddy taking off his belt, but I am sure I deserved it. He ordered me, "Come here boy." I had never tried to run from him or climb a tree, or even escape by crawling under the house. I usually submitted without a struggle. He usually didn't give me many licks, but then it didn't take many from him.

I should have known better than to listen, but that impish little voice said, "Run to the outhouse." I took off running like the wind. I could hear Daddy demanding, "You better come back here boy!" I slammed the door and locked it. I quickly crawled down in the hole and got myself in the ready position.

He approached the door and I warned him, "If you're gonna whip me I'll drop down the toilet hole." I'd show him!

His reply was a short and simple, "Drop!" Needless to say I got my back side lit up good and I never again tried to use the outhouse as a sanctuary.

Most people who had an outhouse could expect to find some unwelcome critters in their privy. Sometimes there would be a little house wren that had built a grass nest in the corner of the wall and roof where the two by fours came together. The little bird would fly out the door when it was opened. It would brush your hair as it made it's quick exit. The little wrens never bothered me, but many times they would force Charlie Bill to seek relief from nature's call somewhere other than the outhouse.

Besides the birds nest, there would usually be other creatures with nests in the sanctuary of the toilet. Sometimes a nest would be built in a corner or along a wall, but the worst place was under the throne. I had no great love for these creatures, in fact, I was even fearful of them. I had just cause, because the red wasp could put a hurting on a bare leg or a bare butt.

After one encounter that forced me to escape with my britches down around my ankles, I always looked the place over before I sat down. If even one wasp was spotted I would call for Mama and she would come and douse him with coal oil. Coal oil, later known as kerosene, served many purposes, from medicine to bug spray, not to mention it's intended purpose, cooking, heating and lighting. With the outhouse properly fumigated, I could get on with my business.

There was one other critter that most people feared even more than the wasp. It was the Black Widow Spider. The spider would build a web in the corners, under the throne and sometimes even in the hole of the throne. A special stick was kept in the toilet for tearing down webs and crushing the spiders. They were very distinct in their shape and color and could easily be spotted if you paid attention to your surroundings. They were a shiny black like satin. They had a round abdomen with a bright red hour-glass on their under side. There were always tales of people being bitten on private parts, but I never knew anyone who was actually a victim of the Black Widow.

Maintenance of the outdoor toilet was simple. Once or twice a year lime was dropped into the holding pit. This helped to keep down the odor and decompose some of the contents. Some people never washed the inside of the toilet, but Mama would give it a good scrubbing about once a week. She believed cleanliness was next to Godliness and she practiced what she preached. She always had a clean house and a clean outhouse.

****

Running water was one convenience we had at our house. Daddy piped water from the Smith's house next door. They had a well and for a small fee to help pay the electric bill, they allowed us to hook on. About the time I was eight or nine, the city of Humboldt ran a water line down Avondale Street and we hooked on to city water. From that time on water was no problem. In the past, however, getting water was sometimes a chore.

One time the Smith's well went out and we were without water. This created another chore for me. I had to go up to the mill and bring back a two gallon water bucket, full to the brim, twice and sometimes three times a day. Two gallons of water is mighty heavy for a seven-year-old, but I would tote and rest, tote and rest, until I finally wagged it home. After about three days of back-breaking work I finally figured out that I could haul the water in my wagon. It took almost two weeks for the Smith's well to be operational again, so I was glad I had the brainstorm. I even shared my wagon with Alvin Smith and he did most of the pulling.

Water was a very important commodity. It was used for cooking, washing clothes, washing dishes, and washing dirty little boys. There were three ways that a boy could get a bath. The one most often used was the tub. I don't mean what most people think of as a bath tub, our tub was a round number two wash tub. Even though we had running water, we did not have a hot water heater. Well, in a way we did have a hot water heater, it was heated on the cook stove. It took two dish pans of hot water and one dish pan of cold water to have enough water for a bath. In the winter time the bath was taken right in the kitchen. I would sit in the warm water and scrub from head to toe with a bar of P&G or Ivory soap.

The heating process for the water was a little different in the summer. The tub was set out in the back yard where the sun could hit it most of the day. When the water got comfortably warm, I would wrap in a towel and go get in the tub and bathe outside. When I got out, I would wrap the towel back around me and make a mad dash for the house. Only Gail and I took the outside bath in the tub of water heated by solar energy. I guess it would have been scandalous for Mama or Daddy to take an outside bath, unless they took it in a bathing suit.

We had another way of taking a bath each night that didn't require as much water as the tub bath. The wash pan and wash cloth bath could be done in about a gallon of warm water. Water was heated in the dish pan on the stove and poured into the smaller wash pan. Soap was applied to the wet wash rag and used to scrub the hide off. After the whole body had been sanitized with the soapy rag, that water was thrown out and clean water was used to rinse off the soap left by the first application. It wasn't as simple and easy as a tub bath, but it worked pretty good.

One favorite kind of bath was the shower bath. It could be taken by two methods of obtaining water. If it was really hot in the summertime, we would go outside in our shorts or underwear and spray each other with the hose. That well water felt like it was forty degrees in the ninety degree heat. Slap on a little soap and we had a shower bath. It was a fun way to get the Saturday bath. The other water source for the shower bath was Mother Nature, herself. A good hard rain and a bar of soap and we were clean as a new fallen snow.

Mama claimed rain water was good for your hair. She, like many other women, kept a rain barrel under the eave of the house to catch rain water to wash her hair. It must have worked, because she had beautiful, wavy, coal black hair. She kept her hair brushed and it shined jet black in the sun. The Cherokee genes really showed in her hair and eyes. She was small of stature at four-eleven, but she was big in my eyes.

****

Water was very important in washing clothes. Mama really had her work cut out for her when it came to doing the laundry, but she was luckier than some women at the cotton mill. They washed clothes outside winter or summer in an iron kettle called a wash pot. Daddy used the scrap lumber I pulled the nails out of, to build a house just for washing. It was called, of course, the wash house.

The wash house was not only used for washing clothes. It was Gail's playhouse, where she pretended to cook and clean. She played with her doll and rocked it to sleep.

To the Cotton Mill Boys it was an army training camp, a fort, a mountain and others assorted things as needed for the day's activities. At night it became a place to hide when we played night games. It was even a haunted house on one occasion.

The wash house had a big walnut tree growing beside it. We had a rope swing in the walnut tree that we could use to swing up on top of the wash house. We could catch the rope and climb upon a post and glide from the top of the post to the top of the wash house. It's a wonder that there was any of the roll-roofing left on the east side where we always landed.

There was a loft in the shed and it was a good place to hide when we were playing games. At the back of the wash house, right at the top where the gables met, there was a triangular shaped hole. It was just large enough for me to squeeze through. It was my secret escape hatch when I hid in the loft. If someone came to look for me in the loft, I would crawl out on top of the wash house roof and escape before they could climb up in the loft. It was a really neat trick, but I pulled it once too often one day when we were playing army.

I was in the loft with my army helmet and army rifle, made of wood of course, and I was surrounded by my cousins Jeep, Doug, and Bobby. They ordered me to surrender or they would toss in a grenade. John Wayne would have never surrendered so neither would I. They thought they had every escape blocked. One was at the door and one at the window. There was only one door into the fort and they had it covered. I knew exactly the maneuver I needed to make. General Patton or General McArthur couldn't have had a better strategy.

I silently crept to the back of the loft, staying low so I wouldn't bump my head or be seen by the enemy. My plan was to sneak out the escape hole on the roof and quietly ease up to the front of the building and look down on the enemy just below me and then turn loose my Thompson machine gun and make mince meat out of them.

First I stuck my rifle out of the hole and laid it on the roof. Next I laid down on my back and stuck my head and arms out of the hole. I reached up and grabbed the roof at it's highest point and pulled all my upper body out of the hole. I had just pulled my head up high enough to see the top of the roof when I felt the first shot hit me in the chest. Then there was one burning sensation after another. I struggled to clear the hole and get on top of the roof. I started screaming and crying because there was so much pain.

ly first reaction was to slap my chest to remove the ng objects, but I had to hold on with both hands or fall ve feet and land on my back or head. I managed to get to roof and I started swatting my chest. I was covered with red wasps. I jumped off the roof into the old walnut tree and shimmied down, all the while screaming and crying. By that time the enemy soldiers had come to my aid and instead of taking me captive, they took me to Mama. She grabbed my tee shirt and nearly yanked my ears off as she pulled it over my head.

There were red whelps all over my chest and two or three on my neck and back. She ran in Little Mama's room without so much as a "Lordy mercy" and returned with a glass of Little Mama's Burton snuff. She proceeded to dab snuff on every sting. Tobacco, like coal oil, had many medicinal uses. It must have worked, because she said if I started to feel faint or have fever she was going to call Dr. Barker, and he never came.

Late that afternoon, when Daddy came home, she had him tear down the big wasp nest that had been built in the eave of the wash house just above the escape hole.

We used the wash house for a lot of things, but its intended purpose was to provide Mama with a place to wash clothes that would be out of the elements. Not only did she have a special place to do the laundry, she also had a set of fancy wash tubs. The two square tubs sat side by side on a stand that had rollers on the legs to make it mobile. One tub would be filled with hot water and one with cold water. Mama had a scrub board that she set down in the hot soapy water. The article of clothing to be washed was rubbed up and down the ribs on the scrub board, then it was twisted so the soapy water was squeezed out. Next it was untwisted and dunked in the clean cold water. It was again twisted. When all the excess water was squeezed out, it was put in a basket to be hung on the clothesline to dry.

The wash tubs had a feature that made life much easier for Mama. Each tub had a hose that came out of the bottom of the tub and hooked at the top of the tub to keep the water in.

When she got ready to drain them, she simply unhooked them and let them drain through a hole Daddy cut in the wall.

About two years later Daddy ran electricity to the wash house and Mama got a brand new ringer washer. She may not have been the first woman at the Cotton Mill to have an electric washer, but she was among the first. I was glad it cut down on her work, but the bad part was, she had more time to supervise me.

I was fascinated by the new washing machine. She filled it up with hot water, put the clothes in, turned it on and the fins on the agitator did the rest. She draped a hose in the hole in the wall and drained the soapy water off and added new water. In no time the clothes were rinsed. To ring out the water, the clothes were fed between two rollers that squeezed them tight. They came out on the other side ready to hang on the line.

I always wanted to feed the clothes into the ringer, but Mama would say, "No, you'll get your fingers caught and it will mash them as flat as a flitter." I never knew what a flitter was, but I figured I didn't want my fingers looking like one.

Once clothes were washed, they were hung on a wire or rope line that was stretched between two poles. Daddy welded two pipes in a 'T' shape and Mama had a double clothesline.

About the only time you will hear the clothesline mentioned today is in a football game. When a player gets caught under the chin with an outstretched arm and the back of his helmet is the first thing that hits the ground, he got clothes lined.

Let me tell you, some of the worst cases of clothes lining came at the Cotton Mill and it wasn't in a football game. It happened most often playing night games or on Halloween. Many a boy had a long red whelp across his neck because he ran full speed into a real clothesline.

****

Mama had an automatic dish washer. She would say, "O'Neal and Gail, wash the dishes," and we would automatically wash them. Washing dishes required some skill, especially in the drying stage. Most of us boys didn't admit to washing dishes, because it was considered woman's work. I usually tried to get the drying job, but sometimes I would come up with dish pan hands. Mama usually did the breakfast and dinner dishes, but after supper, it was our turn. Sometimes if my cousins Shirley and Corky ate supper with us, they would wash the dishes. I invited them as often as I could.

Daddy had Mama set up pretty good for dish washing. He had plumbed a water faucet into the kitchen and installed a sink. It was metal with a white porcelain finish. There was a drain that was piped to the back of the house. There was no sewer or septic tank, so the water from the sink drained out on the ground.

At the point where the water came out he dug a shallow ditch that went down beside the wash house and into the chicken pen. It stayed damp along the ditch, but that wasn't all bad. The moist soil was full of fishing worms. It was an inexhaustible source of bait.

The sink had a rubber stopper to place in the drain to hold in the water. Everyone placed their dishes on the cabinet beside the sink when they finished eating. It was a simple matter to scrape all the left-overs, which weren't many, into the slop bucket. A dish pan of hot water was heated on the stove and poured into the sink on the dirty dishes. A couple of shakes of the box of Ivory Snow dishwashing powders and the washing was on. After all the dishes and utensils were thoroughly scrubbed with the dish rag, the plug was pulled and the dish water drained to the chicken pen. The hogs actually liked the soapy water.

With the soapy water drained it was time to rinse and dry. The dishes were placed one by one under the water from the faucet. They were rinsed off and then dried with a dish towel. That was the most dangerous part. While wiping off all the water, many a dish just jumped right out of the dryer's hand and was broken. Mama even had a fancy rack we could stack the dishes in to drain but she always wanted them wiped dry.

****

Most of our food was either fresh out of the garden, canned from the garden or taken out of the salt box. We did have fresh game and fish in season and Mama would ring a chicken's neck occasionally for a chicken dinner. There were, however, certain items that needed to be kept cold to prevent spoilage. These items were kept in the icebox. The icebox was a wooden cabinet with a metal liner. The top compartment held a block of ice that kept all the compartments below it cool. Milk, cheese, butter, meat, and any other food that would spoil in the heat, would be kept in the icebox. There was also usually a jug of water or tea that could quench the thirst of a dry throat on a hot day. We even stored a Coke or RC Cola in the icebox occasionally. I especially liked the Nehi orange drink.

The icebox didn't run on electricity or have an automatic icemaker. The ice was delivered by the iceman from Bear Ice and Coal Co. It was located at the crossing and even in later years, after we purchased a refrigerator, Daddy would go by and get a block of ice to put in the cooler when we went fishing. There was an ice truck that slowly drove through the neighborhood. The lady of the house merely had to come to the front door and yell, "Iceman!" He would stop and take her order.

"Give me a twenty-five pound block," one would order. Another might call for a fifty-pound block. The iceman was pretty strong because he could take some metal tongs that were sharp on the end and hook around the slippery block and carry it to the icebox. Our icebox was on the back porch so he had a pretty good haul at our house.

Amazingly the block of ice would last almost a week. I think that was because every time Mama heard the icebox door open she would yell, "Hurry up and shut that door, you'll melt the ice." It was such a habit that a few years later when we got a refrigerator, she would still yell, "Hurry up and shut that door, you'll melt the ice."

About the same time Mama got her new ringer washer, she also got a new Hotpoint refrigerator. It must have been about the time Daddy was promoted to foreman at Jones Manufacturing Company. The Hotpoint was a modern-day marvel. It had a small compartment at the top that held four aluminum ice trays. The trays had little dividers that made the ice freeze in cube shapes. You could run water over the bottom of the frozen trays and pull up on a little handle and out would pop the ice cubes. It was the first automatic icemaker I had ever seen. We soon discovered that we could fill the trays with orange, grape or strawberry penny-drink and we had Popsicles.

Below the freezing compartment there were assorted shelves and drawers. The drawers even had names on them to tell you what went where. There was a meat drawer just under the freezing compartment and the bottom two drawers were labeled vegetables. Mama kept the Hotpoint well stocked and we could just about count on something cold to drink or a snack to eat. It must have been a good old refrigerator, because in later years, my kids would hit the refrigerator as soon as they got to 'Maw's' house to see what goodies she had stored in the little Hotpoint. By then she had another newer and larger refrigerator, but she kept the good stuff like peanut butter cake, coconut cake and banana pudding in the little antique. It even lasted long enough for Dalton, my first grandchild, to have a few snacks out of Mama's first refrigerator. Gail still has it today and it still works.

****

If you lived at the Cotton Mill, you could count on three square meals a day. They were all sit-down meals at the kitchen table. Any family members who were home or family or friends who was visiting, were always welcome to join in the meal. We didn't eat a lot of expensive meat, but we usually had vegetables, fresh or canned, and chicken or pork cooked in a variety of ways. Most often it was fried in lard rendered from the hog we raised every year. Homemade biscuits or cornbread was the bread for the meal.

Mama started out cooking on a coal oil stove when I was younger, but by the time I was eight or nine she had an electric range. She could cook everything very well. She had a lot of practice for a woman her age. She took over the kitchen chores for Little Mama when she was about ten years old. Little Mama was in poor health most of her life. Mama could cook beans and taters and a pone of corn bread and I could make a meal out of that. Her cakes and pies were to die for. There were always leftovers to snack on.

After each meal, some of the food on the menu would be left on the table. Each bowl was carefully covered to keep the flies out. From breakfast, a boy could always find some left-over biscuits. There were two mid-morning snacks I liked to grab as I passed through the kitchen. A biscuit, some homemade butter, churned by Mrs. Elam and purchased for twenty cents a pound, and some of Mama's dewberry jelly made a great treat. If there was any middlin meat left from breakfast, I liked middlin meat with mustard on a big fat biscuit. Charlie Bill really liked that combination too, and when he came to play, we always had to check under the table cloth on the kitchen table.

My home-away-from-home was Mamaw Hallie's. I always liked eating at her house because with every meal she made thickening gravy. There was nothing better than a biscuit sopped in gravy, or fresh tomatoes covered with the brown gravy. It always made Mama a little jealous when I bragged on Mamaw's cooking. They both could make almost anything taste good, even liver.

I remember eating at Mamaw's a time or two when I almost lost my table manners and laughed at the dinner table. It was when Alvin Smith was playing with Skeezer and me. Mamaw invited him to eat.

Alvin was part of the Smith family who were my first neighbors to live in the house next door. Alvin was two years older than I, but we were in the same grade in school. He had two older sisters, Maxine and Blondale, and a brother a year younger than him, Charles. His father was Sam and his mother was Beulah. When Sam died, they moved away.

Alvin had a speech impediment and he pronounced my name "I Ni." That was his version of O'Neal. Most other words he could pronounce very well, but the word 'thickening gave him trouble. He, like everyone else, loved Mamaw's thickening gravy. He asked Skeezer to pass the thickening gravy. Only it didn't come out thickening, it was more like 'schiting' gravy. Mamaw was just about to flog him for saying a word of profanity, when we explained what he meant to say.

Whether the food was cooked on a wood-burning stove, or an electric range, if it was cooked at the Cotton Mill, it was good. All the women cooked with lard, either homemade or store-bought. Barrett's Grocery had lard from two pound boxes to twenty-five pound lard stands. There was a constant supply of almost pure cholesterol for our bodies, but we were so active I think we burned up most of it.

At the Cotton Mill, meal time was more than just a time to feed the body the nutrients it needed, it was a time to enjoy the company of the other family members and guests. There was always conversation about the day's events and even world affairs were often discussed. Everyone took their time and enjoyed the meal. It always made Mama happy when someone asked for seconds and she never ceased to ask, "Did you get enough? Are you still hungry? Won't you have another helping?" A lot of the problems with youth today could be more easily solved by sitting around the dinner table than they can be by sitting on some psychiatrist's couch.

****

The storm cellar was a luxury for most people, but it was a necessity for Mama. Very little could frighten her, but a storm got to her. As the clouds turned dark and thunder rolled in the distance, she gathered up her chicks and headed us to the 'storm house'. Sometimes it was kind of neat to go to the storm house if there wasn't something more fun to do.

Daddy built the storm house to put Mama at ease when a storm came. It was dug by hand and was about eight feet by eight feet. Inside the hole in the ground he pored a concrete floor and laid blocks for the walls. The roof was made of concrete and the excess dirt was piled on the top. It created a little hill that we often used in our playing. There was a concrete block stairway that sloped down into the hole at an angle. A metal door, that had been discarded from the mill, closed off the storm house from the elements of nature on the outside.

The inside of the sanctuary from the elements, was furnished with a cot, three or four cane-bottom chairs, a table and a coal oil lamp. The cot was for Little Mama. It was a chore getting her in and out of the storm house. She didn't like going and in her last few years, she refused to go and would ride out the storms in the house.

I couldn't blame her, because the storm house was always damp and musty. We went to the safety of the storm house less and less as I got older. We never had a tornado, or cyclone as Mama called them, just some high winds and thunder and lightning. I was never afraid of storms, except maybe the lightning.

The storm house doubled as a play house for Gail on pretty days. She would take her dolls and go down in the cellar and enjoy the cool air that collected in the underground cavern. It was pretty nice to go down into the cellar when the temperature was in the nineties. The storm house was air conditioned by nature. It was also a really good underground bunker when the boys played army. With the metal door barely cracked open, it was hard for the enemy to get a grenade into the bunker without being shot.

In later years when the blocks began to crack and water began to seep in and stand, Daddy filled in the storm house, but it got Mama through much of her fear of storms. That fear got me one of the worst whippings I ever got.

I asked to go to David Pillow's and play and Mama gave me a flat no. I begged a little hoping she would change her mind. She didn't feel well and told me, "I said no. It's coming up a storm and we might have to go to the storm house." I didn't really think there would be a storm, after all the sun was shining. She had a migraine and she usually had to lie down and sleep to get rid of it. I could go to David's and get back before she knew I had gone, so I crossed the ditch and headed across the field.

When I arrived at David's, he was on his father's Eight N Ford tractor. "Get on and we'll ride over to Stallin's pond," he said with his wide grin. He was proud to get to drive Ezra's tractor. I thought he was the luckiest ten year old boy in the world to be driving a tractor. David had earned the honor of driving the tractor because he had been helping his father farm since he was old enough to walk.

I jumped on with him and off we went riding the field road to the pond. We had not been at the pond long when it started to cloud up. "We better head back to the house, it looks like it might rain", he said with the wisdom of a seasoned farmer. Farmers seem to be able to read the clouds and the wind and make weather predictions, so I didn't argue.

We made it back to David's house and the barn just as a few drops of rain began to fall. It was about that time that Mama realized I had gone somewhere. She went outside and called for me. There was no response. She walked up the road to Charlie Bill's. He said he had not seen me, but he told her that Vanny Dee had seen David and me on a tractor heading toward Stallin's pond.

There was a clap of thunder and her fear of storms kicked in. She headed up to the mill to get Daddy. She caught him in the office and told him I was out in the storm. He tried to tell her that I would be all right, but nothing would do her but for Daddy to go to Stallin's pond looking for me. He headed out into the teeth of the storm. It was easier to face the elements than to face the wrath of Mama if he had refused to go look for her son.

While Daddy was trudging through the rain, David and I were in the nice dry barn playing on a rope that would swing from one end of the hay loft to the other. We were having so much fun that we were oblivious to our surroundings. The rain pounded on the tin roof of the barn, the lightning flashed occasionally, and the thunder shook the barn a time or two, but we were dry and happy. The rain finally let up and we could hear Mr. Pillow yelling something from the back porch. We went to the opening that was used to haul hay up into the loft and looked out.

"O'Neal, your Dad said for you to come home!" he yelled. Uh! Oh! I knew I was in big trouble.

I quickly climbed down the ladder and headed across the fields. All the way, all I could think was, "I'm dead, I'm dead." I got to the ditch and as I crossed the foot bridge and looked at the muddy water swelling the ditch from the heavy rain, I thought I might be better off to just jump. When I got across and looked at Daddy standing on the back porch, I knew it would have been better if I had. He was soaking wet from his head to his toes. His hair that was usually neatly combed to one side was down in his face with water still dripping off it. He had his belt already off and in his hand.

I started to pleading and making excuses. "I didn't mean to stay that long but the storm came up and I couldn't leave," I offered in my defense. I continued walking toward the back porch and tears began to well up in my eyes. I tried, "I'm sorry, I won't ever do it again." But that didn't remove the frown and stare that penetrated right through me.

When I reached the top step he took me by the arm and made the first swat. The belt popped like a gun on my behind. I don't think I felt another lick after that, but the next thing I knew, Mama was there saying, "Don't whip him anymore. That's enough." It was enough because from that day on if it looked like it might storm, I stayed home. I also never argued when Mama said, "Ya'll get in the storm house."

****

We got our first telephone when I was seven or eight years old. Before that time if Mama needed to make a call she would go next door to the Smith's and ask Miss Beulah to use their phone. Sometimes they would send Alvin over to our house to fetch Mama to the phone when someone called for her. Mama never called or had someone call her unless it was really important. Once we got our own phone, we could use it at our leisure. Well, not exactly at our leisure, but at the leisure of the six or seven families who shared the party line.

The party line made for some very interesting conversations. Mama learned to speak in code, when she didn't want the neighbors to know what she was talking about. In her conversation with Aunt Ethel, she might say, "You know that thing we were talking about? Well, it finally happened." The other parties on the line with the receiver to their ear and their hand over the mouth piece would scratch their heads trying to figure out what they were talking about. Mama would have made a good CIA agent. She would feed misinformation to the gossip hotline.

One time just for spite she let out the rumor that a lady in her fifties was going to have a baby. She answered our ring, which was two long rings and two short rings. As soon as she picked it up she could hear the soft clicks as others on the line picked up to get their morning news. It was Sister Barrett, who was just as ready to pull a joke as Mama.

The conversation began, "Hello, this is Alene Henley."

"Hello Alene, this is Sis."

Mama and Sis had a signal when they knew someone else was on the line. Sometimes they would just ask, "Is there someone on this line?" That usually brought a click or two as the extra listeners hung up. If they suspected someone was still on the line, they would shock them with some outlandish story like the one they told that day.

"Sis, did you know that Mrs. 'X' is having a baby?"

"No! You don't mean it?" exclaimed Sis. "Why she's at least ten years older than me," she added.

"I have heard she was fifty," Mama countered.

You could almost hear the gasp of the third and forth parties who were listening to the conversation. Before the day was out Mrs. 'X' was visited by several of the women in the neighborhood. They all asked her how she was feeling and one even brought a stack of baby diapers and asked her if she had any use for them. She told them sure and took them to use for dust rags.

For several weeks she was visited by neighbor women with jars of pickles and other assorted goodies. Each time she had visitors, they fished for news about a coming event. She never understood the strange behavior of her neighbors, but after about six months things got back to normal.

There weren't many secrets that could be kept at the Cotton Mill under any circumstances, but to tell a secret to someone over the phone was the same as having it announced on the radio.

****

Speaking of the radio, it was one of the most used conveniences at the Cotton Mill. Everyone had a radio and everyone had a favorite radio station and a favorite radio show. It was the source of news, weather, sports, music, and shows. The shows were my favorite, especially the westerns.

I liked the Lone Ranger and Tonto. When we played cowboys and played the Lone Ranger, I always wanted to be Tonto. I would get on a stick or cane horse and slap it on the flank and let out a "Get um up Scout", and head out down the trail.

There were other westerns I liked. Bobby Benson and the B-bar-B Riders was one of my favorites also. It was much like the Saturday serials at the movies. Each episode would end with Bobby Benson, or one of his friends, in a bad fix. There was, seemingly, no way out, but in the next episode they would somehow miraculously be saved.

Another show I liked was Sgt. Preston of the Yukon. He was a member of the Royal Canadian Mounted Police. He had a faithful companion, a husky named King. I had never seen a husky, but I was sure it looked about like Trixie. No matter what kind of mess Sgt. Preston got into, King would come to his rescue. He traveled by dog sled and in the winter when it snowed a good snow, I would take one of the old string bottom straight chairs out of the storm house and use it for a sled. It worked pretty good when you laid it down on its back. The runners weren't curved and they would sometimes catch on something and flip, but the overall performance wasn't bad. I even tried to hook up Trixie to the sled, but she refused to pull it.

At night the grown-ups got to listen to their radio shows. Sometimes they listened to Jack Benny and laughed along with him and Rochester as they joked. There were mystery shows like The Shadow and The Green Hornet. I sometimes listenedto those mysteries, but I wasn't very interested in The Grand Ole Opry.

The Grand Ole Opry was Mama's favorite. The show would start with the announcer saying, "It's the Grand Ole Opry! Let her go boys!" From that time until the end of the show, one country music singer after another would come on and sing. I didn't particularly like the singing, but I did like it when Minnie Pearl and Rod Brasfield came on to do their comedy routine. Minnie Pearl would start with, "Howdy! I'm just so proud to be here!" Rod Brasfield ended with, "I'm going to the wagon folks, these shoes are killing me."

One of the singers who was always on the show was Roy Acuff. He would usually sing "Wabash Cannonball" sometime during the program. I did sorta like Little Jimmy Dickens, especially when he sang "I'm a plain ole country boy, a corn bread loving country boy." I would change the words from country boy to Cotton Mill Boy and sing "I'm a plain old Cotton Mill Boy." I also liked Tex Ritter when he came on the Opry. Hank Williams was probably Mama's favorite when he sang "I'm so Lonesome I Could Cry." There were others like Carl Smith and Faron Young. Miss Kitty Wells was considered the queen of country music at that time. She was well known for singing "Honkey Tonk Angel."

The radio was also the only way to hear the St. Louis Cardinals baseball games. There were some great players on the Cardinals, but probably the greatest was Stan Musial. He was known to the Cotton Mill Boys as 'Stan the Man'. Almost everyone had a Stan the Man baseball card. I wasn't into baseball cards as much as some of the other boys, but I had a few. The cards always came in a pack with bubble gum. Some of the boys, like Charlie Bill would spend all their money on the cards and bubble gum. The cards were usually stored in an old shoe box and I think Charlie Bill had three or four boxes full. The play-by-play was done by Harry Cary and on radio's all over the neighborhood, he could be heard to yell, "Holy cow! What a hit!"

****

We had heard about a new invention that showed a picture on a screen much like a movie. It was called television. None of us had seen one of these wonderful inventions until Sister Barrett got one of them. She was the first person at the Cotton Mill to have this magical box, that could bring a moving picture right into your home. Needless to say she had a lot of company. In fact, she had so much company that she couldn't seat them all in her living room. To hold the crowds to a minimum, the neighbors were assigned a night to come and visit and watch the marvel of the ages. The night that was assigned to us was the worse possible night for me.

After supper on our night to go to Sister's house, we would walk up the hill. Sometimes Daddy stayed home, but Mama couldn't wait to go. I wasn't all that excited about going, but at least I would get to see my buddy, Bobby Crocker. When we got to their house and went in, there would be Miss Posey, Carl Scott, Sis and Bobby, all lined up watching the screen. There were kitchen chairs lined up in a row like theater seats. Sometimes Sis had even popped some popcorn. We always timed our visit so we would get there just at the start of the show.

The show would start and the camera would zoom in on a man playing a piano. They would zoom in on his face and his teeth were so big and white, they looked like the keyboard of the piano he was playing. It was the same old show every time we got to visit on our night. The guy's name was Liberachi. Evidently the women thought he was so good

210

looking. Miss Posey even said, "He's purtier than any woman I ever seen." They went on and on about how good he looked and sharp he dressed. They didn't have much to say about his musical talent. I thought he could play a piano pretty good, but when he sang, he was certainly no Roy Rogers or Gene Autry.

As a matter of fact, I thought his voice was down right sissy. He even looked sissy with his hair all long and wavy and he even walked like a girl. Bobby and I almost got kicked out of the theater for laughing at him. After watching Liberachi once a week for about a year, I was sure television would never make it big.

Finally, when I was in the eighth grade, we got a television of our own and I found out that there were some really great shows. Many of the old radio shows were adapted to TV and some of the western heroes moved from the large movie screen to the small screen. It was a pretty good invention after all.

Chapter IX: Sex Education Class

As we grew up at the Cotton Mill and started to school, we came in contact with the real world. We lead a pretty sheltered life at home. Parents never discussed the birds and the bees. If they had tried to tell us about the birds and the bees, we would have probably told them we already knew. After all, we could whistle the call of almost every bird and there were no boys anywhere who could beat us at bumble bee ball. The information that we did receive from our parents about sex was strictly myth and misinformation.

We were constantly having new additions to the family. It was only natural to wonder where they came from. Sometimes a mother would tell her existing children, they were going to have a new baby sister or brother. "When?" would be the question. "Well, it won't be long, just a few months," the mother would answer.

I can barely remember Mama preparing me for a new addition to the family. I noticed Mama's stomach was getting rather large. I asked her why her stomach was so big. She replied, "I swallowed a watermelon seed." It wasn't much of an explanation, but at least it made me very cautious when I ate watermelons.

Sometime later she told me I was going to get a little brother or sister. "When?" I asked. "When the stork brings it," was her answer. I was hoping it would be a little brother so I would have a little buddy to play with. I waited anxiously for the day the stork would come flying to our house carrying a baby wrapped in a blanket in his beak. Somehow I missed the old bird.

I was awakened in the night by Mama groaning and moaning. Daddy was hustling around getting things together to go somewhere. What were they doing? Were they planning on going off somewhere in the middle of the night and leaving me?

I went to Mama and asked her what was wrong. She said she was feeling bad and Daddy was taking her to the doctor. I started to get my clothes on to go with them, but she said I would need to stay home with Little Mama. It wasn't long until my Aunt Ethel came to our house and stayed with Little Mama and me.

"Is Mama gonna be alright?" I asked.

"Sure, she'll be alright and she might even bring you back a little brother or sister," she answered.

"I hope not, because I want to see that stork when he comes," I stated matter-of-factly.

She just grinned. Aunt Ethel looked a whole lot like Mama and I felt comfortable with her.

The next morning I learned that Mama wouldn't be coming home for a few days. They said she was resting in the hospital. It seemed like a long time, but after a few days Mama came home. She came in with something wrapped in a blanket. "I got a surprise for you," she said as she bent down to let me see. I looked with anticipation as she pulled the blanket back.

Was it some kind of toy in the blanket? Then I saw this pretty little baby. It opened its eyes and appeared to smile at me. "This is your baby sister, Gail," Mama said as she introduced my sister to me. Darn, I had missed seeing that big old stork. Of all times for him to come and bring that baby, he would have to come while Mama was resting in the hospital.

For several years I believed that a woman had swallowed a watermelon seed when they got a big belly and that storks brought babies. As I got eight or nine years old I began to hear rumors about other ways that babies came into the world. With no birds and bees at home and no sex education classes at school, the Cotton Mill Boys learned from Mother Nature and each other.

The first hints that having babies wasn't a matter of having the stork fly in on a special delivery came when some of us saw a dog giving birth to puppies. The dog was a stray that just roamed around the neighborhood. We named it Little Bit. Little Bit was a short haired dog that was about half the size of Snowball.

We were up at the big tree playing one day when it seemed like every dog in the neighborhood was chasing Little Bit. They all were trying to jump on her and were snapping at each other. Charlie Bill was sure they were going to hurt her and he was about to throw a rock at the dogs following her, when Bobo made a startling revelation. "They ain't gonna hurt her, they're just making babies," he said as he spit out the brown juice from his Rooster snuff.

"How can they make babies, there aren't any storks around here?" I asked in my innocence.

He laughed, "Ya'll still think storks bring babies?"

"Well, how else would they get here. A stork brought my sister," I insisted.

Bobo proceeded to tell us that there were boy dogs and there were girl dogs. We got our first lesson in the birds and the bees. We found out that not only dogs had puppies by boy dogs and girl dogs getting together, but horses, cows, pigs, and even humans came up with babies by this method.

We weren't sure Bobo was leveling with us about all this until the day we came up on Little Bit laying in a small hole she had dug out. She was on the ditch bank just across from Mrs. Bookers. When we found her we thought she was sick and then we saw a little black puppy that was soaking wet lying under her. As we examined the puppy she began to whine and pant loudly. The next thing we saw was a little black and white ball of fur exiting her body. It was incredible. We watched in awe as she had four more puppies. One of them looked a lot like Snowball. Bobo was right! Babies didn't come from the stork.

It seemed the older the boys got, the more they were interested in girls. I knew girls were different from boys. After all, I had a sister who took baths, and I had seen my girl cousin naked when we were forced to strip off to get rid of the chicken mites. I just didn't understand why Bobo and Skeezer had suddenly become more interested in girls than in playing Robin Hood.

They seemed to be interested in the Sears Roebuck Catalogue. They kept one at Hobo's Mansion. I thought it was there to look at the toys or use when nature called, but they were never looking at the toys. For some reason they were usually looking at the women's underwear. "Boy! She sure is stacked," they'd say. I couldn't figure out what she was stacked on but I would go along and say, "She sure is." Skeezer must have been a leg man because he was always looking at their legs.

One time they told about seeing a woman naked at the Strawberry Festival Carnival. They got in line with some men going in to see the show and the ticket man sold them a ticket and let them go in just like they were grown men. Some music started to playing and this woman came out with some see-through bloomers on and started to dance. She didn't have any clothes covering her belly button. She wiggled around to the music and, to their astonishment, she pulled off the see through blouse and only had on a brazier. "She was really stacked," they added with some degree of excitement in their voice. That was when I realized what stacked meant. Having learned a new vocabulary word, I couldn't wait to use it. Unfortunately, I used it at the wrong time.

Mama, Gail and I had walked to town to buy me a new pair of shoes. We went to Strausburg's and the Black and White Store. We shopped around and finally settled on just the right pair of Sunday shoes. They were never to be worn while playing, especially on muddy, rainy days. I usually wasn't very fond of Sunday shoes, but these were really neat. They had a buckle across the top that had a metal tip on the strap that was arrowhead shaped, much like a cowboy belt. Mama looked around for someone to wait on us and finally a nice lady came to our aid.

The shoes were displayed on top of the box that they came in, so she got a box with shoes my size and brought them out. I sat down on the bench and pulled off my old PF Flyers. Mama frowned at me when she saw that I had worn a pair of socks that had a hole in the heel. I held my foot out for the lady as she bent down and tried to force the new shoe on my foot. It wouldn't go easily so she took a slipper spoon and guided my foot down into the shoe. As I looked down at her as she was bent over, I noticed her sweater had two big bulges. "Boy! She's really stacked," I announced right in front of the lady and Mama.

A cloud came over Mama's face and I knew there was about to be a storm. She grabbed me by the arm and dragged me with one shoe on and one shoe off into the nearest dressing room. I almost got a peek at a woman dressing in there, but she made a quick exit as Mama pulled me through the curtain that covered the door. Once inside she started to frail away with her open hand. Thank goodness there were no plum trees in the store. "How dare you talk like that!" she said, as she continued to whack me. "I have never been so embarrassed in my life." That was where I learned that it was best not to share my knowledge about sex with grown ups.

I did continue to increase my knowledge and vocabulary as I hung out with the older boys. Some words were only to be whispered and certainly they were never to be used in mixed company. We learned what a loose woman was called. I think Charlie Bill must have been looking for an occasion to use this new vocabulary word. We were walking home from school one day. We were in the fourth grade and had become pretty wise about the ways of the world.

He had just recently added the word to his vocabulary. A girl came riding along on her bike, and when she got even with us, Charlie Bill asked her the infamous question, "Are you a whore?" She never missed a stroke on the peddles of her bike as she answered, "No, I'm a Baptist." Evidently she had no desire to belong to that other denomination.

Somewhere Skeezer got some comic books that showed it all. They weren't your regular size comic books, they were small enough to carry in your pocket. They had regular comic characters like Andy Capp, Popeye, and some others. I blushed when I saw them. I had never seen any of these characters with their clothes off. I was offered one of the comic books, but I knew if Mama ever found something like that on me I would be dead. There was a secret hiding place in Hobo's Mansion where some of the books were kept.

One day Skeezer brought a picture of a real woman without any clothes on. He called it a centerfold. I didn't know where he got it, but it was filed away somewhere in Hobo's Mansion also. From time to time boys would get the picture out and look at it. She was really stacked!

For some time I had found these balloons that were in little round packages. Daddy kept them in his closet in the pocket of an old coat that he never wore. I couldn't for the life of me, figure out why Daddy would need a balloon. These were the same kind of balloons that floated down the Forked Deer River, below the raw sewage pipe. Charlie Bill and I had discussed it and he said Louis had some in the top drawer of his dresser. We decided to go to an expert and see if we could find out more about the balloons that our parents seemed to want to keep a secret.

I slipped one of the round packets out of the coat pocket and we headed up to Skeezer's for some answers. "What is this thing?" I asked, as we approached the front porch swing where he was sitting. I held it up to show him. He jumped up and took it out of my hand and hid it behind his back. With the other hand, he placed a finger over his lips to shut us up.

"Mama might see!" he said as he stepped around the corner. "Let's go to the club house," he suggested. When we got to Hobo's Mansion, he proceeded to tell us what it was and what it was used for. I had no idea that Daddy engaged in such conduct.

Our sex education wasn't complete until we saw the real thing, no pictures and no comics. A real live girl in the nude. Charlie Bill got accused of peeping at a nude girl one time and Louis nearly beat him to death. It was all perfectly innocent. I knew because I was with him.

It had just gotten dusky dark and we were walking down the road to my house when this girl named Shirley called to us to come to her house. She was about fifteen or sixteen years old. Skeezer and Bobo liked to sit on her front porch and talk with her. She called us over and asked if we would climb on top of her house and get her kitten down. It was an easy climb, because there was a maple tree right beside the house. It could easily be climbed and then step onto the roof. That's probably how the kitten got on the house to start with. We were good Samaritans and climbed up and retrieved her kitty.

The next day Charlie Bill's dad, Louis, received a call from Mrs. Booker. She explained that she didn't mean to mind someone else's business, but she heard that Charlie Bill was climbing on top of Shirley's house to try to see her without any clothes on. Louis thanked her and headed to Main Street Elementary to get his wayward son. He went in the office and asked Mr. McCarly to get Charlie Bill out of class. When Mr. McCarly came to our room and called Charlie Bill to the office, I just knew he was in some trouble. I never suspected he was in trouble with Louis.

That afternoon, as soon as I could put up my book satchel, I headed to Charlie Bill's. He wasn't outside so I knocked on the door. Opal came to the door and let me in.

"Where's Charlie Bill?" I asked.

"In the backroom," she replied.

I went on back and Charlie Bill was still sobbing. "What's the matter?" I asked. I could sense something was dreadfully wrong. Charlie Bill was tough and he rarely cried.

"Only a flogging rooster could have gotten him this upset," I thought to myself.

"Daddy came to school and got me and brought me home and whooped me," he said between sobs.

"What for?" I pried.

"Cause somebody told him I was peeping at Shirley. I tried to tell him we were gettin' a cat off her roof, but he wouldn't listen," he explained.

I told him I would be right back. I ran two doors down to Shirley's house and explained to her what had happened. She came back to Charlie Bill's with me and explained the whole thing to Opal. Opal hugged Charlie Bill and told him she was sorry, but that didn't remove the stripes from his behind. It just goes to show that no good deed goes unpunished.

Charlie Bill was falsely accused, but we did get to see a topless girl one time. She lived in Zeb Barrett's rental house for a short time and for a thirteen-year-old, she was stacked, to use our favorite vocabulary word for a girl with big breasts. She had spurred some interest from the older boys when she moved into the neighborhood, but rumors that her daddy would shoot you if you messed with her, left her somewhat lonely.

Leenova, Charlie Bill and I were walking behind her house along a hedge row that we often traveled to go to Sherwood Forest, which was directly behind her house. We were surprised to see her in the back yard. She spoke to us as we were passing.

"Where you boys going?" she asked.

"We're going to Sherwood Forest," I answered.

"And where is that, in England?" she came back.

We told her it was just down the hedge row behind Bobo's house. She looked at Charlie Bill and said, "What's your name? You're kinda cute for a chubby boy." Charlie Bills face turned beet red. We talked a while and she invited us to come back and see her the next day.

We were afraid her daddy might shoot us, but we mustered enough courage to come back to her house and see her the next day. The canopy of the hedge apple trees that grew along the fence row made a cool place to play in her back yard.

She was a pretty girl with dark hair and a beautiful smile. As we talked she asked us a question that really blew our minds. "Have you boy's ever seen a girl's breasts?" she asked without the slightest blush. I couldn't believe my ears. We all three stood with our mouths wide open and our eyes staring straight ahead. Slowly she unbuttoned her blouse then pulled it back like Superman, exposing the big 'S', on his chest. What she had was not a big 'S', but two large lumps. We had seen a woman's breast and now we were men!

Well, almost men, because our first inclination was to run. What if her Daddy saw us looking at her breast. He would kill us and skin us and tack our hides on the barn door. It wasn't long after the stripping incident that they moved. I guess it was a good thing because after we told some of the older boys what happened, they again became interested in playing in Sherwood Forest and they always took the trail behind her house.

We figured one day we would hear the bang of a shot gun as one of them got gunned down by her daddy. Fortunately, they moved before anyone got shot.

Chapter X: Church

I must confess, when I was bad, I was really bad and when I was good, I was really good. It all depended on which of the two little voices I listened to. It seemed I had one part of me that would lead me into all kinds of trouble. Mama just came right out and said it was the devil. On the other hand there were times when I was strong and avoided temptation. Mama said that was the Holy Spirit leading me to do the right thing. Religion played a big part in Mama's life, therefore, it played a big part in mine too.

I don't remember going to church until I was five or six. I think Mama probably took me before Gail was born, but after Gail was born, we didn't go until Gail was about two years old. At that time in his life Daddy didn't go to church. On Sunday, he was either fishing or hunting. It was his only full day off from work and he spent it on the water or in the woods. Sometimes he would take me fishing with his men friends. In spite of not having a church at the Cotton Mill, I still got a pretty good dose of that old-time religion.

The Smith's next door would often have prayer meeting at their house. I don't know what denomination they belonged to, but Mama called them 'Holy Rollers'. We could easily hear their whole service in the summer time. Our windows were up and their's were too. The sound carried pretty well. As a matter of fact they were down-right loud. They would start out with one person praying and another would join in and then another. Before long everyone in the house was praying, and some were yelling out. "Halleluiah!" one would yell. "Amen brother!" yelled another.

I asked Mama what all that meant and she said they were

"shouting." Well, I knew they were shouting, but what were they shouting?, was my next question. There would be someone who would start to moan and jabber. I thought some of those folks might be foreigners, but Mama said, "No, it wasn't an earthly language they were speaking. They were in the Spirit and speaking in unknown tongues." She was right about it being unknown; no one could know what they were saying. I later found out they actually had people who understood the unknown tongue and could interpret for the others. It was the night Charlie Bill and I slipped over to the Smith's house and looked in the window, that we saw how the Holy Spirit could move people.

I told Charlie Bill about the prayer meetings that went on at the house next door and he wanted to see it for himself. I told him to see if he could come to my house about seven o'clock on Wednesday night and we would observe the service. Charlie Bill wasn't all that religious, but there was not a single atheist in the Cotton Mill. Not all families attended church, but all believed in God and had a Bible that they read often.

Charlie Bill showed up on Wednesday evening and I asked Mama if we could go outside and play for a while. She agreed and we sat in the front porch swing and waited as the members of the prayer meeting group went into the Smith's house. After a little socializing and hand shaking, they all settled in the living room. There must have been ten or twelve people at the meeting. A man whom I assume was the preacher got up and started the service by leading the congregation in an acapella version of "I was Sinking Deep in Sin". As they sang they clapped their hands and swayed to the rhythm.

As we watched through the window, the preacher asked who had prayer request. One woman got up and said her husband had the gout and needed prayers. Another got up and requested prayer for her mother, who was bed-ridden. As they went around the group that sat in a semi-circle, each one made a request. One woman requested prayer for her husband, who was lost. She began to cry as she stated that she didn't want him to burn in hell. The preacher didn't help her any when he said, "We need to pray for all those lost sinners, cause it is hot in hell." She cried louder and another brother named someone who was lost and going to hell. Then another requested prayer for his brother, who was lost and doomed to hell. The preacher preached on, "The devil is coming to get those lost sinners and throw them in the everlasting fire."

By now Charlie Bill and I were looking over our shoulders to see if the devil was sneaking up on us with his pitch fork. Mrs. Beulah then made a request that probably started me on the road to salvation. "Pray for my neighbors next door, cause I think they are lost," she requested. "That's me, she's talking about me," I thought.

That led me to have a talk the next day with Mama. I couldn't sleep that night for seeing images of the devil. He was red with pointy ears and horns. He had a long red tail that had a sharp point on it. He had a black beard and a smile like the worse villain at the Saturday picture show. He carried a three-pronged pitch fork for serving up little boys to the fiery flames of the underground pit in which he lived. Several times I woke up in a sweat that night.

We continued to watch the service even though we were becoming disturbed by all the preaching about the devil. We were mesmerized by the people talking in tongues. One lady began to groan and speak words I had never heard. Some were more like grunts and yells, than words. Then a man stood up and began to tell the others what she was saying.

"Jesus is coming soon," he relayed to the others. "Repent while there is still time and be saved." I figured she was probably talking to me. Then she did something that rather broke my chain of thought. She fell out of her chair and started to roll around on the floor. She still spoke in the unknown tongue as she wallowed in the floor. That's when I realized how their denomination got the name 'Holy Rollers'.

The day after my experience of watching and listening to the prayer meeting at the Smith's house, I talked to Mama about the sleepless night I had spent in fear of the devil. She reassured me that if I would be a good boy, the devil wouldn't get me. She must have been concerned about it, because shortly after that experience, she started to taking Gail and me to church on Sunday. It wasn't the church of the 'Holy Rollers', but the people at the church we attended did get in the Spirit.

On Sunday morning, Mama would get Gail and me up and get us ready for Sunday school and church. Gail had a little dress with lace on it and a little white straw hat with a ribbon for a hat band. She was cute with her little outfit and white shoes and a little white purse. Mama always gave us a nickel to give at Sunday school and Gail proudly carried it in her little purse. I had on my Sunday shoes, dress pants, and a white shirt. Mama had a Sunday dress that she always wore. After we were all dressed up we were ready to head out to church.

Daddy was usually gone on Sunday morning, but if he was home, he would drive us to church and let us out and come back and get us after the service was over. Most of the time, however, we walked. We headed out down Avondale to the railroad crossing. I always wanted to walk the railroad because it was much closer, but Mama made us walk the road. Eighteenth Avenue was gravel until you got to Connie Dodd's house and there it turned into black top. It was easier walking once we got on the black top portion of the road. We would cut across Campbell Street just past Gibson's Grocery and head to Fourteenth Street. Mama was like a little bannie hen taking her chicks on an outing. "Don't get in the street," she demanded as she motioned us back with a wave of her arm.

"Don't get your shoes dirty! Get out of that yard! Stay close," she clucked out orders to her chicks.

We would finally arrive at the white frame church on the corner. There was a sign on the lawn that read, "Nazarene Church." We were usually a little early, because Mama left in plenty of time to allow for any disaster that might occur on the way. Sometimes we had to wait for a train to pass before we could get across the tracks. There were other hindrances, like the big red chow that we had to pass at the Ellis' house. If Jimmy or June Bug was at home, they would make him come back to the porch, but if they weren't, it was up to the bannie hen to run the big dog off. If he came running toward the road she would pick up a handful of rocks and heave them at the dog. She was a pretty good shot and several times she sent him back to the porch with his tail between his legs. Most of the time there were no major catastrophes and we ended up arriving five or ten minutes early for Sunday school.

We had a children's Sunday school class in a small room that had been added onto the auditorium. The auditorium seated about fifty people and on most Sunday mornings it was full. Our Sunday School Class had about ten children from six to twelve years old. I wish I could remember the ladies name that taught the Sunday school class. She was a real saint. Not only did she teach us about Jesus, she had the patience of Job. She never became angry with us when we cut up or were inattentive to her teaching. She was the kind of lady you didn't want to disappoint so we were pretty good most of the time.

After Sunday school, we would come out into the auditorium for the preaching. The preacher was a woman whose name was Sister Marie. She was a multi-talented lady who lead the singing, sang solos, and preached the message. She truly was God's servant. When she read from the Bible or preached the word, the congregation would voice their approval with a loud "Amen or 'Halleluiah!" She preached some wonderful sermons and much of what I learned about God came from the Sunday school lessons and the preaching of Sister Marie.

Church was not the only exposure to religion that we got. At Main Street Elementary every Wednesday Mr. McCarley had a preacher to come and speak to the whole school at an assembly. The preacher for the week would be from one of the churches in town. All denominations were included in the program. One week we would have the minister from the Church of God. The next week the speaker might be the minister from the First Methodist Church. All were represented at some time during the year, Baptist, Methodist, Presbyterian, Episcopalian, Church of Christ, and Nazarene Church. As far as I know, there was never a protest by any parents. There were no lawsuits by the ACLU, and there was no damage done to any of us who listened attentively to the prayers and sermons of all the different representatives of the denominations.

As a matter-of-fact we were all very aware of our responsibility to the society in which we lived. None of us would have ever thought that in our life-time, students would actually attack and kill their classmates. We lived in an age of innocence where the only guns at school were our trusty cap pistols to play cowboys at recess.

We had the guidance of our parents, teachers, preachers and our heroes to model what a person should be. I never heard of psychological counseling or children going to a psychiatrist unless they were insane. We gave in to the devil's whispers occasionally, but overall, we lived by a code that was instilled in us by those who influenced us most. Children today are at a big disadvantage thanks to the ACLU and the sleazy characters they have for models in the movies, on TV and even in our own government.

It is no wonder so many children go bad. All they see is

the bad of this world. They are never even given a chance to be a child. They have no concept of right and wrong because they are never held accountable for their actions. The belt and the plum tree switch have gone the way of the dinosaur. The preacher preaching fire and brimstone has been toned down in the name of political correctness. Teachers and principals have lost their ability to discipline to the lawyers and their thirst of law suits. Many parents are so selfish, they just don't have time to be proper parents. Thank God we had family and friends who cared when we were growing up at the Cotton Mill.

We were exposed to preaching from other places besides the church and school. Many nights we would sit and listen to the radio for our spiritual inspiration. The great young evangelist, Billy Graham would sometimes have his crusade on the air. Mama thought he might someday be the greatest preacher who ever lived, next to Peter and Paul, of course. He was good. He could preach in such a way that even a child could understand his meaning. His southern accent was reassuring to a plain old Cotton Mill Boy. His voice was clear and carried the enthusiasm of a man with a mission. At the end of his sermon he would ask the people in the auditorium to come down front and kneel and pray. He also invited the people at home to bow and pray right where they were. Mama bowed, so I bowed too.

After one of Reverend Graham's services, I always felt like I should ask Jesus to come into my heart, but I kept putting it off. I'm sure it was the devil that was whispering to me, "You're too young, wait until you're older." He kept on whispering during the invitation of every service I attended, but finally, when I was sixteen years old, I accepted the Lord Jesus as my savior.

There was another preacher we often listened to on the radio. His name was Oral Roberts. He gained great fame because of his ability to heal people. People who came up on the stage with the aid of crutches or a wheel chair, often left by their own means of locomotion. Some jumped and shouted as they left the stage praising the Lord. The good reverend would pray for those at home who had afflictions. He would instruct the listeners at home to place their hand on the radio as he prayed. When Reverend Roberts got to this part of the service, Mama would always say, "Put your hand on the radio and pray for your sight to come back in your eye."

"I was a little reluctant because I didn't consider not having sight in my right eye a handicap. I had already learned to shoot a gun and a bow left-handed and that was the only thing I ever really worried about when I lost my sight. Besides the Bible says that 'all things work for good to them that love the Lord.'

When I got in high school, I tried to shoot pool at the pool room. I wasn't much good left-handed so I dropped out of pool. Now, if I hadn't lost my sight, I might have been a pool shark or a pool room bum and spent all my time and energy at the pool room. I guess if you look hard enough, 'all things do work for good to them that love the Lord.' I did place my hand on the radio as Mama requested, but I just didn't believe strongly enough.

I don't want to leave the impression that Daddy never became a Christian. He was saved about the same time I was. It was at Emmanuel Baptist Church. He went on to help found Avondale Baptist Church, which was the first church established at the Cotton Mill. He became a Deacon and to this day is a devout Christian. Many people who lived at the Cotton Mill or worked at Jones Manufacturing Company were lead to the Lord by my daddy.

Chapter XI: The Thriving Metropolis

Besides Jones Manufacturing Company, there were other businesses at the Cotton Mill. Uncle Bill's store was on the corner, just down from our house. It was a building with a flat roof with a large red and white sign on top of it. On either end of the sign were large red circles with Coke-a-Cola written in white. In the white space between the advertisement, written in red, was Smith's Grocery. On the porch of the store were two nail kegs and one old cane bottom chair. Customers rarely sat on the stools. As a matter of fact, Uncle Bill didn't get too many customers. Those that did do business with him didn't stay long. Almost none of the Cotton Mill Boys patronized his establishment. I think the reason he had so few customers was because of an incident that happened to several customers, including me.

Mama gave me the money to buy a nickel Baby Ruth candy bar. They were my favorite kind of candy. I could taste the peanuts, caramel and chocolate as I walked down the gravel road to the store. Uncle Bill was usually pretty grumpy and I think that added to his lack of customers. I was expecting him to be his usual sour self but when I entered the store, he smiled and asked, "What can I do for you today, Little Man?"

"I smiled back and said, "Gimme one of them nickel Baby Ruth's."

He handed me the candy bar and I handed him the nickel. He punched a key on his cash register and it dinged and the drawer opened. As he dropped the money in the drawer he said, "Thank you. Come back to see me."

I was feeling pretty good about Uncle Bill as I headed out the door and toward home. I couldn't wait until I got home to open the candy. I started to peel back the wrapper. When I uncovered the chocolate, I found there was a fourth surprise in the candy. Not only was there chocolate, peanuts and caramel, there was also some little white worms. My candy was ruined.

I started to go back and ask for my nickel back, but I was afraid Uncle Bill would refuse. If he refused and I told Mama, she would forget she was supposed to turn the other cheek, and go after him. He was an old man and I didn't think he could withstand the wrath of Mama, so I never told her. I did however tell all my friends and they vowed they would never go to Uncle Bill's store again.

That is why he had so few customers. Well, there was one other reason. Our parents didn't like for us to go down there because Uncle Bill sold homebrew. Charlie Bill's Aunt Pauline told us of an incident that led me to believe he would not have refunded my money. She said she had bought a Coke-A-Cola from Uncle Bill, or at least it was in a Coke bottle. She got home and opened it and took a long, cool drink. She spit it out in a hurry. It was a bottle of homebrew he had put in a Coke bottle. She took it back to Uncle Bill to get a refund. Grumpy old Uncle Bill refused and said, "Drink it! It's good for you." Luckily one of his town customers was there and paid Polly for her bottle of homebrew. I am sorry I never gave him the chance to give back my money. I'll never know what he would have done, but he was in a pretty good mood that day.

Barrett's Grocery got most of the Cotton Mill business. It was owned and operated by Zeb and Velma Barrett. Velma ran the store during the week, while Zeb worked at the Milan Arsenal. He helped out on the week ends at the store.

Barrett's was a white block building with a gravel parking lot that would hold five or six cars. In front, on either side of the door, sat a bench and a couple of straight chairs. These benches and chairs were usually occupied by the Cotton Mill Wildlife Society or some other older persons who sat around swapping knives and tall tales. They also often tortured boys who came to the store.

One of their favorite tricks they liked to pull on us was the P&G soap trick. "Bet you can't hold a bar of soap in your hand for five minutes," one of them would say. "I'll buy you an RC if you can hold it." They didn't know it, but a simple, "I dare you to try," would have cost them less.

Some kid would step up for a chance at the prize and they would take two bars of soap off the shelf and hand it to the participant. He had to hold the soap with his arms straight out and his palms turned up. One of the old men would take out his pocket watch and time the event. "Go!" he would say as he dropped his arm in a downward seep.

After about a minute you could see the boy's face begin to develop a little color. After two minutes, the arms would begin to sag and every muscle was straining to hold up those two little bars of soap. Other boys would cheer him on and try to distract him from the obvious pain he was feeling.

I never knew anyone who could hold the soap for five minutes. Bobo almost did it one time, but too much snuff spit collected in his mouth that he just had to spit. The rules stated that the contestant could not move out of his tracks. He couldn't spit on Zeb Barrett's floor, so he moved and went to the door and spit.

Even when a boy didn't reach the time limit, Uncle Whit would go ahead and buy him an RC and a Moon Pie. Most of us knew that, but we tried our best anyway, because we wanted to be the first to ever finish the contest. We had some fun times at Barrett's Grocery, but there were some bad times, too.

When my little sister was about three years old Mama started letting her go with me to the store occasionally. She liked to go with me because most of the time we were allowed to get some candy or bubble gum. I usually tried to talk her into getting baseball cards. That way she would keep the gum and give me the cards. I collected a few cards, but mostly I wanted them because they were legal tender at the Cotton Mill. Cards could be traded for marbles, BBs, comic books, and if you got a St. Louis Cardinal, Charlie Bill would give you money for the card.

We set out on one of our trips to Barrett's Grocery. I usually carried an old stick that also doubled as a horse when we played cowboys. On these shopping trips, I carried it to protect my little sister from any dog that decided to do more than just bark at us. The trip up the hill to the store was uneventful and when we entered the store Velma greeted us with a smile and a "Hiddy, how ya'll doin?" I handed her the paper Mama gave me which contained the list of items we were to bring home. Velma went about the store filling the shopping list.

Bad Eye Elam came in the store and started talking to Gail. "You are a pretty little girl," he said. He bent down and picked her up. I looked around just in time to see her go flying into the air. As she came down he caught her in his arms and pitched her back up almost to the ceiling. I don't know if Gail was enjoying the ride or if she was frightened by the gravity defying trick, but I was her big brother and I was going to stop it before he dropped her on the concrete floor.

I made a move toward Bad Eye with my stick horse in my hand. He tossed her again and as his arm came up, it hit the stick and sent it crashing into my nose. The blood squirted like a leaky water balloon. I felt the warm liquid trickling down my chin. Instinctively I put my hand on the warm wet place and looked at it. "Blood! I'm bleeding!" I yelled out.

I didn't know if Bad Eye had bloodied my nose on purpose or by accident. I only knew I needed to tell Mama. I went running down the hill to my house. The chert gravel pounded the bottom of my bare feet with every stride, but I didn't slow down until I reached the gate to the picket fence. I was crying when I came running into the house. Mama looked at me and exclaimed, "Lordy mercy Honey, what happened?"

She grabbed a wash rag and ran cold water over it and held my head back with the cold rag covering my face. I was trying to tell her what happened, but she couldn't understand the mumbling that came through the wet cloth that covered my face.

"Speak up! Tell me what happened," she demanded.

I tried, but I must have sounded like I was speaking in the unknown tongues. She finally removed the gag from my mouth and asked again, "What happened? Where's Gail?"

I knew she would be worried about Gail so I said, "She's still at the store." I had calmed down and stopped crying so I started telling Mama what happened. "Bad Eye was throwing Gail up in the air and catching her and when I tried to stop him he hit me in the nose", I said. It didn't come out just exactly the way I meant and I know now it made Bad Eye look like a Saturday matinee villain.

Mama stood up, all four feet, eleven inches of her, yanked off her apron and stormed out the front door. I followed behind her as she headed up the hill. She was always a fast walker, but I was having to run to keep up with her quick choppy stride. She was swinging her arms back and forth with each step. Both her fists were clenched and her eyes were staring straight ahead. She mumbled something under her breath that

I didn't understand. It was probably just as well that I didn't. When we were about a hundred yards from the store at the top of the hill, I saw Bad Eye head up the road to his house.

"Wait a minute you sorry, no good, coward!" Mama shouted.

He picked up the pace toward home. His house was less than a hundred yards past the store, but Mama was gaining ground. She narrowed the distance to about fifty yards before Bad Eye reached the gate to his yard.

"Stop you chicken liver!" she demanded.

By the time he got the gate open and got inside, she had gained to within twenty-five yards. When he stepped on the porch, she was at the gate. Mama was angry, but she kept her head and didn't go after him on his property.

When she stopped at the gate, Bad Eye got brave. "You better get on back down the hill where you belong," he ordered.

"Make me!" was her reply.

"Get away from my house," he demanded.

"This is a public road and I'm going to stay here until you come out. You've got to come out sometime," she informed him.

He went inside and every few minutes you could see the window curtain ease back as he checked to see if Mama was still there. Velma had observed the whole thing from the front door of the store and came and brought Gail to Mama.

"They're okay Alene. You don't have to prove anything by beating up Bad Eye. Take the kids and go on home," she pleaded with Mama.

"No! You please take the kids back to the store and I'll be there to get them when I get through with this yellow coward. He can't hit my boy and get away with it," she insisted.

Bad Eye stuck his head out the door and yelled, "You yellow bellied sap sucker! If you don't leave, I'll make you eat this hammer." He had his hammer in his hand waving it in a threatening way toward Mama.

"Well, come on out here and do it! I luuuve hammers!" she growled back at him. It was a Mexican stand-off until Daddy got there. Velma had seen Mama coming up the hill and told Bad Eye he had better get home quick. She sent another customer to the mill to get Daddy. She knew Mama had a temper and would flog like a banny hen if someone messed with her chicks.

Daddy finally calmed her down and walked her back down the hill to our house. He assured her he would have a talk with Bad Eye about my getting a bloody nose and especially about tossing Gail in the air. I don't know if he ever did but Bad Eye was forgiven by everyone. It took Mama a little longer than the rest of us, but knowing the Christian woman she was, I'm sure she finally forgave him.

Barrett's Grocery provided the resident's of the Cotton Mill with a convenient place to shop. It was also the civic center for the older men who needed a hang-out. In 1953, Zeb Barrett closed the grocery store and used the building for a sheet metal shop. Mama and Daddy discussed the possibility of starting a store when they found out Barrett's Grocery was going to close. I'm sure Mama prayed about the decision. She had been working at Jones Manufacturing Company, but the dust from the cotton gave her asthma a fit. She would cough so bad she could not sleep. After much deliberation, they decided for the good of the community, and for the good of Mama's health, they would establish Henley's Grocery.

Daddy went to work on the project. He worked afternoons and weekends to build the store. I helped all I could by handing him blocks and mixing mortar. Bad Eye Elam had been forgiven and Daddy hired him to help with the construction. He could put his hammer to good use, and he did. Uncle Whit and Carl Scott would often work in an advisory capacity. Others in the neighborhood would stop by to see how the project was going. Within a matter of a few months, a new business was ready to serve the Cotton Mill.

When Daddy and Bad Eye finished, we had a nice block building that sat between our house and the ditch. It took up most of the garden spot. I was happy I wouldn't have to hoe and rake as much garden, but I missed all those fresh vegetables and canned green beans.

Daddy painted the blocks mint green to match the asbestos shingles on our house. The store was trimmed in white and had large display windows on either side of the door that took up most of the front. There was a porch roof across the front with a big Coke-a-Cola sign that read "Henley's Grocery"

Daddy built rows of shelves along the walls. He purchased some used equipment from Zeb Barrett and another store that had gone out of business. There were three large wooden tables that formed a 'U' shape in the middle of the store. The front counter held an adding machine and a box filled with credit books. Mama had a stool to set on behind the counter. At the back of the store was a refrigerated meat box. There was also a chopping block where the butcher, Daddy, cut up meat. Besides the meat box, was a scale for weighing meat and produce.

Finally, the store was stocked and ready. The only thing missing was office space for the Cotton Mill Wildlife Society. After a day or two of Carl and Uncle Whit standing around or sitting on her counter, she came up with four mint green metal lawn chairs. Those chairs could write enough books to fill a library from the stories and tales that were told while someone's bottom rested in them. On cold days the old men could sit around the gas stove in the chairs and tell tales or play Rook if there were enough to play the card game. If there were only two, you could hear the shuffling of the wooden dominoes as they played.

Sometimes we boys were invited to play when they didn't have enough adults. We learned to add and multiply quickly by playing dominoes. Children today could benefit from a game of old fashioned dominoes, especially if their parents would take time to sit down and play with them.

Rook was a thinking man's game. It helped to develop one's abstract reasoning. The players had to plan ahead before making a move. There was a lesson to be learned in almost everything that the Cotton Mill Boys did.

On nice warm days, the mint green lawn chairs were transplanted to the outside, in front of the store. The older men then became a greeting committee. "How you doing today?" they'd ask.

The usual reply was, "Fine and how are you?"

Ever now and then they'd ask the wrong person, especially Miss Mary. "I ain't doing so good today," she'd answer. That lead to a long list of ailments and an explanation of what she was doing to doctor each ailment. They politely listened, but I'm sure, inside, they were saying, "Why did I ask?"

Mama got tired of the chairs being shuffled around and got benches for the outside. They sat under the porch roof and were protected from the elements, except a hard blowing rain out of the south. One bench had a metal sign all across the back of the bench that read "Colonial Bread is good bread." The metal sign was cold on your back when you leaned back against it in the winter time. The Henley's Grocery greeters liked sitting on the benches, because they could spit their tobacco without having a spit can and they could whittle and not have to sweep the floor. If weather was permitting, they could be found in their office most any day.

The business received an unexpected boom. Mama and Daddy had looked at all the pros and cons of starting the business and the pros out-weighted the cons. They expected to get most of the local business. Barrett's was closed and people who lived up the hill had to walk past our store to get to Uncle Bill's so they figured they would do pretty well.

What they had not factored into the equation was the business from the mill. Jones' had grown and they were working three shifts of fifty or sixty on each shift.

At first Mama had four or five that would come to get a bologna sandwich or hoop cheese and crackers and a drink for lunch. As others found out, she had more and more customers who took their lunch break at the store. She constantly prepared sandwiches from eleven a.m. to one p.m. and again from five p.m. to seven p.m.. She closed at seven p.m. and opened at six-thirty a.m. It made for a long day, but Daddy pitched in and I pitched in and we had a successful business at the Cotton Mill.

****

The store took up much of the garden space, but everyone had a garden. People were proud of their gardens and the produce they yielded. Mama couldn't stand for one weed or blade of grass to be in her garden. She would take her hoe and chop out every weed on the rows and in the middle. I would come behind with a garden rake and pull out all the grass to the ends of the rows. Sometimes I straddled the rake handle and pulled the rake behind me as I rode Trigger or Champ, depending on which cowboy I was.

Everyone thought they had the best garden in the neighborhood, but I believe Mama and Daddy had the best. I was glad when Daddy borrowed old Flecher's mule and plowed and disked the garden. It sure beat breaking up the whole garden with a shovel and hoe. Every row had to be perfectly straight before Mama would make a little furrow down each row with her hoe. She dropped in the chosen seed and covered it up. It was strictly organic gardening. Chicken manure from the hen house served as fertilizer. Mama's hoe was the herbicide, and I was the pesticide. Mama killed any weed with her hoe and I picked off unwanted insects and worms. The big green tomato worms made good catfish bait and the smaller cabbage worms were death to bream. Mama pointed out the beneficial insects and they were left to feed on the harmful ones.

Miss Posey had an unusual garden. She was the next thing to a doctor who lived at the Cotton Mill. She grew herbs that could cure almost any ailment. Most gardens had the herbs, like dill and mint for seasoning, but Miss Posey grew herbs that, if known today, might be a miracle cure for many diseases. I had some first hand experience with her medicinal practice.

I developed a rash on my side and it spread to my chest. Mama got concerned and asked Little Mama what she thought it was. "Looks like shingles to me," she answered. "You better take him to the doctor or see if Posey has something for it," she added. I don't think Little Mama meant for me to hear her next statement, but she was hard of hearing and often spoke louder than she knew. "If that is shingles and they go all the way around his body, he'll die," she tried to say in a lower voice.

I heard it and looked at my side and chest. "Mama, those

shingles are half way around me now," I spoke up with some urgency.

"Put on your shoes, we're going to Miss Posey's," she ordered. We walked quickly up the hill to Miss Posey's house.

When we got to the porch, Sis came to the door. "Well howdy, ya'll come in," she said as she was pleased to see Mama. "Come in and set down," she invited.

"Can't stay long. Got to get back home and take O'Neal to the doctor if Miss Posey can't help us," was her reply

"Well, go on back to Mama's room and let her have a look," Sis suggested.

We went into her room and she pulled my shirt up and had a look. "Shingles,"she announced. After she made her diagnosis, she went outside and picked some leaves of a plant. She handed the leaves to Mama and gave her instructions as to how the prescription was to be used.

"Beat the leaves and make a poultice. Put a cloth bandage with the leaves on it over the rash," she instructed.

Mama followed directions and within two days the rash was drying up. After four days, it was completely gone. I just wish I knew the name of the miraculous plant, because the secret of it's healing power probably went to the grave with Miss Posey.

The Cotton Mill was bordered on one side by the L&N Railroad, but on the other three sides was a thriving agribusiness. Ezra Pillow had cotton to pick and during the months of September and October, he hired hands to help with the picking. In the month of May, there were strawberries to be picked at the Collingsworth farm. A picker could make a nickel a quart or a dime a quart if the berries were capped. That is when the stems and leaves were pulled off the top of the berry.

The good thing about picking for Edward Collingsworth was he would let you eat all you could eat as you picked. I would dare say I usually ate half of a quart for every quart I picked. I did put the prettiest berries in the container. I wasn't fast at picking, but I could make fifty cents to a dollar a day in good berries.

Old Black Archie had an agri-business that made him money and made us happy. He grew watermelons. He had a secret patch somewhere beyond Stallin's pond. We never found it. He grew some of the biggest and best watermelons you ever put in your mouth. He had a really neat way of marketing his produce.

He had a flat bed wagon with straw on it and it was loaded down with watermelons and cantaloupes. His wagon was pulled by an old mule that had gray hair, just like Archie. As he slowly drove down the road with the load, he would yell, "Watermelons, cantaloupes, watermelons, cantaloupes!" People would come outside and stop him if they wanted to make a purchase.

For some reason Mama would always thump the watermelons until she got just the right one, then she would say, "I'll take this one." It was always good. Old Archie would slowly drive the old mule toward town. When we heard the clippity-clop of the mule coming back home, old Archie's wagon was always empty. At ten cents for a cantaloupe and twenty-five cents for a watermelon, I'll bet he was nearly rich.

There was one other business that was a source of income for the Cotton Mill Boys. The scrap iron man came through the neighborhood about once a week in his old truck. The truck was so old and beat up we figured he bought it for scrap, but it served him well. All week long we'd scrounged iron, copper, and aluminum. Each boy had his own scrap iron pile. Some saved for a big pay-off and only sold about once a month, while others sold what little they had collected each week. I liked a big pay day, so I saved my scrap metal for a month. The scrap iron man came by each Thursday in the afternoon. If you had scrap iron to sell, you simply waited for him to come by and flagged him down. He would stop and purchase the scrap you had. He paid the going price of one cent per pound for scrap iron and ten cents per pound for copper or aluminum.

There were no aluminum cans in the fifties. Soft drinks only came in glass bottles. Beer did come in cans, but they were made of tin. I never bought any beer in cans of course, but we did use them for fishing. The cans had a neck and a cap on them. We tied a line around the neck with a hook and weight on it, put the cap back on the beer can and we were ready to can fish. The brand I remember was Falstaff. We caught a lot of bullhead catfish in the old river at Gibson's Wells on those beer cans.

The scrap iron man would buy almost any kind of iron except railroad iron. I think it must have been against the law or something. It was probably a good law, because some people would take iron anywhere they could find it. Railroad spikes and rails were iron and there probably wouldn't have been a track for the train to run on if the railroad iron had been for sale.

Old copper wire was the real prize. The insulation had to be burned off, but at ten cents a pound, it was worth the effort. There were some months I would make almost a dollar. It sure was good to have a steady income. I always thought the scrap iron man was really nice to pay us for our junk until one day Daddy told me the scrap iron man took our junk to Jackson and got five cents a pound for iron and twenty cents a pound for copper.

Chapter XII: Dares, Double Dares, and Double Dog Dares

When I wanted someone to do something, I used a technique that was almost a guaranteed method to success. Mama always said, "You can catch more flies with honey than with vinegar." I wasn't interested in catching flies, but I did usually get people to do, or at least try to do, what I wanted them to do. I used the 'I dare you' leadership style. It worked better than anything I ever learned in administration classes or leadership academies.

When one of the Cotton Mill Boys balked at becoming involved in one of our schemes, we invoked the "I dare you" clause. If challenged by an 'I dare you', one could hardly refuse. Refusal meant you would be called a "chicken". If that did not stir the person being challenged to attempt the feat for which he was dared, the next challenge would be the double dare. It took an awfully strong person to refuse a double dare. He would be thought to be an absolute coward and he would be issued the final challenge, "I double dog dare you." Death wasn't as bad as refusing a double dog dare. I'm not sure I can ever recall a time when one of the Cotton Mill Boys refused a double dog dare.

Accepting the double dog dare was the cause of many torn clothes, broken bones, and whippings with the belt and plum tree switch. Charlie Bill rarely let a dare get to the double dare stage. He was always eager to prove his manhood. Of course chickens and other assorted birds didn't count in a dare. It was well known that to dare him about a fowl of any kind could get you two black horses and one red wagon. Translated from Cotton Mill to English, that means two black eyes and a bloody nose.

We did get him on one dare that had to go to the double dog dare stage. It had nothing to do with birds. It was a dare about the reservoir. I dared him to climb down the ladder and walk the plank to the island in the middle of the big pool that was once the water supply for the mill and the whole neighborhood. The ladder was a wooden ladder about twenty feet tall. Four or five feet of it was under water and the rest extended to the top of the deep hole. There was a large board that bridged the space between the ladder and the square island in the middle. It was about an eight foot walk on the plank to the island.

The dare started with Leenova. "I dare you to climb down the ladder to the edge of the water," he dared me. I accepted the challenge and climbed down to the last rung above the water. "Hold your foot out over the water," he added to the challenge. At that point I remembered what Mama said about the CCC boys putting an alligator in the reservoir. I started to hold my foot out, but I could almost visualize a fourteen foot gator lying just below the surface waiting for my foot to dangle above the water like a fish being feed to the dolphins at Marine Land. At any minute he would come leaping out of the water and snatch me off the ladder. I quickly climbed back up.

"You chicken," Charlie Bill said.

"I'm not chicken. Leenova didn't make that part of the dare," I argued in my defense. "If you're so brave, I dare you to walk the plank," I came back at him.

"I ain't gonna walk the plank, I can't swim and I might fall in," he offered as an excuse.

"I double dare you!" Leenova countered.

"That ain't fair. I'd do it if I could swim," he said as he squirmed a bit at refusing a double dare.

"I double dog dare you!" I snapped with an 'I got ya' smirk on my face.

"You know I would if I could swim," he pleaded.

"You go and I'll be right behind you," I promised. "I'll save you if you fall in."

Charlie Bill started to descend the ladder and when he was half way down I started down behind him. He reached the plank and looked up at the towering brick walls that surrounded him. He was about to start back up when Leenova reminded him that it was a double dog dare and if he backed out, everyone would know about it.

He stood there for a minute staring at the board. Finally he took a step out on the board. He glanced back up at me and said, "Come on down here in case I fall." He took another step and I came down two more rungs. He was half way across and started to teeter from side to side on the board. Just before he fell he regained his balance and managed to stay on the board.

"Go on just three more steps and you'll be on the island," I encouraged. The island was grown up in weeds but the spot where the board intersected was fairly clean. He stepped off the board and onto land. He had made it.

I don't know what came over me to make me react the way I did, but I must have listened to the devil whispering in my ear again. I reached down and grabbed the plank and pulled it off the island. Charlie Bill was trapped. He had a look of horror on his face as he saw me standing on the ladder holding one end of the board while the other end floated in the water.

"You better put it back or I'll get you," he warned.

I took a step up the ladder as I held on to the plank. Each time I took a step up Charlie Bill threatened more. I left one end of the board dangling in the water and the other lying across the ladder and climbed out of the reservoir. Charlie Bill began to plead with us as his anger turned to fear.

"Come on, ya'll, let me out," he begged.

We added to his misery by taunting, "Don't let the gator get you! Gator bate! Gator bait!"

Leenova and I left with his pleading and begging ringing in our ears. As we walked away my conscience began to bother me and I began to worry about Charlie Bill. What if he tried to swim out and drowned? What if there really was a gator in there and he was eaten? "We better go back and get Charlie Bill," I told Leenova. He argued but we headed back. We couldn't have been gone more than ten minutes but when we got back there was no Charlie Bill on the island. The board was still propped on the ladder and there was no sign that he had escaped.

The first thought that entered my mind was, "He's drowned." We yelled, "Charlie Bill! Charlie Bill!" but there was no answer. We had to have help. I ran beside the switch track all the way to my house and called for Mama as I ran inside gasping for breath.

"Lordy mercy! What's wrong?" she asked as I slid into her as I tried to stop.

"It's Charlie Bill! He's drowned in the reservoir," I blurted out.

I headed back out the door and she was right with me. The only other time I can remember running so fast was when the black racer chased me. When we got to the reservoir, she peered down into the pit. There was no sign of Charlie Bill.

"Go get Louis!" she ordered.

I was about to head out on another mission when I heard a voice from up above saying, "Don't wake up Daddy, he'll give me a whooping."

I looked up in the big catalpa tree beside the reservoir and there was Charlie Bill. Mama made him come down and he explained what happened.

When Leenova and I left, a man who worked at the mill heard his cries and came to his rescue. He thought he would get us back by letting us think we had caused him to drown or be eaten by the alligator. He climbed the tree and awaited our return.

It worked just like he planned, except I ran and got Mama. None of us were allowed to play around the reservoir so when I started to get his daddy, he had to speak up. He would have gotten a whipping for being at the reservoir, but it would have been even worse, because Louis had worked all night and was asleep.

At least everything turned out alright and no one was hurt because of the double dog dare, right? Wrong! When Mama got me to the house, before she set foot on the porch, she reached up in the plum tree and she wasn't picking plums. The switch was three feet long and I had on short pants.

Leenova didn't escape either. Mama told Gertie and Leenova received his just reward for his part in the dare. Mama didn't tell Louis, that is, until he woke up that afternoon. Charlie Bill got a pretty good one, but it would have been worse if Louis had not got his nap out. That broke us of dares for a day or two.

****

The water tank was often the object of dares. There were certain rules on how far a dare could go. The furtherest someone could be dared to go was what was referred to as the first round. The tank had four metal legs that had cross braces on each leg that were about a foot apart. It was possible to climb any of the legs, but one leg had a ladder that started at about twelve feet and went all the way to the first round. Anyone who was dared could use the ladder, or if they wanted to show how brave they were, or maybe how stupid they were, they could climb one of the ladderless legs. The first round was reached just above the area where the legs attached. There was a walkway with a rail that circled the tank at that point. Beyond the first round, which was easily a half a mile high. Well, maybe two hundred feet, a ladder extended to the top of the tank.

Besides the limitation on the height someone could be dared to ascend, they could only be dared one time per year. I always dreaded the time when the year was up. Someone just had to make a dare. The statute of limitation had run out on my exemption from the dare and I knew it was just a matter of time until someone remembered and challenged me. I was very careful to be as inconspicuous as possible and certainly didn't dare anyone during that time.

I was doing pretty good and none of the boys dared me. Then one day my cousin Jeep asked the question I feared, "O'Neal, how long has it been since you climbed the tank?"

I didn't want to lie, but I sure hated to climb that tank. Now, climbing trees was a different matter. I would climb to the top of the tallest tree in Spangler's woods. I didn't have a fear of heights when climbing trees, but I was always leery of the tank. I think I must have trusted God-made objects more than man-made objects. I never liked high buildings or high bridges either. I admitted it had been a year and a month since I had climbed the gargantuan structure.

"I dare you to climb it!" came out of two or three mouths before I could finish my statement. I was no dummy, well, maybe I was in a way, but at least I would climb the ladder.

It was hot near the end of June and my hands were sweaty. It may not have been the heat that started them to sweating, but I claimed it was anyway. After some urging by my "buddies", I thought I would go ahead and get the dare out of the way for another year. I was a year older, a year stronger, and a year smarter, well maybe. "I can do it," I told myself. After some strong concentration and a little silent praying, I started up the tank. There were cross braces about a third and two-thirds of the way up to the first round. I made it a practice to never look down.

I concentrated on the first cross brace as I slowly climbed the ladder. The boys on the ground watched in silence as I slowly ascended the metal ladder. There was no joking or fooling around when someone climbed the tank. It was serious business. A boy could get killed if he made a wrong move. The trick was to hold on tight with both hands as you stepped up a rung. With both feet firmly planted and one hand clamped like a vise, the climber would reach the free hand to the next rung. Some who were more of a dare devil, no pun intended, would climb quickly, but I took my time. All I wanted to prove was that I could reach the first round.

I got to the first brace and then things went bad. The brace provided protection from the elements for my old nemesis, the red wasp. My head was even with a huge nest and I was eyeball to compound eyeball with at least fifty of the creatures who were becoming a bit agitated at the uninvited guest. Now my hands really began to sweat. What do I do? I couldn't continue on up the ladder. They were already stirring around in the nest. If I started down, they would surely swarm me. I didn't believe I could hold on to climb back down if they started to sting. I had experienced the fury of a nest of wasp before and I could already imagine what they could do to me before I could climb seventy-five feet to the ground. I just froze and wouldn't move.

Jeep yelled up, "What's the matter? Are you going to chicken out?" I was wishing I had chickened out. All kind of things ran through my mind. I wished I had the ability that Uncle Whit had. He would find a wasp nest when we were fishing for bream and he would rub his hand under his arm and reach up and pull the nest down. The wasp would dart all around him but they wouldn't sting him. The wasp larvae were bream bait that came packaged. He caught a lot of fish on the little white larvae. If only I had his secret to hypnotize the wasp.

My thoughts kept going back to the time I was covered up with wasp in the wash house. I was frozen and oblivious to my surroundings when a tug on the cuff of my jeans snapped me back to reality. Slowly I looked down and Jeep was below me on the ladder. They knew something was wrong and Jeep had come to check on me. Actually they had concluded that I was frozen with fear of heights and, if they couldn't talk me down, they would call the fire department.

Jeep said, "Come on down and we'll take back the dare."

The dare was the least of my worries now. I whispered, "There's a big wasp nest under the brace and I'm afraid to move or they will swarm."

"A wasp nest!" he said, as he started to descend. Jeep did not like wasp much either.

I let Jeep get back on the ground before I made my move. After all, there was no sense in both of us dying. If I got attacked and fell with him below me, we would both be gonners. The insects had settled down and were quietly resting on the nest. It was almost solid red with the colony as they clung to the nest to protect their precious larvae.

I developed my strategy for escape. It was simple. I would move like molasses in the winter time until I was well below the fierce creatures. It took me a good two minutes to descend each rung of the ladder until I was about ten feet below the brace. I was careful not to make a sound or cause a vibration. The boys stood below gazing up with the expectation that at any second I would fall with a scream like an actor who falls off a mountain in the picture show.

I didn't fall. I made it to earth with one small step for man and a giant leap for all who were dared to climb the tank. With the threat of wasp on the tank, never again was anyone dared to climb the tank. Tank climbing was strictly on a voluntary basis from that time on.

****

Railroad tracks and trains played a major role in the lives of the Cotton Mill Boys. They were often the subject of dares. As many as five or six trains passed the Cotton Mill on a daily basis. In the late forties and early fifties, the trains were going through a transition. The Louisville and Nashville Railroad was gradually replacing their old steam locomotives with the more modern diesel. Within a five-year period, I witnessed the death of the steam engine, but during that period the old steam engine, with black coal smoke bellowing out of the smoke stack could still be seen.

It was easy to tell which kind of engine was coming by the sound of the whistle. The steam engine had the familiar "Woooo! Woooo! Woooo!" sound. The diesel had the sound of a loud horn blowing with a "Harooonk! Harooonk!

Harooonk!" They always blew their horn or tooted their whistle before they got to the crossing where Avondale Street went over the tracks.

There were many dares concerning the train. I'm sure some of our dares gave the engineer of the train a heart attack. One dare was to see how close the daree would let a train get before jumping off the tracks. The objective was to make the engineer blow his whistle. Bobo would stand on the tracks and, just at the last minute, he would leap out of the path of the train. The engineer would pull down on his whistle and let out three warning blasts to clear the tracks. Most of us would abandon the tracks before the whistle blew, but Bobo stood his ground and dared the train to keep coming.

Another dare that was often thrown at someone was, "I dare you to race the train across the crossing." This feat was even attempted by a grown-up in a car occasionally. The objective was to take off on a bicycle down the road that paralleled the track and beat the train to the railroad crossing on Avondale and cross in front of the train.

The person who had been dared would sit on his bike in a ready position, facing toward the crossing. The trains always blew their whistle before they got to the switch track. That was the signal to start the race. The bicyclist had about a quarter mile head start on the train. The race course covered about two hundred yards.

When the whistle blew, we would peddle like our lives depended on it. They probably did, but I don't recall anyone having a real close call until the diesels took over the railroad business. After the diesels replaced the old steam engine, we got away from train racing as a means of recreation. Thank goodness that is one thing Mama never caught me doing.

The most dangerous dare that anyone could do was to hop

a train. I never hopped a train that was going very fast, but I did my share of 'short rides'. Short rides were times when the trains were switching cars on the switch track. We would hop the train and ride from the switch track to the main track and jump off at that point.

The art of train hopping was perfected by the hobos in the late twenties and thirties, during the economic down-turn Mama called the Depression. Hobos and just plain folks traveled around over the country in search of work, using the rails as a means of travel. They had no money for a passenger train so they hopped a freight. There were a few hobos left in the fifties, but they were becoming as extinct as the passenger pigeon.

Mama and Little Mama had lots of tales about the railroad during the depression. One event that they told about was fascinating to me. It was called coal pilfering. The people who lived at the Cotton Mill during the depression had no means of livelihood except working the farms around the area. Mama told of picking cotton all day for a bucket of molasses, or picking strawberries for a quart for every ten quarts picked. She would then go the store and swap the strawberries for flour and lard. They had no money, but they had to survive and that lead to coal pilfering.

The people at the Cotton Mill worked together to survive the depression. If someone was in need, they shared with them. It might only be biscuits and gravy, but they shared. Coal pilfering was a team effort. The word was passed around that the boys were going to pilfer coal that day and everyone would be ready.

The older boys and some of the men would hop a train that was carrying coal. They usually hopped it just as it left the crossing downtown. That way they could get on before it got up a head of steam. They would then climb up on the cars that were stacked with coal. When the train crossed Avondale street, they started to throw off the coal. As quickly as they could, they rolled chunks of coal down the railroad bank.

This process continued all along the mill road that paralleled the tracks all the way to the big curve that went to the old Spangler house. The train began to slow as it entered Hobo's Grade, which was a steep hill. When the train slowed down the men and boys would climb down the ladder and jump off the train.

In the meantime, the women, old men and small children were busy gathering up the coal and putting it on the hoodlum wagon. The hoodlum wagon was a homemade cart that was used to haul the coal home. Mama didn't have far to go with her load. She was only twelve years old, but both her father and Little Mama were sickly and she had to provide for them. She was small, but she was stout. It wasn't exactly honest but the coal kept them warm in the winter.

The Cotton Mill residents hopped trains out of necessity but most of our train hopping was done for fun or on dares. We didn't consider the unauthorized boarding of a freight train to be dangerous and illegal.

Peg Morrison was an elderly man who, in his younger days hopped trains. On one occasion, as he ran along side the train, holding onto the ladder, he slipped and his leg went under the box car. His leg was severed just below the knee and now he had a wooden stump for a leg. I always thought of Peg when I hopped a train. There was also a chance that you would get caught by the railroad men that rode the train. None of us ever got caught, but the rumor was that if they caught you hopping a train, you would go to jail.

There were dares about superstitions. "I dare you to walk under the ladder," one would say. Superstitions ran rampant at the Cotton Mill. Most people believed them enough that they wouldn't tempt fate by deliberately going against a superstition. Mama would turn around and walk out of her way to avoid going where a black cat crossed her path. I don't know if she truly believed they could bring bad luck, or if she had so much bad luck with me that she didn't want to take a chance.

If you broke a mirror, you were in for seven years of bad luck. I once threw a ball in the house and broke a mirror. I don't know if I had seven years of bad luck, but I definitely had seven minutes as Mama whacked away with a plum tree switch.

There was one superstition I believed until I was a teenager. It caused me great anxiety every time we went skinny dipping at Stallin's pond. The Cotton Mill Wildlife Society told us that if a turtle bit you, he wouldn't let go until it thundered.

I knew there were turtles in the pond because I had seen them. I also knew, when we were swimming in our birthday suits, there was an awful lot of white meat to tempt a turtle's taste buds. I was somewhat fearful that I would have a turtle clamp down on some exposed part of my body. To make matters worse, I could visualize myself running down Avondale Street, stark naked, with a turtle hanging on, as I prayed for a thunderstorm. To say the least, this superstition made me nervous when I went swimming. The absence of turtles and the fact that swimming trunks were required made Plu's Slough very attractive.

It was uncanny how some of the superstitions seemed to be true. Mama would say, "My nose is itching, someone is coming to visit." Within an hour of the time she made her prediction, someone would come. It might be our aunt from Texas or Pauline Little from just up the road, but someone would show up.

She also believed that when your ear itched someone was talking about you. Usually when her ear itched and we went to Barrett's Grocery, Velma would say, "Well howdy Alene, we were just talking about you." I didn't believe all those little insignificant superstitions as much as I believed that black cats were bad luck and turtles held on until it thundered, but they did seem to come true.

Chapter XIII: The Nights

The nights at the Cotton Mill were always filled with fun, especially in the summer. There were games and ghost stories from the time the supper dishes were finished until bedtime. In the winter less time was spent outdoors and the radio programs got some attention, but in the summer it was full steam ahead. We played every game known to man and invented a few along the way.

Kick-the-can was a favorite game. It could be played in daylight, but it was more challenging and more fun at night. One person was 'it'. That person had to find and tag all the others who participated in the game. Once a person was tagged, they had to go to a designated place, usually a landmark like a tree or porch post. They had to stand there until all were caught, or someone kicked the can. A Pet Milk can made the best can, because it only had two little holes poked in the top and there were no jagged edges caused by a can opener. The can was set up near the designated place that held those who had been captured.

If someone who had not been tagged ran up and kicked the can, all the detainees could go free, that is if the person who was it didn't retrieve the can and set it up on the spot before the kicker disappeared. If the can wasn't kicked far enough, the person who was it could run get it and set it up on the brick and call the name of all he could see and they had to go back to detention. Sometimes the person who was it would get back everyone who escaped, plus the person who kicked the can.

The need to kick the can as far as possible caused me great pain one time when we were playing at Charlie Bill's grandmother Matt's. We had the Pet Milk can set up on a brick by the big maple tree that was beside their house. It was about eight o'clock and the orange glow in the western sky still gave off enough light to make a shadow as we started the game. Charlie Bill was selected to be it by the 'one-potato, two-potato' method and everyone scattered to hide. I hid under the high back porch, just under the steps. Leenova hid behind the outhouse. Vanny Dee was very fast and wasn't too worried about Charlie Bill catching him. He just leaned against an old walnut tree and waited.

Charlie Bill wasn't swift of foot, but he was pretty shrewd. He knew Vanny Dee could outrun him so he didn't come looking for us, he just waited at the corner of the house. He also knew Vanny Dee couldn't stand the wait and would have to come investigate. His strategy worked like a charm. Vanny Dee came creeping along the side of the house and peeped around the corner. His face met Charlie Bill's hand and he was captured.

Leenova was the next to fall for his strategy. After a ten minute wait with no action, he went on a scouting mission to see what was going on. He spotted Charlie Bill just before he rounded the corner and the race was on. Leenova was gaining on Charlie Bill as they came around back. Unfortunately for Leenova, Charlie Bill's Aunt Polly had thrown the dish water off the back porch and it made a slippery puddle. He hit the puddle and slid like he was on ice. Both feet went into the air and when he hit he skidded five feet on his back. It all happened right in front of me as I peeped through the back steps. Charlie Bill caught up to him before he could get up and tagged him.

Now I was the only one left to kick the can and free my buddies. I peeped out on both sides of the steps then circled around the slop hole created by the dishwater and Leenova. I didn't see Charlie Bill anywhere so I eased around the house.

I was very careful to check behind trees and bushes as I advanced toward the old maple tree. I could see Leenova and Vanny Dee leaning against the tree. The can was sitting in the open on the brick. I had on my Indian moccasins, so I knew he couldn't hear me as I took silent steps closer and closer. When I was about ten yards away I made a mad dash for the can.

Out of the corner of my good eye, I saw Charlie Bill closing ground. He had been hiding behind his grandaddy France's car. I had to beat him to the can and kick it a mile. That was my only hope of freeing Vanny Dee and Leenova. I got there before him and kicked. I must have taken my eye off the can, because I kicked the brick. A sharp pain went through my big toe and I went to the ground. The can rolled about two feet and the brick went about three. Charlie Bill quickly grabbed the can, put it on the brick and called out names. We were all caught, but for some reason that didn't bother me. The pain in my toe got worse. It throbbed with every beat of my heart. I tried to stand and put weight on it, but it hurt too much.

Now came the part I dreaded the most, I had to tell Mama. Charlie Bill and Vanny Dee made a pack saddle and carried me. A pack saddle was made by two people crossing arms and holding on to each other. It wasn't far from Charlie Bill's grandmother's house to my house and they only had to stop and rest a couple of times.

When Mama saw them bring me home on a pack saddle, she knew something had happened. "What did you do?" she asked.

"I think I broke my toe," I answered sheepishly.

I knew kicking a brick with moccasins on was a dumb thing to do and I expected the boys to rib me about it, but I didn't expect it from my own sweet Mama. "How did you do it?" she continued to probe.

"I kicked a brick," I answered.

"That was a dumb thing to do," was her response.

I didn't sleep much that night with all the throbbing, so the next morning Mama called a cab and we went to see Dr. Barker. We usually walked to town. A cab ride was very rare, but in this case I couldn't walk. Dr. Barker confirmed that my toe was broken. He taped it to the toe next to it and told me to stay off my foot for a few days. That was bad news, because there was supposed to be a big game of kick-the-can that night.

****

We played hide-and-go-seek, but we usually added something to make it exciting. We sent out the word through the neighborhood that everyone would meet at my house after supper for some night games. Word got around and we anticipated having ten or twelve boys there to play. This was while my cousins Bobby, Doug and Jeep lived next door in the haunted house. That afternoon my cousins and I got our heads together to see what we could do to spice up the game. Bobby came up with an idea that would become a ghost story for years at the Cotton Mill.

Bobby had an old rubber mask that was a white skull. It looked authentic when it was in the dark. His idea was to dress up in the mask and hide in the wash house before the game of hide-and-go-seek started. My job was to convince as many as possible to hide in the wash house. Doug volunteered to be it. That should have been a tip-off that something was up, but no one seemed to suspect anything.

Doug started to count to one hundred and we all scattered to hide. Charlie Bill had brought two new boys who had just moved into the neighborhood. They didn't stay but about a month or two before they moved. I can't help but believe what happened that night had something to do with their moving.

Bobby was in the very back corner of the wash house. He had on Blubbers long black trench coat and a black hat. He kept the white mask covered with his hands that were in black gloves. He was invisible in the darkness of the wash house. There were no street lights and the only light was the light that shined through the side window of the living room.

As we ran to find a hiding place, I told Charlie Bill to follow me. He, in turn, told the new boys to follow him. Jeep went along with us for good measure. The older of the two boys was named Ed. I can't remember the younger brother's name. We disappeared in the darkness of the wash house. I assured them Doug would never find us in there. We all settled into the darkness at the back of the little building. The youngest of the two boys squatted down in the corner where Bobby stood. Doug yelled, "Here I come, ready or not!" There was total silence in the wash house.

Bobby reached down and lay his hand on the boy's shoulder. There was no reaction. He put his other hand on his other shoulder and squeezed in toward his neck. "Stop it Ed, He's coming," he whispered. We got a glimpse of Doug as he passed through the light that shined out of the living room window. Bobby tightened his grip on the boys throat. "I said stop it," the boy demanded. He then reached back and felt of the hand that had him. "Ed! Stop it!" he said in a louder voice. His hand slid on up the arm as he stood up. As he searched for some familiar feature, his hand touched the rubber mask. "Ed? Ed, is that you Ed?" he questioned with doubt in his voice. He slowly turned and he was face to face with the skeleton. He screamed out, "Ed, that ain't you!"

All eyes turned to the back corner of the wash house. All that could be seen was the bony white face. There were screams and banging and ranting. I got to the door first. I knew what was going on, but when Bobby let out a moan, I wanted out of there, too. We were all stumbling and tripping and hung up in the door until Charlie Bill finally saw the ghost and decided to exit. He hit us like a bowling ball hitting the pins and it was a strike as we all scattered. He was screaming "ghooooost!" and sprinting like an Olympian. He didn't bother to pass me, he just ran over me and flattened me.

Mama had been watching out the window in anticipation of the ghost sighting. She heard us hatching up the scheme. What she saw was hard to believe. Charlie Bill, who was much more of a tortoise than a hare, was leading the pack. She said his hair was standing straight up on his head and he was as white as a ghost himself. He rounded the house, jumped on the porch and jerked open the screen door so hard that he broke the door spring. He ran inside and began to tell Mama that she had a ghost in her wash house. Mama played along with us and told him she would be afraid to wash clothes in there from now on.

While everyone was in the living room telling about the encounter with the spirit, Bobby slipped out and went next door and changed. Others who had found a hiding place someplace besides the wash house, began to come out of their hiding places to see what the commotion was. Bobby slipped in with the others as we related the story. "Ya'll didn't see no ghost," Leenova said with skepticism.

"I not only saw it, I felt it," the new boy shuttered.

Everyone who was in the wash house swore they saw a ghost. Charlie Bill even crossed his heart and hoped to die if he had not seen a ghost. The skeptics wanted to see for themselves and I lead them back behind the house to the place of the sighting. We approached very cautiously and peered in the open door, which by the way, had one busted hinge. There was no ghost to be seen which led Vanny Dee to be brave and volunteer to go inside. He took a step or two into the dark building and reported, "No ghost in here. Ya'll just saw a shadow or something." He was brave now but later he would get his.

The next day bright and early Mrs. Booker came to see Mama. "Heard ya'll had a ghost in the shed last night," she said as she fished for information.

"That's what all those boys said," she answered.

"What did it look like?" she further inquired.

"I don't know, I didn't see it," Mama answered with a little sarcasm in her voice.

By noon, anywhere you went in the Cotton Mill neighborhood, people would ask, "Did you know there was a ghost in Alene's wash house last night?"

As far as I know, none of the co-conspirators, including Mama, ever told anyone the origin of the ghost. After fifty years, I guess the statute of limitations has run out, so I can tell you that the ghost in Mama's wash house was my cousin Bobby.

****

There were some nights when we would just sit around and tell ghost stories. The ghost in Mama's wash house would always be told. Sometimes we would sit on one of the boy's front porch, and at other times we would go to Hobo's Mansion and build a camp fire and tell ghost stories. Most of the stories were actual accounts of events that took place at the Cotton Mill. Occasionally someone would make up a big tale, like Bloody Bones, or some other fictitious ghost, but most of the stories were actual ghost encounters. Well, at least they thought they were ghost encounters, as in the case of the wash house ghost. I only had two real encounters with a ghost, where I could personally vouch for their existence.

The sun had set on the western horizon behind our house and only a light yellow streak remained of the daylight. Daddy was slopping the hogs when he heard a strange sound that seemed to come from a big hollow sycamore tree on the ditch bank behind the house. He called for Mama to come and listen.

Naturally, I was curious when he said, "Alene come here and listen to this spooky sound." I followed her out the back door and paused on the back porch to listen. What I heard was hard to describe. It was like someone gasping for breath. There was the sound of air being sucked in, then a pause, then the air was let out. The sound was amplified as if it were coming over a loud speaker. I stood frozen in my tracks as I listened to the ghost, or whatever it was.

Daddy and Mama stood silently and listened. Then Daddy asked, "What could it be?"

Mama didn't have an answer or comment, which was unusual in itself. The sound of the labored breathing gradually got higher. It had started at the base of the sycamore tree and in a minute or two the sound seemed to be coming from the top of the tree.

If the sound had stopped at the top of the tree, I could have easily explained it away. It could have been one of the boys climbing the tree and making the sound as a prank. It could have been a possum or coon with distemper making the sound. However the breathing didn't stop at the top of the tree. The sound went higher into the night sky. The higher it went, the softer the sound of the breathing got. It must have taken ten or fifteen minutes for the sound to get completely out of hearing.

We never knew what the belabored breathing sound was, but the next day our next door neighbor, Sam Smith was found dead in his bed. I truly can't say that there was a connection between the sound and Sam Smith's death, but most of the neighbors who heard the story agreed that we had heard Sam's spirit going to the hereafter. I do know one thing for sure, you couldn't get one of the boys to climb the old sycamore tree, even for a five dollar bill.

****

When we sat around and told stories, one ghost would always come up, the ghost of Jack Beasley. Jack Beasley was walking the railroad tracks and was killed by a train. It sounds gruesome, but his body was scattered all down the railroad tracks. I was only three or four years old when it happened, but I can remember people talking about finding fingers several days after the accident. Most folks speculated that he got caught on the trestle with no place to go and tried to outrun the train. It was a horrible accident that lead to a ghost legend.

A couple of years later one of Uncle Bill's customers was returning to town after having partaken of some of Uncle Bill's homebrew. He got on the tracks at the railroad crossing and started across the trestle. The next thing he knew, there was a man walking along beside him. It was dark and only the light of the quarter moon allowed him to see the man.

Being in a jovial state of mind, he said, "Hi pardner. Where you going?"

The figure he supposed to be a fellow traveler, didn't say a word.

"I'm headed to town, how bout you?" he restated his question.

Still there was no answer.

By now they were across the trestle and almost of the big white concrete post with the big black 'W' on it. It was the sign for the engineer to blow his whistle before he got to the railroad crossing. The man was becoming impatient and agitated by the strangers failure to answer his questions. He turned to the stranger and stuck out his hand.

"Let me introduce myself, I'm Leonard," he said.

The other traveler turned to face him and stuck out his hand, or should I say stump. Leonard looked in horror first at the wrist that had no hand and then at the face that was half gone. He couldn't tell what happened after that because he passed out. Luckily he awoke before the eleven o'clock passenger train came by.

He said he was reluctant to tell what happened because people would think he was drunk or crazy, but he told a few people and the word got around. Sure enough, some people said he was drunk and passed out and dreamed the whole thing. Others said he was drunk and imagined things. One man said he hadn't told anyone before now because he didn't think they would believe him, but he had also seen a mysterious man walking across the trestle like he was looking for something. I don't know about the adults, but that cinched it for us boys. There was definitely a ghost walking the railroad tracks.

There were other ghost sightings on the railroad. Several people who crossed the tracks at night would get a glimpse of a man in their headlights. He would disappear as the lights hit him.

On another occasion, a group of boys who were walking back home from the little league games, decided to take the shortcut down the railroad tracks. Just before they got to the trestle they saw a lone figure standing in the middle of the tracks. Right before their eyes they saw a dull red glow in front of the figure. The man or ghost disappeared as the red light ascended into the air. They turned and ran back down the tracks and got on eighteenth street. After that it was rare for anyone to cross the trestle at night.

It was that event that lead Charlie Bill, Leenova, and me to pull a ghost prank. It wasn't that we were not afraid of ghost, but our love of a good joke outweighed our fear.

The prank would involve our being at the trestle after dark but if things went as planned it would be worth it. Besides, the ghost had never been sighted off the tracks and we would be beside the tracks instead of on them.

Our plan involved much preparation during the daylight hours, so we went right to work that afternoon. We knew there would be a large delegation of Cotton Mill Boys going to the little league ball games. They would leave while it was still light, but would return in the dark.

I had a small lantern I had won at the Strawberry Festival Carnival. I had three different colored bulbs in it. One was clear and the other two were red and green. Our plan involved the red light, since the ghost had been observed disappearing in a red light. The glow of the little lantern was perfect. It didn't give off enough light to illuminate the surroundings, but it could easily be seen at a distance.

That afternoon, I climbed the tallest tree on the ditch bank. It was about thirty feet from the trestle. We took some trotline string that Daddy had and unrolled about one hundred yards of it. I tied it to the top branch of the tree. Leenova and Charlie Bill stretched it tight as it sloped from the top of the tree to the cotton patch that ran beside the tracks. I tried to get Leenova to stretch it to the bank of the railroad, but he wasn't about to be on the railroad after dark.

The lantern was given a test run to see if our plan would work. I hooked it over the string and let gravity do the rest. The little lantern slowly slid down the string and landed where Leenova and Charlie Bill had staked it at the edge of the cotton field.

"It worked just like we planned," I announced.

"It'll scare the pants off them," Charlie Bill added. We left the string in place and went home to await the night.

The little league games were usually over by nine o'clock and most of the boys had to be home by nine-thirty. Just to be sure we didn't miss the chance to scare them, we went back to the set up about eight-thirty. I climbed the big sweet-gum tree with the little lantern strapped to my belt, and Leenova and Charlie Bill hid in the Cotton Patch where the string was staked down. We waited patiently for the boy's return. About nine-fifteen, we heard Vanny Dee's laugh. They were walking the road instead of the tracks. The road went parallel with the tracks until it crossed the wooden bridge, then it turned at a ninety degree angle and crossed the tracks. We were set up where they would see the light just before they crossed the bridge.

Vanny Dee had been with the bunch that saw the ghost and the red light. He was constantly looking in the direction of the railroad tracks. He was fleet-of-foot and relied on his legs to get him out of most jams. When they were almost even with us I let out a moan to get their attention. At the same time I flipped on the red light on the lantern and started it on it's decent. The little red light slowly hovered over the field and appeared to be coming toward the boys on the road. It disappeared behind the railroad bank and as it touched down,

Leenova flipped the switch and turned it off.

The whole group, except for Vanny Dee, was frozen with fear. They couldn't believe they had actually seen a ghost come down out of the air and land in the field beside the railroad track. Vanny Dee, however, had crossed the tracks and was headed home as he scratched gravel on Avondale Street. There were screams, and one boy even squealed like a girl, as the paralysis left the rest of the group and they began to run. They pushed and shoved each other as they tried to clear a path home.

I cut the string so there would be no evidence the next day. I was sure they would return in the daylight to show others where the ghost encounter took place. Leenova rolled up the string on the stake and Charlie Bill brought out the lantern. I was all smiles, as I climbed down. We didn't tarry for very long on the tracks, because there was the possibility that we might have a visit from the real ghost. We hurried back to my house and once in the safety of home, we sat in the porch swing and bragged on a job well done.

The next day when we gathered across the street at the old elm tree to play cork ball, the stories were flying about the ghost. Vanny Dee swore the red light had the shape of a man and swooped down right on top of them. Then Pee Wee told something that made our hair stand on end and kept us from performing an encore of the ghost act. He said, "You know, I wasn't all that afraid of the red light, but when I looked on the trestle and that ghost was standing there holding it's head in it's hand, I really got scared."

I glanced at Leenova and Charlie Bill and both had their mouths wide open. We got our heads together later and decided we had upset the ghost with our joke and we would never do it again. Heck, we would probably never walk the railroad again.

****

The house next door was well known for brushes with the paranormal. Every family that lived in the house had some unexplainable event to happen while they were there. Mama even had a brush with the mysterious house.

It happened late at night. She had awakened with a case of the cotton mouth and got up and went to the kitchen sink to get a drink of water. Our kitchen window faced directly across from their kitchen window. At the time, my Uncle Blubber, Aunt Linnie Mae, and my cousins lived in the house.

Mama thought she saw a light in the kitchen window, but on further examination, she realized she was seeing flames. The flames leaped out the window and up the side of the house to the second floor window. She ran and got Daddy, screaming, "The house is on fire! The house is on Fire!"

Daddy woke up from a deep sleep and thought she meant our house was on fire. He woke up Gail and me and was about to get Little Mama out, when Mama finely explained that it was the house next door. He ran out on the porch in his underwear, but when he looked in the direction of the house he didn't see any fire.

Mama was totally shocked when she ran out and looked. There was no fire at all. She told Daddy, "Herbert, I know I saw that house on fire."

He was a little upset that his sleep was disturbed so he said, "You're just seeing things. Go back to bed."

She dropped her head and went back to bed. She wasn't used to being wrong, but there was no way to explain how she could have seen a burning house and yet it didn't burn.

The only time I recall something similar happening, was a burning bush and God spoke to Moses. Since Mama didn't hear a voice coming from the house, it couldn't have been the same situation. The only logical conclusion was that the house was haunted.

I had a direct encounter with the haunted house when my Uncle Joe and Aunt Ethel moved into the house. I was always leery of the house, but I was forced to stay over there one night while Mama, Daddy, Joe and Ethel went to a dance. Shirley, my older girl cousin, was in charge of Corkey, Johnny, Gail and me. She wanted to keep us at their house, so I had no choice but to stay until Mama and Daddy got home.

Everything was going just fine as we listened to the radio and ate popcorn. Shirley had popped the corn and poured it in a large bowl. We sat in the floor and on the bed in Joe and Ethel's bedroom, while we listened to "The Shadow". Shirley reached on the night stand and turned the radio down as she thought she heard something. The rest of us froze in silence and strained our ears to hear what she heard.

There was a stairway that led from the back porch up into the attic. The rooms had been used for bedrooms when the Smith's lived in the house, but they were only used for storage after Joe and Ethel moved in. There was a creak at the foot of the stairs, as if someone had just stepped on the bottom step. After that, there were a series of creaks in succession, just like the creaks made as pressure was applied it each ascending step. The footsteps went right on up into the attic.

I was already thinking ghost, but Shirley was pretty mature for her age, and much more practical than the rest of us. "Someone just went up into the attic," she said in a whisper.

My first reaction was to run, but she tried to keep us calm.

"Be very quiet and I'll go see if the door to the stairway is still locked," she instructed us.

Corkey, Gail, Johnny and I all huddled up together, much like a covey of quail about to explode into the air. Shirley was only gone a minute, when she returned visibly shaken. "The door's still locked," she informed us.

It couldn't be a human up there. It was just as I suspected, it was a ghost. The popping and creaking continued as the wandering spirit walked across the floor and was directly over us in the attic. Chilly air spilled down from the ceiling like someone had opened an ice box. There was a sound much like the wind moaning through a grove of trees. It was all we could stand.

Shirley was mature, but she wasn't about to take on the spirit world. She grabbed Johnny up in her arms and said, "Let's get out of here!" Without any hesitation, the rest of the covey scattered. I grabbed Gail by the hand and literally dragged her out the door. We followed Shirley to the safety of our house next door.

We sat and waited until Mama, Daddy, Joe and Ethel arrived. "What are ya'll doing over here?" Ethel asked.

"There's a ghost at our house," Corkey blurted out.

"Now, there are no such thing as ghosts," Joe added.

"I'll tell you, there was a ghost and I'm not going back in that house tonight", Shirley flatly announced.

"We heard it climb the stairs and moan in the attic," I said in her defense.

"It was probably a cat or something in the attic," Joe countered.

Mama jumped in, "Joe, there have been some strange goings-on in that house. Let me make them a pallet and let them spend the night over here."

Joe and Ethel agreed to let them spend the night that night and the next night they spent at home. Johnny slept with Joe and Ethel and Corkey and Shirley slept in their room on the floor. They eventually got over the ghostly visit.

Shirley was glad when they moved and I was glad I didn't have to live in that house. However, I sometimes worried that the ghost next door might get lonely and come visit us.

As far as I know, there was only one time we had a visitation from a spirit in our house. It was later when I was in junior high. It was after the death of Little Mama and when my little sister, Booger, was about three years old. Mama was working at Henley's Grocery from sun-up to dark and had little time for house work. She hired a black lady named Iona to come in once a week and clean and wash clothes.

One day Iona came out to the store and asked Mama who that little gray-haired lady was that came in the house. Mama said, "What did she look like?"

"She was about this tall," she said as she held her hand at about five feet. "She was a little heavy set, with gray hair in a bun, and she had on a light blue night gown," she added.

Mama wasn't the least bit startled when she said, "That's my Mama. She's been dead over a year, but she comes back to see me." Mama had told us that Little Mama talked to her when she was sleeping, and we just figured it was a dream. Mama pointed to the apron around Iona's waist and said, "That's Mama's apron you have on. That's probably why you saw her."

There has never been an apron untied and removed with

such speed. She yanked it off and threw it on the counter where Mama stood. "Miss Alene, you gonna have to get a new house-keeper. I quit!" she exclaimed as she left the store in a hurry. I sure hated that Iona quit because she made a great chocolate pie.

Ghost sightings and ghost stories were not uncommon at the Cotton Mill. As I grew up and reflected back on some of the incidents, I tried to rationalize and explain away the stories. I wanted logical explanations to some of the things that happened. Some, of course, were pranks. Some could have been the over-stimulated imaginations of people who had too much homebrew. But there still were some unexplained occurrences. Sometimes the only explanation was, it was a ghost.

Epilogue

To look at the Cotton Mill Boys in the early fifties through the eyes of a social worker today, we would have seemed to have been poor, underprivileged, children. They would look at us and think we had no chance to succeed in life. Well, maybe none of us became rich and famous or powerful politicians, but the whole bunch turned out pretty well.

We owe a lot to parents who practiced tough love with a plum switch or belt. We owe a lot to each other as we taught and supported our friends. We owe the most to the Cotton Mill neighborhood. The people who lived in this small mill village helped to mold and shape us. Some of the molding might have left us a little lop-sided in some areas, but by and large, you could always count on friends and neighbors.

Almost all the older people are gone, but they live in the memories of the Cotton Mill Boys. I have to blink to keep back the tears as I see their faces. I know they are all sitting in heaven around a pot-bellied stove made of gold and looking down on me as I write. I can see Mama's smile as the ghost scared Charlie Bill. I can hear Mamaw Hallie's laugh. I can see Uncle Whit standing in his old rubber knee boots. Carl Scott is up there with his old World War I Calvary hat on.

Some of the Cotton Mill Boys are there too. Charlie Bill left us when he was 42 years old. After high school, he worked at Jones Manufacturing for a while, then he moved to Detroit and worked in heating and air-conditioning. He came back to visit almost every summer, but in the fall of 1985, he had a heart attack and died.

Jeep graduated from high school and joined the Army. He

became an accountant after his service time, but a car accident ended his life in 1985.

Jeep wasn't the only Cotton Mill Boy to join the service. I don't know what influenced the Cotton Mill Boys the most, our movie heroes or our real live heroes at the Cotton Mill. Love and service of country was high on the priority list of the Cotton Mill Boys as they became men. They were true patriots.

Skeezer joined the Navy and after he served his hitch, he worked at Jones Manufacturing for a while, then went to work for a printer. The only pay he asked of the old printer was to teach him the trade. He went on to establish Henley Printing which was the most successful printing business in Humboldt.

Bobo joined the Air Force and made it a career. He returned to the Cotton Mill for a visit, but finally ended up in Las Vagas.

Bobby also joined the Air Force and came back to Humboldt. He worked as an executive for American Olean Tile until it shut down. He moved to Big Sandy, Tennessee and owns a restaurant there.

Vanny Dee joined the Air Force after high school and married while enlisted. He came back for a visit a time or two, then never returned.

Doug came real close to signing a baseball contract with a minor league team but didn't quite make it. After that he signed up for the Army and spent a hitch in there. He returned to Humboldt, where he lives today, on the other side of the tracks from the cotton mill.

Alton "Fats" Morris joined the Air Force and served a hitch. Bill Wages, my cousin who shot me with the BB gun, joined the Marines and got a medal for sharp shooting. Anyone who could hit someone in the eye through the crack in the door of an outhouse, deserves a sharp shooter medal. After Billy got out of the Marines, he moved to Texas.

Andy Collinsworth joined the Air Force and married while in Scotland. He returned to Humboldt for a while but now lives in Arizona.

David Pillow married right out of high school and worked in Humboldt at Century Electric for several years before he retired. He still lives in Humboldt with his wife who was his high school sweetheart.

Pee Wee went to work at Jones Manufacturing right out of high school. He was promoted to fixer and then to foreman. He still lives in Humboldt.

Leenova went to work for Jones Manufacturing and worked for them several years. He was promoted to fixer, which is a machinist, who keeps the mill running.

Colin graduated and went to work at a service station. He always loved working on cars. He was a good business man and before long he owned the service station and a wrecker service. He was elected to the Board of Aldermen for the City of Humboldt.

I went to work for Jones Manufacturing right out of high school. My daddy was the plant superintendent. After a hot summer of loading boxcars and tractor-trailer trucks with one-hundred-pound balls of mop yarn, I decided there had to be something better. I think that was the conclusion Daddy wanted me to draw, because he gave me the hottest, dirtiest jobs at the plant. I decided college might be good.

I wanted to play college football but there was no demand for a one-hundred-fifty-five pound center. After college I got the chance to do the thing I loved the most, coach football.

So I guess none of us were warped by our upbringing at the Cotton Mill. We all turned out to be a pretty good bunch of ole boys.

Main Street Publishing, Inc.

206 E. Main Street Suite 207
P.O.Box 696
Jackson, Tn 38301

Toll Free #: 866-457-7379
or
Local #: 731-427-7379

Visit us on the web:
www.mainstreetpublishing.com
www.mspbooks.com

E-Mail: mspsupport@charterinternet.com